The English Newspaper

Keith Williams

The English Newspaper

an illustrated history to 1900

Springwood Books

Published by
Springwood Books Limited
11 Garrick Street
London WC2E 6AR

First published 1977

ISBN 0 9059 4715 0

Printed in England by
Butler & Tanner Limited
Frome and London

Contents

The First Papers

There is a popular view that journalists are persons with the words 'scoop' and 'probe' deeply scarred on their hearts. It is assumed that they are professionally dedicated to making public every kind of scandal, infidelity and corruption, both of private persons and official organisations. When the one will not suffice to fill their pages, the other will.

The modern newspaper scribbler commands something of a distinct swagger before the public gaze. He is that roving buccaneer of print whose published words strike daily at the very core of infamy, with interviews on television and the radio to sharpen his attack.

Yet his sole weapon is the typewriter across the battered keys of which his nail-bitten, nicotine-stained fingers scramble to write him clear of all those dangers to which he is so vulnerably exposed. Whether he is an editor being sued for libel, or a more humble performer being placed in jail for refusing to divulge to the authorities those sources from which his most wounding stories come, his life as a journalist is one fraught with constant peril. Any rise to fame that he may achieve can be cancelled in a few short weeks if his nose for news loses its sharpness, or if his prose fails to gleam.

Like any other merchant adventurer, risk is what challenges him, and reward supplies only a taller pinnacle from which to tumble. That being so, journalism as a way of life, and the manner of its origination raise a number of serious questions. Why do newspapers exist? What is their appeal? What role do they play? What attracts ordinary people to them so strongly that they will, when the necessity arises, pay relatively high prices to secure them?

Common human curiosity, of course, needs to be constantly satisfied. And as the range of human affairs spread ever more widely, so there were more and more distant matters about which the enquiring person required to be informed.

Furthermore, it can be safely assumed that the activities of any government are antagonistic to the interests of the individual who needs, by any means available, to obtain advance information as to their plans, sources of information, what they know or think they know, and thereby to protect himself against whatever inroads they plan on his life. So that one explanation for the appearance of newspapers and journalists in England during the seventeenth century could be that an increasing number of people wanted to know what was going on in the country, and that the government of the day was increasingly reluctant to tell them. Between the years 1620 and 1660, something over 400 newspapers made their first ventures into print, most of them to sink almost instantly into oblivion. Such publications had editions running from as few as one hundred copies, to as many as five hundred, these generally being the practical limits of the hand presses then available.

The desire of the government to preserve secrecy in the conduct of its affairs was not without reason. The Tudor years had not been tranquil ones. Apart from the political and military involvements in Europe, there were many difficulties at home. A rising, merchant-backed, middle class was steadily eroding the autocracy of the central government in London, annexing to its control many local, domestic matters that had previously been Crown prerogatives, or under central control.

Resulting from the considerable inflow of Spanish gold to the European money markets, England suffered a more-or-less galloping inflation from 1580 to 1620, during which period the annual price rise was about 15 per cent.

With government centred in London, immediately proximate to the Royal Court, a comparatively limited number of people had any detailed knowledge of the full range of government affairs. Only the government had the physical and financial resources necessary to organise a flow of detailed information concerning matters generally in the country and elsewhere in Europe. It was, therefore, not difficult to control the dissemination of that information to the country at large.

The custom grew up for certain persons with access to the inner cabals of power to write long informative letters to notable persons in the provinces. These in turn would hand such letters round to a few chosen associates. In this way the authorities could ensure that a chosen few knew all that it was considered expedient for them to know.

Later, this letter-writing activity grew to the point that it became a kind of profession. Hangers-on of various sorts, took to putting together the overheard gossip of the better-class taverns, clubs, private gatherings, and larding these with whispers and rumours of government matters into news letters. These were copied by scribes and distributed to subscribers in the country towns and provincial centres. Yet, these never grew to the point where they caused the government any serious concern that their bastions of information were being breached.

Just as printing came to England from Europe, so now a new use of printing was introduced. For it is an odd fact that the first English newspapers – that is, papers printed in the English language – came not from England itself, but from Europe. It is possible that either Germany or Holland can claim that distinction.

The reason is clearly stated: in England the Crown claimed for itself the rights to publication of all English matters. To avoid treading on Royal toes, therefore, English papers were printed in Holland and, rather openly, smuggled into England. In order not to arouse too much official restraint, they concentrated exclusively on foreign news. This policy was to remain an escape route for editors – a way of avoiding entanglement in sensitive domestic issues – for some two hundred years.

The English Crown backed up its claim with a crude licensing system. Any printer rash enough to transgress by publishing matter without a licence was liable to arrest and imprisonment.

The Dutch newspapers, once inside the country, were widely distributed in geographical terms. But the number of literate people able to afford such an expensive luxury twice a month was not large.

Just as in wartime technical innovation receives a speeding shot in the arm, so in those turbulent times the growth of the newspaper industry was accelerated. As the Royalist position declined, and the gap between the King and Parliament grew wider and deeper, more and more people felt themselves impelled to know what was happening at a fundamentally more understandable level than that provided by meagre official sources. And, cynical though the view might be, bad times are invariably good times for newspapers. Indeed, many proprietors of papers were later to find that they flourished when the news was bad, and went out of business when there was no bad news to report. One of the first expedients of survivalism for journalists was to find acceptable forms of substitute bad news with which to hold their readership.

It is a paradox typical of the confusions to which the mid-seventeenth century was subject in Britain, that the Civil War, supposedly fought to break the absolute power of the Crown, and thus liberate ordinary people to the enjoyment of every manner of decent freedom, was fought by a Parliament that made of itself the repository of all those absolute powers that the King had previously claimed for himself. So far as the newspapermen were concerned the licensing arrangements under which they had been curtailed by the King were continued in just as restrictionist a form by the Parliamentarians.

However, whatever may be said and done under public scrutiny, politicians are essentially practical people. Although those who would write, print and publish newspapers were officially frowned upon in the early 1640s, privately many Members of Parliament found that they could be used to good purpose. Not only was it possible for particular members to put into public circulation views and news that were advantageous to their careers and causes, but a modest income could be made on the side at the same time.

Thus, a composite view of the life of a journalist then can be built up. Firstly, he would be a great one for hanging about useful places, including the Parliamentary precincts, where he could chat up useful and willing persons, picking up a mixture of rumour, gossip and hard news – the latter almost certainly from government sources and generally what the government wished to have released. In addition, he might have access to some confidential papers, letters, drafts, notes and other documents. From the foreign embassies in London there was a constant outflow of information of a confidential nature, gleaned by agents and paid informers. Some of this found its way into foreign newspapers, and copies of these came back to London to be (badly) translated and republished.

Once a week, he would gather this material together to produce four, eight or twelve poorly printed pages, lacking organisation, headings, headlines and most of the other attributes of the modern newspaper. In this role, he would now have put on his second hat, that of the editor. His writing, compilations and editing all now completed, he would turn his hand to yet a third task, that of printing the pages on a small, wooden hand press of a type that had barely changed from that introduced into the country by William Caxton two centuries earlier. Finally, with anything up to five hundred copies to sell, he would hand these over to hawkers and peddlers who would cry these wares through the narrow, crowded streets of London.

Monday was the normal day of publication because the mails left London on Tuesdays, allowing papers to be sent thereby all across the country.

It is clear, therefore, that while many papers were officially banned, such edicts were seldom prosecuted by the authorities with any severity. In practice, during the first years of the Civil War, the practical freedoms for editors grew, regardless of whatever regulations to control them might be introduced. Both the Royalist side and the Parliamentarians recognised the value of having access to effective organs of publicity and information, often making of these outright instruments of propaganda.

The political division of the country did not result in a geographical division of the kind found in Korea and Vietnam. Once the final breakdown had taken place, the King removed himself and his erstwhile Court to Oxford, while the Rump Parliament remained in London. Both created powerful press houses that were to set the foundations for modern partisan journalism. Indeed, the techniques of anti-Catholic reportage as practised by the London press of 1642 closely parallel those of anti-Communism used in the USA some three hundred years later. And, not only were the London papers widely available in Oxford, but those from the Royalist camp were fairly openly sold in London.[1]

---

[1] *Mercurius Civicus* – issue dated June 8/16, 1643.

'In my last weeks intelligence concerning Oxford occurrents, I related the devices which many Carriers had to releeve the Cavaleers and to convey things to them, which course it seems is not yet stopped: on Thursday last two carts full of several commodities were carried to Woodstocke, which were brought from London by severall Carriers: Also divers packs with Paper (for Mercurius Aulicus to vent his falsities and querks in) came into Oxford, which were brought from London by long Compton Carrier.'

Perhaps, to some degree, there was very little distinction between them. Because of official hostility, it was in any case difficult to sell papers openly on the streets of the capital. This hostility arose from typical confusions and muddlements. Whilst one bureaucratic department doggedly pursued the newspapermen according to the strict letter of the law, others blandly winked a blind eye in order to enjoy the benefits of publicity.

The first vendors were so-called news-boys – the term covered both men and women – who hawked their bundles of papers through the streets, dodging the prowling government agents. The published price of a paper was one penny, but the news-boys collected more than this whenever they could.

Those entrusted with the task of keeping the papers in check had a far from easy task on their hands. Apart from the difficulty of rounding up peddlers in the streets, the elusiveness of the editors made them a difficult mark to trap. Their hand presses might have been crude, they were also easily demountable. It needed but a few moments to break down and load a press with its founts of type onto a handcart. Any dark, dingy room was adequate for the purpose, and all that was needed, in addition, to put a newspaper into production was a modest supply of paper such as a man could carry himself, and a small quantity of ink. London's honeycomb of closely packed streets provided innumerable hiding places for such secret presses that could be moved every few days.

In the face of a range of daunting regulations, an almost entirely illicit publishing industry grew up, sometimes conforming to the licensing requirements, at others wilfully ignoring them. So that, by the early part of 1644, any prospective reader in London had a choice of some twelve regularly produced papers. He could indeed purchase a different paper every day of the week, except Sunday.

Monday	A Perfect Diurnall
	Certaine Informations
	Mercurius Aulicus (from Oxford)
Tuesday	The Kingdomes Weekly Intelligencer
Wednesday	The Weekly Account
	A Continuation of Certain Speciall and Remarkable Passages
Thursday	Mercurius Britanicus
	Mercurius Civicus
Friday	The Parliament Scout
	The Scotish Dove
	Occurrences of Certain Speciall and Remarkable Passages
Saturday	The True Informer

The men who founded, wrote, edited and published these early news sheets were noteworthy in their stubborn dedication to what must often have seemed the most hopeless of causes. Most official hands could be assumed to be turned against them. Even those who,

from time to time, favoured the press for various reasons were mercurial in their attachments, waxing hot one week and cold the next. Some editors were able to secure some measure of official approval and recognition, and to have their papers licensed week by week, as each issue appeared. But the confusions in government were such that even then an editor might unwittingly offend with some item, and find himself in jail anyway.

What provoked such dedication is hard to explain. It can hardly have been monetary gain, although most editors and publishers proclaimed themselves to be in the business of making a living by their activities. Yet the rewards from publishing newspapers were so meagre that few editors were able to lift themselves far above the poverty line. And into the early years of the nineteenth century it was customary for newspapermen to supplement their incomes by selling proprietary medicines, imported items of many kinds, by teaching and other enterprises.

Nor can it be suggested that such men sought to gain social status, political or social influence, since they were commonly regarded as little more than common rogues.

Fortunately for society, men who have it in mind to introduce new ideas are seldom put off by practical considerations. The excitements and challenges are reward enough: and they have also the belief, against all reasonable odds, that some ultimate recognition of their work and its value may be possible.

Some idea of the see-saw lives to which these first editors were subject can be given by a description of the careers of two men. With the King entrenched in Oxford, there appeared in that city, on the first day of the year 1643, the first issue of a paper calling itself The Oxford Diurnall. The following week, its second issue came out under a new title – The Mercurius Aulicus (i.e., The Court Mercury) – and thus it remained until its closure in September, 1645. Needless to say, the paper was pro-Royalist, and was published each week, in Oxford, on Sunday, thus publicly snubbing the Puritan belief in the sanctity of the Sabbath. However, Sunday publishing was not just a churlish taunt. It had the practical effect of allowing time for the paper to be transported to London, to be sold there on the Streets, on Monday.

The editor of the paper was John Birkenhead, an Oxford graduate, the son of a saddler. John Aubrey described him as 'exceedingly bold, confident, not very grateful to his benefactors; would lye damnably. He was of middling stature, great goggli eies, not of a sweet aspect.'

At the age of twenty-seven Birkenhead became the most formidable journalist in England, a past master at the craft of partisan journalism. His strategies of attack were boundless, his tactics of endless guile. A favoured technique was to draw threads of discord through the anti-Royalist ranks, exposing the natural disharmony that existed between the various factions, setting Parliament against London, contriving quarrels between Parliamentary generals, dividing the war party from the rest of the House of Commons, the Commons from the Lords, both of these from the commercial interests in the City, London from the rest of England, and England from Scotland. These dissensions may, to a degree, have originated as suppositions in Birkenhead's mind. But there was enough reality in them for the digs, gibes, taunts, and whispers of rumoured scandals to have a continuously disruptive and demoralising effect.

He innovated the atrocity story, ascribing all manner of horrible acts to the Parliamentary forces, which may well, for the most part, have been true. But acts which were in no way distinct from those performed by the Royalists, Birkenhead conveniently overlooked.

For the best part of that year, Birkenhead had things pretty much his own way. No London paper had a pen as forceful at its command. Then, in his thirty-fifth issue in September, Birkenhead referred briefly to the appearance of a new London weekly – 'All other Newes (I mean Lyes) you must expect from a fine new thing borne this week called Mercurius Britanicus. For Mercuries (like Committees) will beget one another.'

Birkenhead could have had little idea then of the strength of the journalistic adversary about to face up to him in print. His name was Marchamont Nedham. At first only an assistant editor, he soon took over control of the paper from Captain Thomas Audley. Four years younger than Birkenhead, Nedham was also an Oxford graduate, but with very strong pro-Parliamentary views. After a brief period as a teacher, he tried his hand as a law clerk, studied medicine (studies that were to support him in later life), and then found his way into journalism where he quickly gained a reputation for a sharp wit and a ready pen. Devoting most of his paper's space to countering Birkenhead's thrusts, *Britanicus* quickly became a best seller and, so far as that was ever possible, the darling of the Parliamentarians. By a curious paradox, as the battle of words between the two editors unfolded, and as each week the bite of one was matched and turned by the counter-bite of the other, *Aulicus's* sales in London also shot up to about five hundred copies a week – not bad going for a paper produced laboriously on hand presses, and which had then to be transported into enemy territory some sixty miles away.

As the Royalist cause weakened, so Birkenhead's tone became more strident, his literary devices less subtle, more blatant. Typical of his style in the summer of 1645, the last months of his paper, is this rather crude piece –

The Cathedral at Lincolne hath lately been prophaned by Cromwell's barbarous crew of Brownists: who have pulled down all the brave carved workes there ... and (for which all Christians will ever abhorre them) have filled each corner of that holy place with their own and horses dung ...

Nedham countered with –

But harke ye, thou mathematicall liar, that framest lies of all dimensions, long, broad and profound lies, and then playest the botcher, the quibling pricklouse every weeke in tacking and stitching them together; I tell thee thou art a knowne notorious odious forger: and though I will not say thou art (in thine owne language) the sonne of an Egyptian whore, yet all the world knowes thou art an underling pimpe to the whore of Babylon, and thy conscience an arrant prostitute for base ends.

Journalists have always enjoyed the opportunity to demonstrate their skill in the play of words, and it would be a mistake to assume that this bombast resulted from anything other than professional prowess. When the Royalist cause collapsed, it seems that Birkenhead came to London where Nedham helped him to revive *Mercurius Aulicus* in 1648 with introductions to useful Parliamentary contacts. In turn, when the Parliamentary regime came to an end twelve years later, Nedham was obliged to flee to Holland, where he languished for a few months, returning to England again under guarantees of amnesty negotiated, in part, by John Birkenhead, who by that time had been appointed by Charles II as his chief press censor.

Apart from the occasional pamphlet, Nedham never again turned his hand to writing, supporting himself to the end of his days by the practice of that knowledge of medicine which he had providentially gained earlier.

For those men running these seventeeth century London papers, the greatest editorial problem was undoubtedly trying to achieve an equable balance between readership interest and Parliamentary sanctions. There were many things going on in Parliament, or under governmental jurisdiction that an educated, literate public would want to know about. But to dare to publish them would spell disaster for the reckless editor who did so. Again and again the briefest hint of some important topic is concluded with the suggestion that it was not appropriate to write about such matters any more fully.

In such circumstances, editors were often faced with the problem of finding some way of filling their pages that would not contravene the censorship dictates and that would yet persuade readers to buy the paper. One way of solving the problem was to print extensive reports of European news. This had two advantages. Sometimes, matters that were of delicate concern in England, somehow found their way into the pages of Continental papers. When this happened, it was generally a safe defence for an editor here to print a verbatim translation, and to claim that he was merely reprinting what had already appeared elsewhere.

Secondly, such items directed readers' attention to events of great drama abroad that were capable of skilled journalistic expansion over a number of weeks. The opportunities for doing this were steadily improving. By the middle of the century, a trans-European post system was reasonably well established. Even in the depths of winter it took no longer than nine days for reports to travel from Rome to Paris, from whence they could be readily passed on to London. Commercial and political expansions were taking educated men to the most remote parts of the earth. For more than a century it had become the custom for such men to send back to England long reports of what they observed, these to be included in the early handwritten news letters. Now such men sent their reports back for publication in the newspapers. As a matter of interest, it seems that generally they received no payment for this service, but that they were usually glad enough to do it because a well balanced report could be advantageous to their careers.

Yet again, for a lonely man in a lonely place, one way of pressing for the support that he might feel he lacked from London was to describe the dangers he faced.

Such a report occupied almost all the space in an edition of the *Mercurius Civicus* in May 1645. It came 'from Virginy' and presented the longest report on American affairs yet to be published in England. It told of attacks on their homes, families and crops by the hostile Indians, and the measures they were taking to protect themselves. It concluded with this striking anecdote:

... I shall onely set down the words of the Letter comming from an honest and knowne hand in that Plantation, to a person of good repute in this City: Gods goodnesse hath beene lately very eminent in delivering me and my family from the Indian massacre. Upon the first day of April my wife was washing a bucket of clothes, and of a sudden her clothes were all besprinkled with blood from the first beginning to the rincing of them, at last in such abundance as if an hand should invisibly take handfuls of gore blood and throw it upon the linnen. When it lay all of an heape in the washing-tub, she sent for me in, and I tooke up one gobbet of blood as big as my fingers end, and stirring it in my hand it did not staine my fingers nor the linnen. Upon this miraculous premonition and warning from God, having some kinde of intimation of some designe of the Indians (though nothing appeared till that day), I provided for defence, and though we were but five men and mistrusted not any villany towards us before, yet we secured ourselves against 20 savages which were three houres that day about my house.

By the early weeks of 1646 the prospective newspaper buyer in London was faced with the conflicting and confusing claims on his attention of sixteen regularly produced weeklies in addition to the transitory appearance of many others whose life might be as brief as a single issue. The sheer physical production of all these must have placed a great strain on the resources of, not only the journalists and editors who compiled them, but also on the printers. And the already noisy streets must have been made yet more clamorous by the calls of the raucous news hawkers on every corner, calling their wares.

Although news from as far afield as China and Russia was regularly received in London, often there was not enough material of sufficient interest to capture the attention of readers. If, at the same time, there were particularly rigid restrictions as to what items of domestic concerns could be printed, editors were likely to find themselves caught in a tight clamp. If they risked not bringing out an edition in a difficult week, as some did, they risked losing their hold, ephemeral at the best of times, on their regular readership. Some actually flaunted their difficulties publicly by putting out issues in which there were one or more blank pages that could not be filled. But the buying public had little interest or sympathy to bestow on these problems, and were unwilling to pay money for incomplete papers.

It was these pressures that led some resourceful paper men to discover the appeal of the human interest story. Papers began to feature prominent crimes, omitting not a single one of all the most gruesome details. Matching these in prominence were sex crimes, or any affair that exploited the peccadilloes occurring between husbands and wives, men and women. A nice example is to be found in the pages of *The Kingdomes Weekly Intelligencer*. The report tells of –

... a Yeoman not farre from Warwick who for want of discretion or other discourse would sell his wife to his Companion. He asked what he would take for her. The Yeoman answered five pound. The other looking on her (for she was present) and conceiving with himselfe that a good wife is worth gold, he thought that she was worth five pound ... whereupon he presently layd down the money, and tooke his purchase in his Armes and kissed her. Not a quarter of an hour after, the Yeoman repented of his bargaine, and offered to restore the money, and desired to have his wife returned. His companion left it to her choyce, not without some intimation that he was loath to leave her. The good woman assured him that she was well content to live with him and had rather goe with the buyer than the seller, and accordingly expressing a courteous farewell to her Husband, she went along with his Companion.

The uncertainties of the news and of their position, the instability of those years of civil war, the fierce competition for readers, all contrived to press the more lively editors towards yet a further innovation. With so many constraints upon their earning capacity, other ways of exploiting the printed word were considered. One to make its first showing, during 1647, in the pages of the *Mercurius Civicus*, was the paid advertisement – in this case, a notice for the recovery of three stolen horses. The editor also made a few additional shillings each week by inserting paid items vindicating the activities of a particular individual or group – public relations in embryo.

One other journalistic device made its first showing in these years – the feature article. *The Moderate Intelligencer* published in 1648, as a report from Warsaw, what must surely be among the first items about flying.

There is at present in this (Polish) Court a certain man lately come from Arabia who is come hither to the King of Poland, to whom he proffereth his head for security of that which he propoundeth, which is that he hath brought from that Countrey the invention of a Machine, being Airie & of a construction so light, nevertheless so sound and firm, that the same is able to bear two men, and hold them up in the

Air, and one of them shall be able to sleep, the whiles the other maketh the Machine to move, which thing is much after the same manner as you see represented in the old Tapistry hangings . . .

With the ending of actual fighting the King fled abroad, and the Rump Parliament seeming likely to be well established, it could have been assumed that a regime dedicated to increasing and protecting the freedoms of men might have treated with the newspaper publishers more liberally. But this was not to be the case. The old licensing and censorship laws were continued. And as the Parliamentary cause steadily lost support throughout the country, the application of these steadily degenerated into chaos. Official censors, who might also be editors in their own right, often had no idea which issues Parliament would allow in print, and which they would not. Ludicrous positions arose in which such men were seemingly in conflict with themselves as well as their Parliamentary masters.

Furthermore, by contrivance and guile, so many counterfeit issues of established newspapers were coming onto the streets, that when material offensive to authority appeared, it was impossible to establish who had committed the crime.

While some papers escaped from these toils by limiting themselves exclusively to crimes or bawdiness, the more responsible editors pressed for the freedom to deal with key issues. These included:

The abolition of the House of Lords
The ending of traditional honours and payments
Decentralization of the judicial system
Elimination of class distinctions before the law
A more equitable redistribution of land
The ending of tithes
The ending of imprisonment for debt
The creation of a democratically elected Parliament
The rights of free speech

These were years of economic stagnation in England. Increasing financial stringency afflicted the newspapers ever further. *Perfect Occurrences* set up an advertising office in London to handle notices for insertion, at four pence each, about lands and goods for sale or lease, jobs offered and wanted, coach and shipping terms and timetables, and the sale of other commercial items of which proprietary medicines were an important element.

From September 1649 to September 1651 the London press was restricted and held down by the 'Act against Unlicensed and Scandalous Books and Pamphlets'. In various forms, this legislation continued until the collapse of the Cromwellian era in 1660. Nedham fled to Holland, and another former school teacher stepped into the journalistic arena—Henry Muddiman. More cautious and impersonal in style than Nedham, he was the first journalist to step carefully aboard the returning Royalist bandcart. In November 1660, Nedham's old adversary Birkenhead was made the appointed licenser or censor of what was left of the once ebullient weekly press. Muddiman was careful to toe the guidelines.

This circumspection paid off. Muddiman was attached to the office of Charles II's senior Secretary of State, placing him in a privileged position for access to official papers. From then onwards, the papers that he edited were marked 'Published By Order'.

Five years later Muddiman became the editor of what has proved to be the longest surviving newspaper in the world.

London Gazette and Lloyd's List

The oldest surviving London newspaper is today such a model of absolute rectitude that it is almost invisible. Indeed, to most English readers it is invisible, as they never see it and do not know it exists. The paper is the *London Gazette*. And it is salutary that such uprightness and moral certitude should have had such a sordid start in life.

It can be assumed that in a seventeenth-century newspaper, circumspection, caution and conformity were the natural consequences of suppression, persecution and tight control. With the ever-present risk of being clapped in jail should a word appear in print out of line with official policy, editors were more inclined to curb their pens.

But courage and a rush of words to the page are regular temptations in the lonely life of the writer, when physical threats seem remote and only the empty page is a challenge. And so, even the dying days of the London press before the Restoration had a certain vitality – vital enough to stimulate the Parliament to strive to put it down.

When General Monck was formulating his plans for the bloodless return of the King, he was clearly mindful of the advantages to be gained from a powerful, effective, popular press in favour of the Royal Cause. The man chosen to fill this role of spokesman for the revived Monarchy was Henry Muddiman.

At that time, in 1659, Muddiman had two papers, the most important of which was *The Parliamentary Intelligencer*.

The Long Parliament dissolved in March 1660. Monck's Council of State took over, pending the King's return from France. For his good offices, the King subsequently confirmed Muddiman's monopoly of the news – granting licences only to his two newspapers – and, in addition, gave him a job in the office of one of the senior Secretaries of State, Sir Edward Nicholas, a department that would now be considered a part of the Foreign Office. Furthermore, Muddiman was awarded – for life, as it turned out – free postage on both his incoming and outgoing mail. By this right, not only could he send whatever material he chose to any destination in the Kingdom, but any correspondent could also write to him without payment of postage.

This was an opportunity too great to be missed, and Muddiman took it. He continued to run his newspapers, but set up a further service of manuscript news letters for private subscribers, employing a team of copying clerks at his home at The Seven Stars in the Strand, and later at The Peacock.

Consider his position: by reason of his official appointment he had access to official documents. The Parliamentary proscriptions only applied to printed, and not hand-written, news sheets. Any items that he could not risk publishing in his papers, he could safely insert in the news letters. Moreover, he could organise a nationwide spread of contacts and regular correspondents who could send him their information through the post without cost. By this same right, Muddiman could despatch his news letters to subscribers, charging them five pounds a year, but not paying a pennyworth of postage for the service.

Exploring a new trend in his second newspaper, the *Mercurius Publicus*, he published, in May 1660, what is probably the first toothpaste advertisement. It seems oddly familiar – '... most excellent Dentifrice to scour and cleanse the teeth, making them white as Ivory: Preserves from the Toothach, fastens the Teeth, and sweetens the Breath, and preserves the Gums from Cankers and Imposthumes...'

In that wilderness beyond the protection of official patronage a few of the old journalists were still scrabbling for some way to support themselves by the exercise of their pens. Already, as the Commonwealth had begun to crumble towards collapse, certain specialised forms of newspaper had been tried. Samuel Peake, in the mid-1650s, had included reports of ship movements in his paper, and made a first attempt to produce a commercial/economic/financial business paper that would attract the custom of merchants and businessmen.

At the same time, the seventeenth century had seen the generation of many new writers who sought to augment their precarious income and their influence by journalism. These included John Dryden, Samuel Butler, Daniel Defoe, Joseph Addison and Richard Steele.

Muddiman was, therefore, poised – whether he knew it or not – on the brink of an explosive situation. The first dangerous shift under his feet came when the Printing Acts were reaffirmed in June 1662. The press licensing system was retained, and the Secretaries of State made responsible for controlling the publication of news.

Nicholas was an indolent, easy-going man with little taste for the minutiae of administration. As often happens, one of his subordinates, his Under-Secretary Joseph Williamson, had a great grasp of detail. He was a greedy, ambitious man, determined to extract from his position every opportunity for gain and advancement. And Muddiman, with all the profit he derived from his privileges and the influence he gained from his writing and publishing, stood four-squarely in his path.

Williamson's first move was an obvious one. Pre-empting the lackadaisical Nicholas, he made himself responsible for the licensing of Muddiman's newspapers. But the next move in his little game is not clear. Williamson was such a devious, secretive man that at this

Numb. 24.

The London Gazette.

Published by Authority.

From Thursday, February 1. to Monday, February 5. 1665.

Harwich, January 30.

THe Four Convoy ships from *Hamburgh*, (which were for some time missing) viz. The *Monke*, the *Amity*, the *Breda*, and the *Guift*, were concerned about Sunday noon, going to Anchor at *Oasley Bay*, where at present they remaine.

Dublin, Jan. 27. On Tuesday last the Court of *Claimes* sate, heard some motions, appointed daies of hearing several causes, and adjourned the Court till the 31 instant. Two Gaboards were sunck in this Harbour, and a Ship laden with Canary wines bulged, of which, it is feared, little can be recovered.

Kingsale, Jan. 23. On Saturday last here arrived 2 great Ships from the *Barbadoes*, the *Daniel* of *London*, Captain *Samuel Randall* Commander, of 12 Guns, and the *Adventure* of *London*, Capt. *Etherton* Commander, of 14 guns, the latter of which meeting with a *Flushinger*, killed and wounded 22 of them, as we are assured by several Vessels, and more particularly by that Ships Company, who (as you were lately told) regained their Vessel, after they had been in the power of this *Flushinger*. Five other *Barbadoes* Ships were in fight with a *Flushinger* of 36 guns, one of which was taken, and 4 escaped. A Ship of *London* from *Bermudas*, Capt. *Bargrave* Commander, and a Ship from the *Maderas* came in this day.

Marseilles, Jan. 19. The St. *Malo* Ships are now at *Toulon*, attending Monsieur *de Beauforts* Order for their departure, whose Fleet being intended to carrene, it is thought they will be disappointed of their Convoy, in regard they cannot be ready in a Moneth, and what course they will then take, most conceive is yet unresolved.

This day came in a Ship of this Town from *Alexandria*, in 25 daies, who adviseth, that the Grand Signor has stopt several Ships for his service to carry Men and Provisions for *Candia*.

Legorne, Jan. 16. On the 12 instant the *Tunis* Merchant arrive here, coming from *Algier* in 11 daies, who adviseth that an *Algier* Ship had burnt the *Charity* of *Hamburgh*, bound hither from *Archangel*, with 106 packs of Hides, &c. He saies farther, that the *Algier* Men had sunck a *Dunkerke* Fregot with 300 Souldiers coming from *Spaine* and *Naples*, and several Dutch and French. The Peace which the French have concluded with *Tunis*, is reported here with much dishonour to the French; and the Italians understand it so, the humor of *Tunis* being chiefly to follow Trade, in which they found themselves so much debarred, that they were in consultation to deliver up the French Captives gratis; and indeed they might have been brought to any termes, had the French not been so forward to patch up a Peace with them. Since *Genoa* made their Agreement with the Grand Signor for Traffique, they are endeavouring to make all forts of Cloth to send for *Smyrna* and *Constantinople*. The Grand Duke hath for some time been deteined by an Imposthume at *Florence*, from whence he is weekly expected, with the Court at *Pisa*.

Cleve, Jan. 26. Monsieur *Beverling* is arrived here, and Monsieur *Colbert* shortly expected, who brings with him a rich Furniture of a Chamber, as a present from the King of *France* to the Electress. *Beverling* has been offered as is reported, to be put into the States General for his life, and to be made Burgomaster of the Town of *Targo*, but excuses all upon pretence of his want of health to undergoe those employments; though it is suspected he hath other reasons for not mixing in the present Government.

Hamburgh, Jan. 13. The Swedes are now in earnest upon their march over the *Elve*, and the Country people

about us, though they have no cause for it, are so jealous of suffering from the Soldiery, that yesterday they sent into this City above 200 Waggons, laden with Houshold stuff for security. Some would have it that *Bremen* is not yet fully agreed, but they cannot but see the necessity of falling into the Swedes hands, if they should offer to oppose them. Some farther design, 'tis certain they have in hand, supposed to besiege *Embden*, and we have received from a very good hand, that the Swedes have sent to the Duke of *Lunenburgh* to consider well how he engages, or disposes of his Forces against the Prince of *Munster*, or in aid of the Hollanders. And surely there is something more then ordinary in it, at least, those of *Munster* apprehend it to 3 for in the Prince of *Munster's* Court, in their general Healths, 'tis observed, that, next to that of His Majesties of *Great Britain*, they remember the King of *Sweden's*, and then Gen. *Wrangels*.

Warsaw, Jan. 7. We are now again at a stand, to judge what will be the end of the affair with *Lubomirski*, who instead of sending his Plenipotentiaries to the Treaty, according to his promise, on the 15 of *December*, has in his Letter sollicited that the High Mareschal, the Master of the Horse, and the Referendaries of the Crown, might be sent as Commissioners to the Frontiers of *Silesia* to Treat with him: This Proposition is not accepted by His Majesty, but referred to the Lord Bishop of *Cracow*, who has all along treated with *Lubomirski*, to confer farther with him concerning it, according to the Declaration, published in *Rawa* and *Palczin*.

Rome, Jan. 16. In the Consistory held the 1r instant, his Holyness represented to the Cardinalls the great apprehensions he had, that Christendome would break out again into Warrs, and desired the assistance of their Prayers for preventing them. The Cardinal *Corrado*, the Datary, took the Popes chiding, you heard of, so much to heart, that he is now reduced almost to the last gaspe. Here are come to this Town a company of Ordinary Players, who acted a play Entituled *Scaramuccia soldato a Gigiri contro Mori*, which reflecting upon the Frenches late disgrace there, Monsieur de *Burlemont*, who acts here for the French King, complained to the Popes Nephew of this designed insolence and Nationall dishonour, as he called it; upon which the poor Players are laid by the heeles, which the Town takes very ill, as being in this time of Recreation denied the contentment of a peice of mirth, which was acted it seems at *Florence*, and other parts of *Italy*, with great applause. Here is in Town the Prince of *Baviere*, Brother to that Elector, the younger Brother of the Duke of *Longueville*, and a son of the Count of *Harcourt*, who came to see the curiosities of this City.

Durham, Jan. 27. Wednesday last was buried here Mr. *Anthony Pearson*, a man particularly noted in these parts, for having passed heretofore through all the degrees of Separation and Phanaticism, in all of which he was ever observed as a principal leader; but having lived to see his Error sometime before his death, he himself, with his children and family, had received Episcopal confirmation, and did now at last upon his Deathbed very solemnly confess his former Errors, and the party that first seduced him into them, declaring that he now dyed a true Son of the Church of England.

Falmouth, Jan. 27. A Vessel of about 80 Tuns arrived here from *Dublin*, bound with Tallow, Hides, and provision, for *Cadiz*, which proves so leaky, that she was forced to run ashoare here, and appears to be so unable to performe her voyage, that the Master will be obliged to sell Ship and Goods. Several of the Ministers, &c. of this County have made their subscriptions required by the late Act of Parliament. A 2

Smyrna,

Issue No. 24 is the first to appear under the title the 'London Gazette'. England did not adopt the Gregorian calendar until 1752. As a result, calendar dates were out of phase with the seasons. It was the custom, therefore, not to alter the numbering of the year until the end of March. Consequently, although the date shown is 1665, it is properly 1666. Three days after its publication, Muddiman resigned as editor.

distance it is difficult to follow the exact line of his schemes. For reasons that are not entirely clear, at some time between 1662 and 1663, Muddiman was replaced as the privileged journalist by Roger L'Estrange, a Cavalier whose past service to the Royal cause was now rewarded with this post. In fairness to Williamson, it may have had nothing to do with him. There may have been the feeling elsewhere in the administration that too much power and privilege was concentrated in the hands of one man. Muddiman does not seem to have done anything to offend anyone other than Williamson. And even after the change he still retained many of his previous perks.

To accommodate L'Estrange the post of Surveyor of the Press was especially created. Later he took over Muddiman's exclusive right to publish newspapers. Muddiman, however, continued to be attached to Nicholas's office, and to enjoy the rights of free postage. And as the patent granted to L'Estrange concerned printed news only, Muddiman was able to keep up the very profitable and influential circulation of hand-written news letters.

It was very galling to Williamson. He could find no way of budging Muddiman from his post in Nicholas's office, nor of moving in on the news letter business. When his direct approaches were rejected, Williamson employed a postal clerk named Hicks to scrutinise Muddiman's letters and so compile a list of his correspondents. But so long as Muddiman remained in London he was powerful enough to prevent Williamson from taking any effective action against him.

Williamson's opportunity came in 1665. In the summer of that year the plague raged through the narrow streets of London, and the Court removed itself to the untainted air of Oxford. As members of the official entourage, Muddiman and Williamson went also. L'Estrange remained in London where, bereft of official professional support, his editorial and journalistic incompetence were nakedly exposed.

On 15 October, Williamson sent him a nastily oily letter –

I am sorry the distance in which we are from you deprives me of the occasion of helping and directing you in the composing of the publick news as would be better for His Majesty's service and your own reputation. I have often advised you to agree with Mr Muddiman in this matter, who having had the good luck and opportunity of falling into the channel of these things would have been very useful to you and in despair of seeing this effected in the future I take the freedom to propose to you that if you will relinquish to me your whole right in the composing and profit of the newsbook I will procure for you in recompense of it a salary from his majesty of £100 per annum, which shall be paid through my hands...

L'Estrange squealed like a stuck pig, protesting volubly that his patent was worth at least £400. But his complaints fell on deadened ears, and in any case, his position was a weak one.

Meanwhile, in furtherance of his plans, Williamson enticed Muddiman to become the first editor of a new Oxford newspaper with the bait that, in sending it out, he would have the right to enclose also his own news letters. Muddiman might have seen his offer as a personal concession to him. He should have known better. Williamson never proposed anything lightly, and this was all an integral part of his larger scheme to unseat Muddiman from his profitable position.

Thus, on 16 November 1665 there appeared the first issue of this new bi-weekly entitled the *Oxford Gazette*, written by Henry Muddiman. A London edition was separately printed there. And this publication was, in effect, a direct challenge to L'Estrange's patent, in that no agreement had been made between him and Williamson. But as the new paper was published in Oxford, L'Estrange could not raise the matter as a clear issue. For Williamson could always claim that it came under the special exemption extended by Parliament to the University.

Muddiman, preserving his own rights, designed the *Oxford Gazette* to be the same size and shape as his news letters, so that the two could be posted together, thus extending, as it were, the range of his postal privileges.

When the plague abated, the Court returned to London. And, as a logical consequence, on Monday 5 February 1666, the *Oxford Gazette* became the *London Gazette*. Three days later, Muddiman got out, refusing to have anything further to do with it. It seems that some of Williamson's schemes were beginning to come to light.

Having made his offer of postal concessions to Muddiman, Williamson had bribed the same postal clerk named Hicks to supervise the franking of the combined newspaper/news letter mail and continue to compile a list of Muddiman's correspondents and subscribers. Every day these lists were sent directly to Williamson.

Muddiman, discovering this, resigned from the paper, and arranged for all his news letter correspondence to be re-routed via another department of the Secretary of State's office to which neither Hicks nor Williamson had access. Thereinafter, he confined his journalistic activities to the running of his news letter enterprise.

On Muddiman's resignation, which was undoubtedly a blow, Williamson tried to counter its effects by arranging for Hicks to send out a circular letter to all Muddiman's correspondents of which he had knowledge, stating that Muddiman was

...dismissed from the management of that correspondence he formerly was intrusted with for that he hath contrived and managed that correspondence to his own particular advantage and not for the service of his majestie and those persons of honour, as he ought and they expected he should have done.

While it was true that Muddiman used his postal privilege for the running of his private business, it would seem that he did so openly enough for the authorities to have stopped him if they wished to. Perks of this kind, as rewards for past and present service, were common enough then, and it can only be assumed that Muddiman's use of his privileges was considered legitimate according to the standards of those times. But, in any case, the claim that Muddiman had been dismissed was untrue.

A journalist of Muddiman's stamp and experience does not take an affront of that kind without retaliation. A few days later, on 24 February 1666, he issued a counter-blast in the form of a circular letter of his own.

Upon a misunderstanding between Mr Williamson and myself about the Gazette which I wrote at Oxon and till the last week in London I thought it most advisable to quit that office wholly and turn my correspondents to Sir William Morice, his Majesty's first principal secretary of State. I shall write as fully and constantly as formerly and with the same privilege and post free.

Urged on by Williamson, Hicks attempted to compile his own news letter, which forgery he attempted to pass as Muddiman's own work. When Muddiman exposed him, he drew up a petition claiming redress from Muddiman for the charge of being a forger. But he got nowhere with it.

Even worse, Hicks's debacle exposed Williamson's involvement. He was officially rebuffed, and Hicks silenced.

Muddiman was authorised to publish a second official paper in competition with the *London Gazette*, which he called the *Current Intelligence*. All that summer the rival papers jostled for pride of position. Then, in the first week of September came the Great Fire of London. Muddiman was burnt out. Williamson jumped in and took the opportunity of negotiating a settlement. And, having lost only one issue, the *London Gazette* reappeared again on Monday 10 September, with a notable scoop: an eyewitness account of the Great Fire. *Current Intelligence* was not seen again.

But Muddiman continued with the news letter which had gained an authority among an influential readership that the *Gazette* could not match. In a complaining letter to Williamson, Hicks reported – on 27 December 1667 – that twenty dozen fewer *Gazettes* had been sent out. People preferred the news letter and would only accept the *Gazette* as second best. Even though Williamson, by now knighted, stooped to the level of stealing Muddiman's news letters while they were in transit through the post, he was never able to damage it seriously, or to stop its distribution.

Not until 1692 when Muddiman died at his house in Coldhern, near Earl's Court (London), did the *Gazette* finally come into its own.

In his editorship of the *Oxford Gazette*, Muddiman had concentrated on two main categories of news: foreign reports and announcements of shipping movements. The tradition for these choices, stemming from

the Royal Prerogative, and the licensing system, has already been described. Additional to these, Muddiman included the weekly Bills of Mortality – listing all the causes of death in London for the preceding week (this gruesome morsel was later to become one of the staple items in the popular press), legal matters and reports of crime.

By means of his postal organisation, he was able to receive regular reports from a dozen English sea ports of the arrival and departure of trading vessels, captured prizes and other maritime matters. This reflected a preoccupation with trade that was to be turned to great journalistic advantage elsewhere.

With the lapsing of the Newspaper Licensing Act in 1695 a great stimulus was given to the appearance of many new papers. Yet, on the evidence of past experience, the writers and publishers of these felt inclined to advance with caution. Parliament was certainly turning no blind eye on their activities. A sharp distinction arose between those papers which featured 'news' – relatively uncoloured reports of events – and 'views' – which reflected, often strikingly, the desire of a new generation of editors to comment on the passage of affairs and so attract a coterie of like-minded readers to the support of their paper. Between these two extremes, other more specialised papers came into being to explore 'safe' areas of news coverage.

Towards the end of the seventeenth century Edward Lloyd was the proprietor of a coffee house in Lombard Street, London. It was the 'in' place for merchants of every kind. They came to Lloyd's Coffee House to meet colleagues, competitors, clients, to discuss and conduct their business. It became a centre for the sale of ships and wines, and an informal club for the City business set. Shrewdly judging what would be of useful service to his clients, Lloyd organised a private network of correspondents. These were mostly other coffee house owners in commercial or shipping centres who would send him regular reports which he posted as bulletins in his establishment. More and more, it became the custom for the leading merchants, ship owners, bankers and those with other financial interests to drift along to Lloyd's each day, to meet their cronies, browse through the newspapers, and to check for news of any enterprise in which they had a financial stake. About 1696 Lloyd began to publish these daily bulletins as a weekly news sheet under the title *Lloyd's News*. Oddly enough, it does not seem to have been a great success, and died out.

Increasingly, the clientele of the Coffee House consisted of those merchants who made a business of sharing proportions of marine risks. They would inscribe their names one under another at the bottom of a policy – and thus were dubbed 'underwriters'. After Edward Lloyd's death the Coffee House came into the hands of a succession of 'Masters', but no further development of the news sheet took place until Thomas Jemson took it over. He did all the spadework necessary to revive

Numb. 85.

The London Gazette.

Publiſhed by Authority.

From **Monday**, Septemb. 3. to **Monday**, Septemb. 10. 1666.

White-Hall, Sept. 8.

THe ordinary courſe of this Paper having been interrupted by a Sad and Lamentable Accident of Fire lately hapned in the City of *London*: It hath been thought fit for ſatisfying the minds of ſo many of His Majeſties good Subjects, who muſt needs be concerned for the Iſſue of ſo great an Accident, to give this ſhort, but true Accompt of it.

On the Second inſtant at One of the Clock in the Morning, there hapned to break out a Sad & Deplorable Fire, in *Pudding-Lane* near *New Fiſh-Street*, which falling out at that hour of the night, and in a quarter of the Town ſo cloſe built with wooden pitched houſes, ſpread it ſelf ſo far before day, and with ſuch diſtraction to the Inhabitants and Neighbours, that care was not taken for the timely preventing the farther diffuſion of it by pulling down houſes, as ought to have been; ſo that this lamentable Fire in a ſhort time became too big to be maſtered by any Engines or working neer it. It fell out moſt unhappily too, That a violent Eaſterly Wind fomented it, and kept it burning all that day, and the night following ſpreading it ſelf up to *Grace-Church-ſtreet*, and downwards from *Cannon-ſtreet* to the Water-ſide as far as the *Three Cranes in the Vintry*.

The People in all parts about it diſtracted by the vaſtneſs of it, and their particular care to carry away their Goods, many attempts were made to prevent the ſpreading of it, by pulling down Houſes, and making great Intervals, but all in vain, the Fire ſeiſing upon the Timber and Rubbiſh, and ſo continuing it ſelf, even through thoſe ſpaces, and raging in a bright Flame all Monday and Tueſday, notwithſtanding His Majeſties own, and His Royal Highneſs's indefatigable and perſonal pains to apply all poſſible remedies to prevent it, calling upon and helping the people with their Guards; and a great number of Nobility and Gentry unweariedly aſſiſting therein, for which they were requited with a thouſand bleſſings from the poor diſtreſſed people. By the favour of God the Wind ſlackned a little on Tueſday night, and the Flames meeting with Brick-buildings at the Temple, by little and little it was obſerved to loſe its force on that ſide; ſo that on Wedneſday morning we began to hope well, and his Royal Highneſs never diſpairing or ſlackning his Perſonal Care, wrought ſo well that day, aſſiſted in ſome parts by the Lords of the Council before and behind it, that a ſtop was put to it at the *Temple-Church*, neer *Holborn-Bridge*, *Pie-Corner*, *Alderſgate*, *Cripple-gate*, neer the lower end of *Coleman-ſtreet*, at the end of *Baſing-Hall-ſtreet*, by the *Poſtern*, at the upper end of *Biſhopſgate ſtreet*, and *Leaden-Hall-ſtreet*, at the *Standard* in *Cornhill*, at the Church in *Faw-Church-ſtreet*, neer *Clothworkers-hall* in *Mincing-Lane*, at the middle of *Milk-Lane*, and at the *Tower-Dock*.

On Thurſday by the bleſſing of God it was wholly beat down and extinguiſhed; but ſo as that Evening it unhappily burſt out again afreſh at the *Temple*, by the falling of ſome ſparks (as is ſuppoſed) upon a Pile of Wooden Buildings, but his Royal Highneſs, who watched there that whole night in Perſon, by the great Labours and Diligence uſed, and eſpecially by applying Powder to blow up the Houſes about it, before day moſt happily maſtered it.

Divers Strangers, *Dutch* and *French*, were, during the Fire, apprehended, upon ſuſpicion that they contributed miſchievouſly to it, who are all impriſoned, and Informa-

tions prepared to make a ſevere Inquiſition thereupon by my Lord Chief Juſtice *Keeling*, aſſiſted by ſome of the Lords of the Privy Council, and ſome principal Members of the City; notwithſtanding which ſuſpicions, the manner of the burning all along in a Train, and ſo blown forwards in all its way by ſtrong Winds, makes us conclude the whole was an effect of an unhappy chance, or to ſpeak better, the heavy hand of God upon us for our Sins, ſhewing us the terrour of his Judgment in thus raiſing the fire; and immediately after, his miraculous and never enough to be acknowledged Mercy, in putting a ſtop to it, when we were in the laſt deſpair, and that all attempts for the quenching it, however induſtriouſly purſued, ſeemed inſufficient. His Majeſty then ſat hourly in Council, and ever ſince hath continued making rounds about the City in all parts of it where the danger and miſchief was greateſt, till this Morning that he hath ſent his Grace the Duke of *Albemarle*, whom he hath called for to aſſiſt him in this great occaſion, to put his Happy and Succeſsful Hand to the finiſhing this memorable Deliverance.

About the *Tower*, the ſeaſonable Orders given for plucking down Houſes to ſecure the Magazins of Powder, was more eſpecially ſucceſsful, that Part being up the Wind, notwithſtanding which, it came almoſt to the very Gates of it, ſo as by this early proviſion, the ſeverall Stores of War lodged in the Tower were entirely ſaved: And we have further this infinite cauſe particularly to give God thanks that the fire did not happen in any of thoſe places where his Majeſties Naval Stores are kept, ſo as though it hath pleaſed God to viſit us with his own hand, he hath not, by disfurniſhing us with the means of carrying on the War, ſubjected us to our Enemies.

It muſt be obſerved, That this Fire happened in a part of the Town, where though the Commodities were not very rich, yet they were ſo bulky, that they could not well be removed, ſo that the Inhabitants of that part where it firſt began have ſuſtained very great loſs: But by the beſt Enquiry we can make, the other parts of the Town, where the Commodities were of greater value, took the Alarm ſo early, that they ſaved moſt of their Goods of value, which poſſibly may have diminiſhed the loſs; though ſome think, that if the whole induſtry of the Inhabitants had been applyed to the ſtopping of the Fire, and not to the ſaving of their particular Goods, the ſucceſs might have been much better, not only to the Publick, but to many of them in their own Particulars.

Through this ſad Accident it is eaſie to be imagined how many perſons were neceſſitated to remove themſelves and Goods into the open Fields, where they were forced to continue ſome time, which could not but work compaſſion in the beholders; but His Majeſties Care was moſt Signal in this occaſion, who, beſides his Perſonal Pains, was frequent in Conſulting all wayes for relieving thoſe diſtreſſed perſons, which produced ſo good effects aſwell by His Majeſties Proclamations, and the Orders iſſued to the Neighbour Juſtices of the Peace to encourage the ſending in Proviſions to the Markets, which are a publickly known, as by other Directions, that when His Majeſty, fearing leſt other Orders might not yet have been ſufficient, had Commanded the Victualler of his Navy to ſend Bread into *Moor-Fields* for the relief of the Poor, which for the more-ſpeedy ſupply, he ſent in Biskot out of the Sea Stores; it was found that the Markets had

been

the paper, but the first issue of *Lloyd's List* did not come out until 1734, several weeks after Jemson had died.

Those early issues were stark by modern standards. The earliest surviving copy, dated 2 January 1740, contains no text other than a bald announcement that 'this list which was formerly publish'd once a Week, will now continue to be publish'd every Tuesday and Friday . . .'. There follows the Exchange Rates for various European Ports, Aids in the Exchequer, Gold and Silver Prices, Annuities, Lottery payments, Prices of Stocks, and other commercial information. On the reverse side of the single sheet is the Marine List giving ship movements – arrivals and departures – for Gravesend, Leostoft (Lowestoft), Harwich, Leverpool, Bristol, Penzance, Falmouth, Dartmouth, Pool, Cowes (Isle of Wight), Southampton, Portsmouth, Dover and The Downs. It notes the prevailing winds for the previous three days (30 SW, 31 W, 1 NW) and ship movements at Dublin and Cork.

What is interesting to us now, in the more general context of the development of newspapers, distribution services, and postal facilities, is the time taken for reports to reach London. These are shown in the following table covering a thirty-year period from 1740 to 1771.

PORT	NUMBER OF DAYS TO REACH LONDON								
	1740	1747	1748	1749	1750	1768	1769	1770	1771
Appledore				5					
Bristol	2	3		2			3	4	3
Cork	12		11	11		10	11	11	9
Cowes	4	3	4	2	2	2	2	3	3
Dartmouth	3	4			3			6	5
Dover	2	3		1	1	1	1	2	1
Downs	1	1	1	1	1		2	1	1
Dublin			10	8			9	11	10
Falmouth	6	5	4	4	4	4	4	4	5
Glasgow				7					
Gravesend	1	1		same day	1	1	1	1	1
Leverpool					4				
Londonderry				8					
Milford		9		5					1C
Orkneys				22					
Plimouth		4	6	5	3	6			4
Pool	2	3		4	2	2	2	2	3
Portsmouth	3	4		2				1	1
Saltcombe									4
Southampton	3	3	3	2	1	4	2	1	2
Spithead				2			1		
Torbay									4
Waterford							12	11	11
Weymouth						3	2	3	

From 1742 onwards, with a tumult of events in Europe and on the high seas keeping merchants on the edges of their seats, it grew to be the practice that brief news items, mostly gleaned from captains returning from voyages, concerning English ships in distant and perilous places were reported in a crisp, laconic style:

Tuesday, 10 February, 1746. The Lovely Betty, Wane, from Jamaica for London, last from Plymouth, was taken off Beachy Head by a french Privateer; she was afterwards lost near Callais, but the People were sav'd.

Tuesday, 9 February, 1747. A French Ship, one of the Outward bound West India Fleet, is Taken by the Anne and

Numb. 8.

LLOYD's NEWS.

London, *September 17. 1696.*

SR.

Berbadoes, June 30. Capt. Barret Commander of a small Vessel carrying only 4 Guns and about 10 Men, having in his company 2 other small Vessels of little force, coming hither from New-England, met with a French Privateer (a Sloop) of about 50 Men off of this Island, who immediately came down upon Barret and discharged several Volleys of small shot at him, and forthwith boarded him : Barret retiring to his close Quarters kill'd them several Men, which obliged them to repair to their Sloop and unlash from him ; which done, Capt. Barret plied them with his great Guns and presently sank the Sloop down right : He hath brought 26 of the French Men Prisoners hither (most of which being wounded) 2 or 3 more were drowned, and the rest killed in fight; Capt. Sunderland Commander of one of the other small Vessels, before the Engagement, took 2 of his Men and went on board Capt. Barret, giving orders to the rest to make the best of their way, which they did ; he also fought bravely on board Capt. Barret, who lost not one Man in the Engagement.

Coronna, September 4. O.S. The French Ship Laden with Salt (mentioned in my last to be brought in by a Dutch Caper) was a Prize, first to the Macclesfield, Rising-Eagle, Tuscany, Prince George and Slaughter, Gallies ; who together Sail'd the 9th of August, for Torbay, and had besides her taken 3 other Prizes ; and to rid themselves of their Prisoners, gave them this Vessel to carry them whither they thought fit : but was afterwards taken again by the aforesaid Dutch Caper.

Edenburgh, September 8. This Day the Parliament met, pursuant to their Adjournment and his Grace the High Commissioner made a Speech to this effect, Declaring how forward His Majesty was to Expose His Royal Person for the Good of His Subjects ; rehearsing the Plots and Designs of His Enemies laid against Him ; and letting them know, That the Subsidies for carrying on the War which His Majesty was at present engaged fell short ; that there was Arrears due to the standing

Title page of 'Lloyd's News', issue No. 8, published by Edward Lloyd

Mary, Johnton, from Leverpool, for Tortola, and sent into Antigua – Soon after, the above Anne and Mary was Taken by a French Privateer, and sent into Martinico.

Friday, 9 February, 1749. The Two Brothers, West, with Corn for the Streights, put into Milford in a shattered Condition, having lost her Foremast, all her Head Sails, and narrowly miss'd being wreck'd on the Wolf. After she got in, with a Pilot on board, she was drove ashore, the Cargoe is much damag'd, and one Man was washed over board.

The Pike Gally, Green, of Pool from N. foundland for Leghorn, were taken by the Algerines, and Men put on board in order to carry them to Algiers; but a strong Gale of Wind at East springing up near Cape de Gatt, the Captains with the Remainder of their Crews left on board, overpower'd the Turks, and carried both their Vessels to Gibraltar.

By 1769 the standing of the original establishment had seriously declined, and New Lloyd's Coffee House – under new ownership – opened in Pope's Head Alley on 21 March, attracting to its doors a majority of the leading merchants, brokers and underwriters. A *New Lloyd's List* was started, and for several years the Old and the

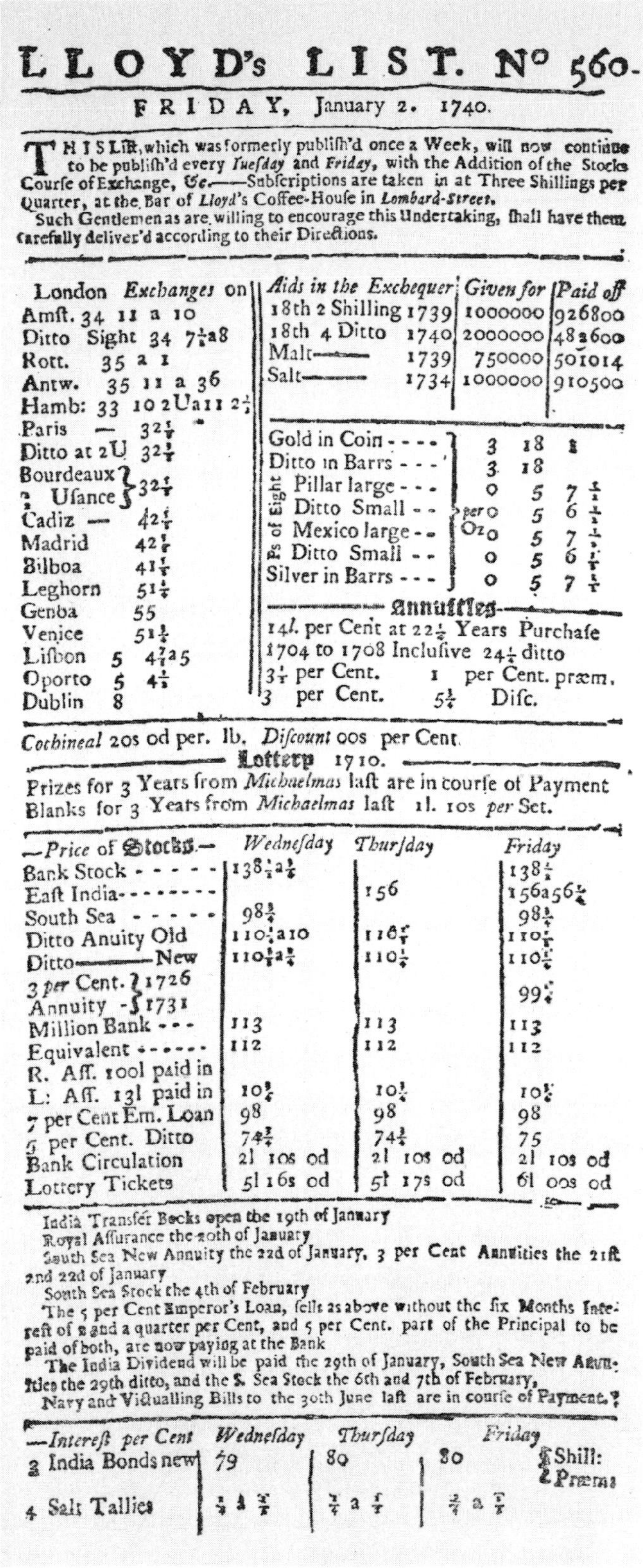

LLOYD's LIST. N° 560.

FRIDAY, January 2. 1740.

THIS List, which was formerly publish'd once a Week, will now continue to be publish'd every *Tuesday* and *Friday*, with the Addition of the Stocks Course of Exchange, &c.——Subscriptions are taken in at Three Shillings per Quarter, at the Bar of *Lloyd's* Coffee-House in *Lombard-Street*.

Such Gentlemen as are willing to encourage this Undertaking, shall have them carefully deliver'd according to their Directions.

London *Exchanges* on	
Amst.	34 11 a 10
Ditto Sight	34 7½a8
Rott.	35 a 1
Antw.	35 11 a 36
Hamb:	33 10 2Ua11 2½
Paris —	32½
Ditto at 2U	32½
Bourdeaux 2 Usance	32½
Cadiz —	42½
Madrid	42½
Bilboa	41½
Leghorn	51¼
Genoa	55
Venice	51¼
Lisbon	5 4⅞a5
Oporto	5 4½
Dublin	8

Aids in the Exchequer		*Given for*	*Paid off*
18th 2 Shilling	1739	1000000	926800
18th 4 Ditto	1740	2000000	482600
Malt——	1739	750000	501014
Salt——	1734	1000000	910500

Gold in Coin - - -	3	18	1
Ditto in Barrs - - -	3	18	
Ps of Eight Pillar large - - -	0	5	7½
Ditto Small - - per Oz	0	5	6½
Mexico large - -	0	5	7½
Ditto Small - -	0	5	6½
Silver in Barrs - - -	0	5	7½

Annuities

14*l*. per Cent at 22½ Years Purchase
1704 to 1708 Inclusive 24½ ditto
3½ per Cent. 1 per Cent. præm.
3 per Cent. 5¼ Disc.

Cochineal 20s 0d per. lb. *Discount* 00s per Cent.

Lottery 1710.

Prizes for 3 Years from *Michaelmas* last are in course of Payment
Blanks for 3 Years from *Michaelmas* last 1l. 10s *per* Set.

—*Price of* Stocks.—	*Wednesday*	*Thursday*	*Friday*
Bank Stock - - - - -	138½a¼		138½
East India- - - - - - -		156	156a56¼
South Sea - - - - -	98¾		98¾
Ditto Anuity Old	110½a10	110½	110½
Ditto——New	110⅛a¾	110½	110½
3 *per* Cent. Annuity 1726 1731			99¾
Million Bank - - -	113	113	113
Equivalent - - - - -	112	112	112
R. Aff. 100l paid in			
L: Aff. 13l paid in	10¾	10¼	10¾
7 per Cent Em. Loan	98	98	98
5 per Cent. Ditto	74¾	74¼	75
Bank Circulation	2l 10s 0d	2l 10s 0d	2l 10s 0d
Lottery Tickets	5l 16s 0d	5l 17s 0d	6l 00s 0d

India Transfer Books open the 19th of January
Royal Assurance the 20th of January
South Sea New Annuity the 22d of January, 3 per Cent Annuities the 21st and 22d of January
South Sea Stock the 4th of February
The 5 per Cent Emperor's Loan, sells as above without the six Months Interest of 2 and a quarter per Cent, and 5 per Cent. part of the Principal to be paid of both, are now paying at the Bank
The India Dividend will be paid the 29th of January, South Sea New Annuities the 29th ditto, and the S. Sea Stock the 6th and 7th of February,
Navy and Victualling Bills to the 30th June last are in course of Payment.

—*Interest per Cent*	*Wednesday*	*Thursday*	*Friday*	
3 India Bonds new	79	80	80	Shill: Præm:
4 Salt Tallies	½ a ¾	¼ a ½	¼ a ¾	

Title page of the oldest surviving copy of 'Lloyd's List'

New ran side by side, until the newer version drove the older one to the wall.

The competition between the two papers sparked off a rapid multiplication of overseas correspondents, so that by 1771, in addition to domestic reports, the paper carried records of sightings and ship movements from Smyrna, Nice, Alicant, St. Andero, Barcelona, Cadiz, St. Lucas, Malaga, Seville, St. Sebasstians, Amsterdam, Rotterdam, Elbe, Hamburgh, Konigsberg, Habredegrace, Honfleur, Rochelle, Rouen, St. Vincents, Ostend, Barbadoes, St. Christophers, Dominica, Tobago, New-York, Rhode Island, Philadelphia and Senegal.

The ending of the licensing control of newspapers coincided with a great uprising of writing talent that found its way into journalism. Daniel Defoe founded the *Review* in 1704, and was also a prolific contributor to other papers. Milton both wrote for and licensed papers. Dryden and Bunyan wrote for the press, as did Swift and Pope. But without doubt, the two most fertile writers were Joseph Addison and Richard Steele.

In the strictest sense, neither of them were journalists. They did not grub about for news stories, hovering in the extremities of favoured places where the latest rumours, scandals, and hints as to forthcoming Government policy were likely to be bandied injudiciously about. Their forte was the social and/or political essay, an experimental trial or testing of an argument in a public setting – a form of newspaper literature today preserved in the leading article or editorial.

Addison and Steele were born in the same year – 1672 – and their inclusion in these pages can be justified by a summary of their careers and influences. The two boys met first, at the age of twelve, at Charterhouse School. They do not seem to have made any striking impression on each other, for seemingly no attempt was made to keep in touch.

For those with a flair for writing the opportunities must have seemed more prime then than at any time previously. Many new publications were springing up. The first English daily paper – *The Daily Courant* – was started in 1703. For the rest, the old leisurely pace of weekly issues had been accelerated to three a week. By 1709 eighteen papers were being published regularly in London:

Daily	*The Daily Courant*
Monday, Wednesday and Friday	*The Supplement*
	The British Apollo
	The General Remark
	The Female Tatler
	The General Postscript
Wednesday only	*The Observator*
Tuesday, Thursday and Saturday	*The London Gazette*
	The Post Man
	The Postboy
	The Flying Post
	The Review
	The Tatler
	The Rehearsal
	The Evening Post
	The Whisperer
	The Postboy Junior
	The City Intelligencer

This then was the sea of opportunity upon which Captain Steele, not long out of the Army, sought to cast himself at the age of 35. The opportunity came his way to become the Gazeteer, that is, the editor of the official paper, the *London Gazette*. At that time he had a few plays to his credit and what the diarist Hearne describes as 'several romantic things'. By comparison with other papers, since the ending of licensing and therefore the loss of its monopoly of news, the *London Gazette* had been selling very badly. Steele was brought in to brighten the paper's image and make it more competitive. Typically, the authorities were not prepared to allow him the freedom of control that would enable him to do this. He was hedged in by every kind of restriction and stipulation. His overlord in this operation was Lord Sunderland, one of the Secretaries of State. And who should happen to be most usefully placed in Sunderland's department, as an under-secretary, but Joseph Addison – his schoolboy companion.

Addison was a cold, rather calculating kind of genius – Steele the exact opposite, warm, spontaneous, erratic, and a genius of a different kind. It would seem, therefore, that Steele made the first approach. Addison made himself responsible for guiding Steele in the selection of news that could be safely published in the *Gazette* without arousing official displeasure. Naturally, many matters came to Steele's attention that could not be published in the official organ. To provide himself with an outlet for these, he started *The Tatler* in 1709, running the two papers in tandem. Possibly in an attempt to make his implied affront to authority less conspicuous, Steele chose to write a 'views' rather than 'news' paper. By writing essays and critiques of a social and political character Steele could control his form more completely, make it a more personal vehicle for the opinions that generated within him as a result of being subliminally exposed to official peccadilloes. And he invited Addison to join him in the enterprise.

Addison's motives for doing so are interesting. He was an ambitious man, securely and advantageously placed. Whilst he undoubtedly had a thirst for words, he was careful enough not to expose himself too vulnerably to the invitation Steele extended. During the following two years Steele wrote 188 of the 271 issues of the paper, Addison wrote a mere 41, the remainder being contributed by a variety of writers.

In 1710 Steele was dismissed from the *Gazette* – not for anything which he had allowed to appear in its pages – but because of an incautiously critical article that he had published in *The Tatler*. And in January 1711 that paper also came to an end.

Steele was certainly an enthusiastic and persuasive man, for two months later he had talked Addison into joining him full time on another venture – *The Spectator*. The two men wrote like beavers, and this time the newcomer outwrote his senior. The paper ran from March 1711 to December 1712. In that period 555 issues came out – virtually it was a daily paper. 236 came from

Steele's pen and 274 from that of Addison. As Steele ruefully wrote in later life of his partner – 'I fared like a distressed prince, who calls in a powerful neighbour to his aid; I was undone by my auxiliary; when I had once called him in, I could not subsist without dependence on him.'

Following the closure of *The Spectator*, Steele went on to publish *The Guardian* (1713), *The Englishman* (1713), *The Lover* (1714), *The Reader* (1714), and a number of lesser known works – *Town Talk, Tea Table, Chit Chat, Plebian* and *Theatre*.

Despite the nominal relaxation of press control, any idea that Parliament had relinquished what it regarded as its essential right in this regard was a false one. Various other enactments – such as the Stamp Act, to which I will return in the next chapter – made it abundantly clear that the Establishment was firmly entrenched behind sanctions of intransigent severity to be applied against journalists who published unacceptable material. The most striking case of a writer who fell foul of these was John Wilkes who, in issue No. 45 of the *North Briton* published in 1763, commented adversely on the King's Speech to Parliament. He was arrested and placed in the Tower. On application to Chief Justice Pratt he was released, it being ruled that his prosecution was illegal. That omission was speedily remedied at the next meeting of Parliament when a special Bill was passed to sanction his prosecution. In addition, in 1764, Wilkes – who was himself an M.P. – was expelled from the House of Commons.

This had no immediate effect as, by then, Wilkes had prudently removed himself to France, and as he did not appear for sentencing at his trial, he was outlawed. Four years later, assuming the storm to have abated, Wilkes returned to England to take part in the General Election of 1768, and was duly returned by his faithful constituents as the Member for Middlesex. But Parliament has a long memory. When he tried to take his seat in the House, he was expelled, arrested and imprisoned. Three times Wilkes was re-elected to the same constituency, but the House persisted in keeping him out. Great public agitation was focused on the slogan 'Wilkes and Liberty', and he was finally released from prison in 1770, having already been elected an alderman of London. He was next appointed Sheriff of Middlesex, elected Lord Mayor of London, and became again the Member for Middlesex in 1774. This time he was allowed to take his seat – and his story virtually comes to an end in 1782 when the resolutions respecting the disputed Middlesex elections were formally expunged from the Journals of the House of Commons.

It is against this kind of background that one must view the activities of newspaper men during those years. There was no official encouragement for those seeking to create a vital and radical press. Yet, there was much public support, and provided the challenges to authority were not too blatant it is instructive how far a disciplined and well commanded pen might go. Specialisation proved to be a valuable screen behind which every kind of critical faculty might find expression so long as it was suitably, chastely and discreetly veiled.

The rise of London as a mercantile, commercial, financial centre, the growth of the coffee house trade and the success of papers such as *Lloyd's List* were not to be overlooked.

John Newbery, the scion of a publishing house going back to 1563 (and of whom we shall hear more later) joined forces with William Bristow and William Faden to found a new commercial paper in 1760. It was called *The Public Ledger*.

Editorial policy recognised the growing cultural sophistication of the merchant classes. The paper set out to serve these by combining accurate market information with articles of a high literary standard. Among the first contributors, especially commissioned by Newbery to write for the paper, was a young Oliver Goldsmith, whose writings in the paper formed the basis for his later 'Citizen of the World' series. Laurence Sterne's Tristram Shandy appeared in its columns for the first time. Later, William Makepeace Thackeray was its Paris correspondent.

Perhaps the first literary record of the paper is to be found in James Boswell's *London Journal* where – convalescent in his lodgings, he wrote on 9 February 1763 –

My landlord took a great anxiety that I should read the news, thought it would divert me much, and begged me to take in one of the papers. I expressed my fondness for his scheme, but said I did not choose to be at the expense of it. So I put it off. However, his anxiety was so great that he made a bold push at the Office, where a number of papers are taken in, and regularly every day does he bring home The Public Ledger, which is most duly served up to me. I joked with him and said, 'You see, Sir, when I put you to your shifts what you can do.'

Of all the great outflood of newsprint in the seventeenth and eighteenth centuries, the *London Gazette*, *Lloyd's List* and *The Public Ledger* – one the official journal of the Crown, and the other two papers serving business interests – are today the oldest and only surviving papers in London.

Still, in the 'Casualties' page in *Lloyd's List* – covering marine, weather and navigation, fire and explosion, and aircraft disasters around the world, there is preserved that same casual, offhand, unemotional style born more than two and a half centuries earlier.

Monday, July 21, 1975 – RECLEZ (yacht) British. Niton Radio, July 19 – Following received on 2,182 kHz at 1345 GMT: 'Mayday (distress signal), this is yacht Reckless (? Reclez), dense smoke, no flames, position 30 miles from shore on course 189 deg Cherbourg for Needles.' No further communication with vessel, broadcast action being taken. Following received from motor vessel PERTINENCE (Eristano for Boston, Lincs): At 1440, GMT: About six miles from distress area and proceeding to investigate. Estimate time of arrival 30 minutes. Visibility three and a half miles. At 1450, GMT: Sighted dense smoke in approximate position lat 50 08N, long 01 46W. We are three miles from this position but have engine trouble and cannot proceed. There is a large vessel in vicinity of smoke. Following received from motor vessel Cabo San Roque at 1516, GMT: Motor vessel Sauzon, FOQD, embarked survivors. Proceeding on voyage. Vessel is still burning fiercely. Following received from PERTINENCE at 1530, GMT: Yacht has just sunk in approximate position lat 50 08N, long 01 46W. Following received from Boulogne Radio: At 1531, GMT: Following received from Sauzon: Bound now for Cherbourg with English survivors on board. At 1555, GMT: Estimated time of arrival Cherbourg 1800 hours with crew of Reckless (? Reclez). Needles, July 19 – Poole lifeboat and Search and Rescue helicopter from Lee-on-Solent returning to base after proceeding to yacht Reckless (? Reclez), on fire 30 miles SSW of Needles. All survivors picked up by French motor vessel Sauzon, which is now bound Cherbourg – Coastguard. Cherbourg, July 19 – Three people and two children who were on board British registered yacht Reclez, which sank near here, were brought back safely to Cherbourg by motor vessel Sauzon, port authorities said tonight. The Reclez, owned by M. Jacob Zelcer, a Belgian living in London, caught fire and sank almost immediately some 30 nautical miles off Cherbourg. M. Zelcer, his wife, their two children and a friend escaped in a rubber dinghy and were later sighted by a British Navy helicopter. – Reuter. Cherbourg, July 20 – British yacht Reclez sank pm, July 19, further to fire in position lat 50 08N, long 01 46W. Five crew members recovered safe and taken ashore at Cherbourg at 1830, July 19, from motor vessel Sauzon.

Numb. 267. *Worcester-Arms.*

THE
WORCESTER
Post-Man:

Semper Fidelis.

CONTAINING

The Heads of all the Remarkable Occurrences, both Forcign and Domeslick.

From *Friday,* July 30, to *Friday,* August 6, 1714.

From the News-Letter and other Intelligence.
Saturday's and Monday's Post.
Two Foreign Mails bring us the following Advices.
Rome, July 14.

WE are advis'd from Marcho, that there has been a Hail there of an extraordinary Bigness, some of the Hail-Stones weighing 3 Pounds: It has done great Damage in the Fields and kill'd several *Men* and *Beasts.* Last Monday a great Tempest happen'd at Frascati, where the Thunder falling, kill'd a Capuchin as he was discoursing, at a Window, with the Ambassador of Malta; the Ambassador himself seem'd to be struck dead, and continu'd 2 Hours without any Motion, and one of his Domesticks was kill'd with the same Blow.

Milan, July 21. The Mortality begins to rage again, and make great Havock among the Cattle in these Parts and in Piedmont, which added to the continual Rains, that have spoil'd the Fruits of the Ground, have reduced this Part of *Italy* to great Misery.

Baden, July 24. The Imperial and French Plenipotentiaries have held their 28th Conference, touching the Affairs of Cologn and Bavaria, and those of Lorrain. The Ministers of France have signify'd to those of the Protestant Princes, that they must not hope for the Abolition of the 4th Article of the Treaty of Ryswick, nor the least Modification thereof, it having been confirm'd by the 3d Article of the Treaty of Rastad.

London, July 29. We have advice from Genoa, That Sir James Wisheart who was at Port Mahon with his *Squadron* is sailed for Algiers to renew the Peace, and demand Satisfaction for the
English

Birth of the Provincial Press

The relentless attack on press freedom by the Government in seventeenth-century England was of a quality that if brought into operation today would merit a description in very ugly terms. It could be compared with the measures used by authoritarian regimes now. Agents were employed to infiltrate the ranks of journalists and printers and provoke outbursts of disaffection. These, finding their way into print, led to instant imprisonment.

The night-time arrest, with its brutish and brutal overtones, was commonly employed, and is vividly described by Thomas Gent, printer and publisher from York. Laid low with a fever, he had taken a hot cordial one night and retired to his bed. Between one and two o'clock in the morning he was awakened by heavy knocking at his front door.

I asked who was there, and what they would have? They answered they must and would come in; and without assigning any other reason, they violently burst open the door. Being undrest, and all over in a sweat, in miserable pain, I looked in a woeful condition; when Mr Crawford, one of the King's Messengers, took hold of my hands, and seized a pretty pistol that lay near me, a pair of which I had procured, from Holland, as a defence against thieves or housebreakers, which was never after returned me; but the insolence of Kent, his companion. I could scarce bear, when, helping on my clothes, he went to search my pockets for what written papers he could find therein. I called him a blockhead, and told him, had I been in another condition, I might, perhaps, have laid him by the heels; at which he scornfully said, he never should fear a ghost, intimating that I seemed little better than a spirit at this time.

No evidence could be offered by the prosecuting authorities against Gent, and he had to be released from Newgate Prison. This was a common device. By unjustified arrests of this kind made on the basis of vague, unsupported allegations, the authorities could have newspaper men in and out of prison. The cost of this, of paying for food and other necessaries in prison, of securing the services of lawyers to obtain a release, and the loss of income whilst in prison were just as effective in bringing many of them to their knees as any warrantable prosecutions.

The broad basis of official hostility towards the press was the appearance in print of any critical or injudicious comment that happened to be out of harmony with the administration's thinking at that moment: this was interpreted as the publication of a libel against the State and Crown. In later years (as in the case of John Wilkes) most of the arrest and prosecution procedures used by the authorities against presumed offenders had no basis in law.

Other government agents were employed to purchase copies of any publication, including newspapers, that seemed to them of a scandalous or seditious nature. When these arrived at the offices of the Secretaries of State, with the offending passages carefully marked, the arrest of the printer, publisher or author, whenever their identity could be established, generally followed, regardless whether the issue of a warrant on his basis was legal or not.

London papers were beginning to find a market in the provinces. The only effective way in which they could be distributed was through the post. And so postal clerks were paid to remove secretly from the mails any papers they deemed offensive, and to replace them with others favourable to the governmental cause. In later years, the authorities bought up, or heavily subsidised, antagonistic papers, so that their hostility was thereby muted. This forced the competing critical papers to operate under a severe financial disadvantage.

Whilst these conflicts were waging in London, the rest of the nation was not inert and inactive. Many provincial centres were expanding into thriving communities. With so much hostility towards them at the hub of national life, there was a natural encouragement for printers to move out towards the rim. Particularly, as in London, printers had less and less command of the papers they printed, this now being dictated by the proprietors. But in any real or illegal prosecution, the printers, being the best known and the only individuals with an actual establishment, were the most vulnerable. Often, they were hounded for material which they had printed but did not control.

As printers moved away from London, so apprentices moved in. Any smart young man seeking a career in the printing trade must virtually obtain an apprenticeship in the capital, before he could return to his own shires and establish himself there. After about a century of discord in London, then, the doors slowly opened on the first thrusting sheets of a provincial press. Many were founded and failed, a few survive to this day, and it is through them that I intend to sketch in the history of the rest.

But first we have yet to examine one further weapon in the Government's armoury of assault against the expansion of the press. This was the notorious Stamp Act of 1712 – the first of a series of enactments extending over some one hundred and forty years, and known collectively as the 'taxes on knowledge'. Ironically, to begin with, it was not especially at the popular newspaper that the Stamp Act was aimed, but at the political pamphlet. Yet it was the newspapers that were the most seriously affected.

By the original legislation, pamphlets were required

to pay a tax of two shillings per page on each complete edition. Under the same Act, 'newspapers, or papers containing public news, intelligences or occurences' had imposed on them a half-penny tax on every copy printed on paper of half-sheet size, and a penny on every copy printed on paper 'larger than half a sheet, and not exceeding one whole sheet'.

This meant, in practice, that a newspaper had to pay a duty on each copy, whilst the pamphlets only had to pay a charge per edition.

The effects of the tax were severe. By the end of 1712 about seventy country papers had ceased publication. This rot continued until some ingenious mind found an escape door in the legislation. The wording therein seemed to imply that newspapers were periodicals printed on either a half or full sheet. No larger size was specifically mentioned. Printers drew from that the implication that anything bigger was not a newspaper, and therefore paid tax at the lower pamphlet rate. By this interpretation, while a half sheet paper – folded to form two pages of print – could be charged twelve shillings and six pence on 300 copies, and a full sheet paper – folded to form four pages of print – could be charged twenty-five shillings, the large one and a half sheet paper or 'pamphlet' was only liable to pay three shillings on an entire edition of whatever size. This difference more than made up for the increased cost of paper and printing.

Many newspapers thereby adopted this new format – six pages which when printed on both sides gave twelve pages of reading matter. Not for thirteen years was this escape route closed. But in 1725 a new Stamp Act made it clear that the duty was $\frac{1}{2}$d for every half sheet on which the paper was printed. The ingenuity of the newspaper men was not yet exhausted. For the new Act had omitted to define the size of a sheet. Nothing prevented the printers buying much larger sheets of paper, slicing them in half to produce the broadsheet paper that was still, within the Act, only chargeable at the $\frac{1}{2}$d rate, and yet contained as much material as a paper three times that size in the old format.

The printing trade, however, accepted this new burden with such comparative equanimity that it is clear other, more weighty considerations, were beginning to bear on them. The 1720s were tranquil years compared with those that had gone before. Events, both at home and abroad, had for the time being settled into a more quiet run. There was a distinct absence of hard news of high drama by which the popular press prospers. So, of greater concern to the newspaper publishers than the impositions of the Stamp Act, grave though these were, was the more fundamental problem of finding material with which to fill their pages, issue after issue. Many remedies were tried. They included long editorials, the printing of books and novels as part works (this was also used as a tax dodge), and the reporting of non-political, soft news matters, such as crime, sex offences and other scandals. The number of advertisements was greatly in-

Newspaper Revenue Stamps

creased. And gradually these adaptations and innovations moulded the form of the newspaper as we now have it.

By the late 1730s the problem reversed itself. These new items had claimed the attention of a new readership, and occupied so much space in the papers that when the turn of events became more lively, the alternatives to hard news could not be removed and papers were once again hard pressed for space.

The average page size crept up, step by step, 18 inches by 12 inches in 1730, until by 1757 it had spread out to 22 inches by 16½ inches. To gain even more news room, the size of type face used had been steadily reduced in order to cram more onto each page. When a new Stamp Act of 1757 raised the tax even higher to a penny per paper regardless of size, pages grew even larger, and print smaller. Readers of the Newcastle Journal protested at 'the Injury thereby done to the Sight, and of the Difficulty they find in reading so minute a Character'.

Needing money to pay for the American War of Independence, Lord North pushed up the tax again to 1½d in 1776. William Pitt considered the Newspaper Duty a luxury tax and upped it to two pence in 1789. The war with France forced it up to 3½d in 1797. It became four pence in 1815: but that was the peak. Twenty-one years later the force of public opinion was so strong that the tax had to be drastically reduced to 1d, and was finally abolished in 1855.

These were not the only fiscal measures that, by tradition and custom, came to be applied against the newspaper trade. In addition to a paper duty, there was also a tax of one shilling on each advertisement, rising to two shillings, and to a maximum figure of three shillings and six pence, before it was removed in 1853.

These general, and very much summarised circumstances, formed the backcloth to the growth of an active provincial press. In the early years of the seventeenth century those few pioneers who began to publish papers in the country towns could do so on the simplest 'scissors-and-paste' basis. Arrangements were made by a local printer for a selection of the most notable papers from London and abroad to be sent to him directly through the post. On arrival, these he would hastily scan for suitable news items. A selection of these would be printed verbatim, acknowledging the source – by this means the printer sought to evade responsibility and possible prosecution for any item he might print that should cause offence to private individuals or to officialdom. And, by and large, this proved to be a workable evasion. The authorities found it, on the whole, less costly and time-consuming, to lock away the original London publisher and thus cut off the supply of offensive news at source.

One of the first of the provincial papers to be founded, and certainly, the longest surviving paper today, is Berrow's *Worcester Journal*. Although claims for its first appearance in 1690 have been made, these

probably cannot be justified. It is much more likely that its first publication as a regular journal was in 1709. Stephen Bryan, its founder, proprietor, printer and editor, had served his appenticeship in London. He gave his paper the title of *The Worcester Post-Man*. It cost 2d, but when the stamp tax was imposed in 1712, he increased the size of the paper, and raised its price to 2½d.

Bryan also sold patent medicines, a sideline associated with many of these early newspaper barons. These included an elixir for the dropsy, powder for gout, Hypo drops, the Royal Chemical wash ball and Dr Egton's Balsamick. Despite the availability of all these sovereign remedies, his own health began to fail in 1748, and he sold out to Harvey Berrow, whose name the paper now bears.

One gathers that competition between rival papers was fierce and business methods had few restraints. In one issue, Berrow wrote of 'the mean, scandalous wretches' who went around his district spreading false rumours that his agents had given up selling the paper, or had absconded with the money they owed him.

If money, or cash flow, was always a problem, time was equally pressing, as noted in 1769.

The Journal is published very early in the morning (by

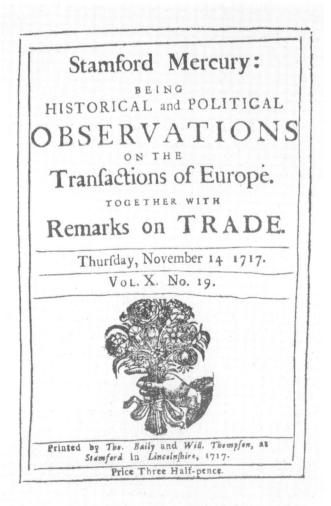

means of an express) and circulated with so much expedition as to precede in many places the arrival of the London Mail by several hours, and yet will contain, as usual, the most material occurrences from the papers published in London on Tuesday night.

This speed, in advance of the ordinary mail service, was achieved by employing post-boys who collected the papers in London and rode with them through the night with all haste directly to the provincial printer concerned. Because the early delivery of the London papers was crucial, it was not unknown for competing printers to attempt to waylay, delay and by whatever means hold up a rival's post-boy.

Travel, even under ordinary circumstances, faced these messengers with many hazards. The winter of 1747 was a particularly hard one, and the *Reading Journal* reported that a post-boy had 'froze to death'. Two years later, the *Worcester Journal* excused itself 'that the Person employ'd to forward the Packet of News for the Use of this Paper, not being return'd, 'tis fear'd some Accident has befall'n him; and (after waiting several Hours for him) we are oblig'd to publish with the News that came Yesterday.' Again, in 1755, the *Derby Mercury* declared that 'this Morning the Post came in without the Mail, and brought Advice that the Post Boy who rides betwixt Harborough and Leicester had been robbed of the same.' One of the most dramatic episodes comes from Farley's *Exeter Journal* of 1726 – 'the Western Post coming from Yeovil in Somersetshire being oblig'd to swim his Horse at a River ... was unfortunately drown'd; but the Horse got safe to Shore with the Mail...'

Typical of the express items thus received appears in an extra sheet attached to issue No. 267, dated Friday 30 July, to Friday, 6 August 1714 of *The Worcester Post-Man*

Thursday's Post. London, August 3. On Sunday between 7 and 8 in the Morning, Her Sacred Majesty Queen Anne (to the great grief of her Subjects) departed this Life in the 50th Year of her Age, and the 13th of her Reign; a Princess of exemplary Piety and Vertue.

The report continues to print in full the Proclamation

Whereas it hath pleas'd Almighty God to call to his Mercy our late Sovereign Lady Queen Anne, of blessed Memory, by whose Decease the Imperial Crowns of Great-Britain, France and Ireland, are solely and rightfully come to the High and Mighty Prince George, Elector of Brunswick-Lunenbourg... To whom we do acknowledge all Faith and constant Obedience, with all hearty and humble Affection, beseeching God, by whom Kings and Queens do reign, to bless the Royal King George with long and happy Years to reign over us. Given at the Palace of St James's, the 1st Day of August, 1714. God Save the King.

Almost the entire history of the 'taxes on Knowledge' applied against newspapers can be told through the experience of one paper – *The Stamford Mercury* – first published in 1713 (claims to an earlier date of 1695 can probably be discounted). It was started by two printers

in partnership – Thomas Bailey and William Thompson. The essence of what we know of the latter is contained in an obituary notice published in 1732.

Mr William Thompson, one of the Aldermen of this Town, who in the Year 1708, set up a Printing House and Bookseller's Shop, by which and other Large Dealings, he has been able to leave his Widow a handsome Annuity; after whose Death it descends to a Nephew. The Widow has dispos'd of all Effects in Trade to Cluer Dicey, eldest Son of Mr William Dicey of Northampton, who has, by his indefatigable Care and Industry, raised within a few Years, against strenuous Opposers, two of the most popular Country News-papers, viz the Northampton and Gloucester Mercuries, both remarkable for their Impartial and disinterested Collection of Intelligence.

This would seem to have broken the continuity of the paper's life. But a Stamford chemist, and a friend of Thompson, began publishing in that same year *Howgrave's Stamford Mercury*. Exactly how much of the Thompson estate was sold to the Diceys by his widow is not clear, and the claim is made (which cannot be challenged) that, in effect, or by purchase, Francis Howgrave kept the original paper alive.

Nothing more cumbersome and impractical, from the printer's point of view, can be imagined than the method by which the tax stamps were printed on the sheets of newsprint. Blank sheets had to be delivered to the Stamp Office in London – first at Lincoln's Inn and later at Somerset House. On these, stamps were printed in batches of 25. The printer was required to prepay the tax. He had then to transport the sheets back to his printshop. For a printer situated 91 miles from London – since we happen here to be speaking of Stamford, other printers were even further away – involving a journey each way occupying the best part of a day and a half, this procedure was a ludicrous waste of time and money. Furthermore, the printer had to guess how many sheets he would require. If he paid for too many, he would tie up his limited resources in unwanted stamped sheets. If he secured too few, he might have to turn away custom for his paper, being forbidden to print on unstamped sheets.

This was not the end of the government's impositions on him. Whenever he bought supplies of paper from the mills, an additional paper tax was charged. And, as we have already described, any advertisements published in his paper had to pay a separate tax which he had either to collect from his clients and bear the brunt of their disapproval, or absorb the cost himself. The only alleviation of these tax burdens came from the growing custom of allowing papers to pass and repass through the general post provided they bore on the postal wrapper the name of one of that galaxy of persons granted the privilege of free mailing. One category of such people thus privileged was local postmasters, who often thereby acted as local distributors of papers as a sideline to their official functions.

In defiance of the Stamp Act, many printers published

Stamford Mercury, &c.

London, November 7.

Bills of Mortality, from October 29. to November 5.

Abortive	1	Fever	68	Rifing of the Lights	2
Aged	30	Flux	1	Small-Pox	24
Ague	1	French-Pox	1	Stilborn	18
Apoplexy	2	Gout	2	Stone	1
Cancer	4	Griping in the Guts	10	Stoppage in Stomach	5
Childbed	6	Headach	1	Suddenly	2
Chrifoms	1	Jaundies	1	Teeth	23
Colick	1	Impofthume	1	Thrufh	3
Confumption	55	Loofenefs	2	Tiffick	7
Convulfion	127	Meafles	1	Tympany	1
Dropfie	10	Rickets	3		

C A S U A L T I E S.

Drowned accidentally in the River of Thames 3, One at St. Dunftan at Stepney, One at St. John at Wapping, and One at St. Paul at Shadwell.

Chriftened ————— 305
Buried ————— 418
Increafed in the Burials this Week 25.

From Fox's Letter, November 7.

Letters from Italy and France affure us, that the War in Italy will go on, the Spaniards having fent more Forces thither, and demands a free Paffage for them through the Territories of Genoa. The Emperor at the fame time demands a Paffage for his Troops through the Pope's Territories, at which the Pope and Cardinals are alarmed, becaufe the Seat of the War is fo near them.

The Spaniards are building and purchafing Frigates and Men of War againft the 'pring, to make them formidable in the Mediterranean, and the Regent of France has ordered 15000 Men to march towards Italy, and obferve the Motions of the Spaniards and Savoyards.

This Day the Lord Parker committed Mr. Yates, *Cuftos Brevium* of the Common Plea, for not returning a Writ in Time.

Bills of Mortality

papers on unstamped sheets. Despite a constant barrage of prosecutions, the Government were unable to stop this practice and, eventually, as Governments generally do, allowed themselves the opportunity of giving way to popular demand, or what is presented to them as such. The Stamp Act was modified to become a postal concession, that is, papers were now obliged to be franked with a special postal stamp. This, it was judged, would in any case be more easy to control. As an instrument of that control, power was given to the Stamp Office to withhold stamped paper from any printer until the duty on advertisements had been paid by him. To ensure that defaulting printers could not get supplies of paper elsewhere, it was laid down that each paper should carry a special stamp on which would appear its name.

Yet, with newspaper circulation increasing rapidly, even these arrangements had to be modified. The Stamp Office could no longer cope with the quantity of paper being sent to it for stamping. And so, certain papers, with appropriate precautions, were allowed to print their own stamped postal wrappers. The Post Office Act of 1870 confirmed these as being *The Times, Illustrated London News* and the *Stamford Mercury*. Both of the London-based papers have long since given up this practice. And now the *Stamford Mercury* remains the only paper in England still to have this privilege.

An early issue of the paper, dated Thursday, 14 November 1717, indicates the wide range of interests for which the early newspapers had to cater. Following the ever-present London Bills of Mortality (see illustration), there is an extract from Fox's Letter (dated 7 November), a collection of despatches from Hamburgh

(5 November), Leghorn (25 October). Madrid (29 October), Brussels (15 November – the apparent impossibility of a report from Belgium being dated a day later than the newspaper in which it appears resolves itself when it is realised that the publication date is intended to be read as – the week commencing 14 November, thus covering the period up to and including the 20th), Hamburgh (a second despatch dated 12 November), Barcelona (24 October), Vienna (3 November), Fox's Letter of 9 November, Miller's Letter of the same date, London (7 November), and again (12 November). Prices of Grain are listed, and there is a final page of advertisements, two for stolen horses, stolen cows, three houses to be sold, and one announcing the arrival of a travelling Goldsmith.

One of the news items gives an interesting sidelight on crimes of violence –

Letters from the Devizes, in Wiltshire, of the 9th Instant, say great Search is making in those Parts after the Persons concern'd in a barbarous Robbery lately committed at Shepherd-Shord, about 3 Miles from the Devizes, in the Road from Sandy-Lane to Marlborow. The Person robb'd came to the Devizes stark naked with his Tongue in his Hand, and was generously relieved by Mr Eyles, a Justice of the Peace there, who sent for a Surgeon to dress him. He is suppos'd to be a Devonshire Man, and signify'd as well as he cou'd by Hems, that he was met at the Place aforesaid by two Men and a Woman, who robb'd him of about 5l. stripp'd him, and to prevent Discovery, cut out his Tongue.

That, at least, is one form of criminal violence made irrelevant by a universal literacy.

Another of the early provincial papers that still survives, began life as the *Kentish Post and Canterbury Newsletter*, first published in 1717. It was founded by James Abree, a printer in that town. However, its development into the present *Kentish Gazette* has been a purely local affair.

Of more consequence to our history is the *Northampton Mercury*, the first issue of which is dated Monday, 2 May 1720. It was 'printed by R. Raikes and W. Dicey, near All Saint's Church'. The second of these men we have already met in the sale of the *Stamford Mercury*. Of the first we shall discover much more in the growth of the *Gloucester Journal*.

Raikes and Dicey had originally joined forces to start a paper at St Ives in Huntingdonshire. Rumour suggests that they were obliged to leave that small market town in some disarray, having aroused the displeasure of a local dignitary with an item in their paper, for which they had been fined heavily. Their second venture, the Northampton paper, however, did well, and became one of the greatest of all the provincial press.

Two years later, they founded another great paper – the *Gloucester Journal*. The two men now divided the management of their publishing interests, Raikes moving to Gloucester while Dicey stayed in Northampton. They remained partners in other business interests, also. Because of the precarious nature of their trade, printers customarily set up subsidiary enterprises. And, as they had access, virtually without cost, to press advertising, one type of business to attract their attention was that to do with patent medicines.

Nostrums of every kind were pressed upon the gullible public. A typical announcement in the *Reading Mercury* (1746) states that the printer of it sold:

Dr Hooper's Female Pills, Anderson's Scotch Pills, Aurea Medicine: or Boerhaave's Scots Pills improv'd, the True British Oil, Frier's Balsam, Daffey's Elixir, and Squire's Grand Elixir, Greenough's Two Tinctures, the one for preserving the Teeth, the other for curing the Tooth-Ache, a Tincture to cure the Itch by smelling to, Golden and Plain Spirit of Scurvey Grass, Godfrey's Cordial, Hypo Drops, Golden Cephalick Drops, Lady Moor's, Bateman's, Stoughton's and Chymical Drops, Pile Ointment, The Liquid Shell for the Stone and Gravel. The best Sort of Issue Plaisters, Hungary and Lavender Water...

One of the best known of these remedies was Dr Bateman's Pectoral Drops. In 1730, it is recorded in the *Northampton Mercury* that William Dicey had entered a partnership with Benjamin Okell, Thomas Cobb and Robert Raikes to market this product. For many years these four men owned the sole rights to sell the medicine. Later, in 1761, Raikes's son, also Robert, went into partnership with John Newbery of Reading to sell the famous Drops – and that carries us ahead to yet another powerful newspaper dynasty.

John Newbery, the son of a Berkshire farmer, began his career in printing apprenticed to William Ayres of Reading. He, later edited the *Reading Mercury*, founded in 1723. An energetic man with a lively mind, he moved on to London where he exerted a thrusting influence on most aspects of the publishing industry. At his death, in 1767, he had an interest in *The London Chronicle*, Lloyd's *Evening Post*, *The Public Ledger*, Owen's *Chronicle*, *The Westminster Journal* and the *Sherborne and Yeovil Mercury*. All these were inherited by his nephew Francis who, in 1774, sold his interest in the Sherborne paper for two hundred pounds, having in his own right purchased a twelfth share in the *Gentleman's Magazine* from Benjamin Collins, the Salisbury printer.

Copies of the *Reading Mercury* published in 1747 give an indication of the concerns aroused by the Scottish Rebellion. Long reports of the activities of the rebels ('It is currently reported that the rebels have made themselves masters of the castle of Inverness', and '...a French transport is taken in the coast of Scotland', etc) are followed by an editorial

Wednesday, March 5. The state of affairs both abroad and at home are at present so uncertain, the imagination of mankind so bewilder'd, and their inclinations so hard to be discover'd, that it is impossible to form any notion of the consequences of our own perplex'd situation. We were overjoy'd the other day at the news of the dispersion of the rebels, and now we are as much alarm'd as ever by the fresh advantages they have gain'd, and the succours they have receiv'd: It was but a few Weeks ago that we were assured, that the

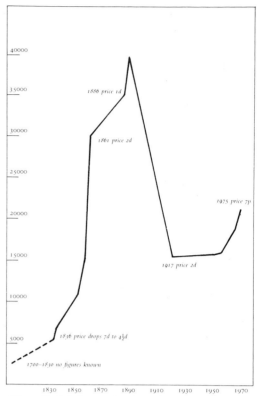

'*Stamford Mercury*' – *Circulation Graph*

Dutch would declare themselves in earnest against the common enemy, but now every mail brings fresh marks of the uncertainty of their resolutions.

Yet humour was not absent, either. 'A Townsman and a Countryman having met together in the Street the other day, the Townsman asked the Countryman what news? Upon which the honest Countryman answered, I hear nought but that Willie of Cumberland is pursuing Charlie of Plunderland.'

And rebellion or no, threats of invasion or not, other concerns continued to exercise the attention of some.

Letter from a Country Clergyman to a Bishop concerning the proposed tax upon Coaches, etc. My Lord, As there is now no reason to doubt but that a Tax upon Coaches is really intended, give me leave to represent to you our thoughts of it here. My Living, your Lordship knows, is under 70 l. a year, yet out of this, four years since, I made shift to lay out 6 l. on an old chariot, which, with the help of my ploughman and a pair of old cart-horses, has drawn my wife, etc. half a mile to church, who, for the future, must go in a cart, or stay at home. Repairs have cost me, one year with another, for eleven years I have had it, about 7 s. so the interest of my Money at 5 per Cent on the 6 l. and 7 s. in repairs, is 13 s. a year which with the Tax on this my pompous luxury, will be increased to 4 l. 13 s. a year, almost the prime cost of setting up my equipage. I am afraid this is not my case singly, but will be found nearly so, of most of the small Clergy in England.

The Reverend Gentleman then goes on to compare his own modest conveyance with those more lavish and expensive coaches of the exalted aristocracy (but taxed, none the less, at the same rate) and comments on those other nobles who keep stables full of horses for racing and hunting on which they pay no tax at all. He concludes –

''Tis, I must own, my Lord, with regret I should see the poor Parson, with his wife and children reduced to the wretched alternative of being in the dirt, or loaded with a burden these Squires do not touch with one of their fingers.'

Heavy taxation provokes the suggestion that to raise money it is only necessary to –

Take the tax off soap and candles and lay it upon kept Mistresses. Every Duke to pay for each lady of pleasure 500 l., every Marquis and Earl 400 l., every Viscount and Baron 300 l., every Baronet 200 l., all Esquires 100 l., and every private Gentleman 50 l. a year. The venerable Judges, the reverend body of the Clergy, and all above Dukes (to avoid giving offence) are to be exempted.

Benjamin Collins started the *Salisbury Journal* in 1729, and with Robert Goadby, a printer from Sherborne and Yeovil, was another of the provincial newspaper proprietors who was able to get his foot in the door of the influential London publishing world.

Sherborne was the starting point of the *Sherborne Mercury*, set up there in 1737 by William Bettinson. The present *Western Gazette* is its direct descendent.

No eighteenth-century paper was free for long from the often complained of, shortage of news. In times of war, civil or otherwise, papers flourished. With peace, the readership tended to melt away unless editors could find replacement material. A master of that craft was Robert Walker who may be justifiably dubbed – the

first press baron. In London he was the Northcliffe of his day, conquering the cheap newspaper market with journals costing as little as $\frac{1}{4}$d, a price he achieved by the simple expedient of not paying the Stamp Tax, for which offence he was arrested and charged in 1741. He was probably the first publisher to issue popular books as part-works in cheap weekly instalments, in which he conveniently ignored the simple law of copyright prevailing then. Part-works also served as a tax-dodging device. They were published as pamphlets – the news being enclosed with them as a kind of free give-away sheet.

Noting the growth of the provincial newspaper market, he made a bid for this also, printing in London and distributing to selected country areas. He started the *Warwick and Staffordshire Journal* in 1737, the *Shropshire Journal* the same year, the *Lancashire Journal* a year later, and the *Derbyshire Journal*, also in 1738. He opened his first provincial printing office at Birmingham in 1741, selling out to Thomas Aris two years later.

The time, he judged, was ripe for a fresh venture. The war with France was just beginning, and the first rumbles were to be heard of Scottish unrest. Taking into partnership Thomas James, Walker began the *Cambridge Flying Weekly Journal*, renamed later the *Cambridge Weekly Flying Post* (and known to its rivals as the 'Lying Post').

In these years there was steady progress in the building of a national trunk road system to carry mail from

29

The English Newspaper

THE

HARTFORD MERCURY.

Price Two-Pence Halfpenny.] FRIDAY SEPTEMBER 18, 1772. N°. 18.

Saturday *and* Sunday's *Posts*.

FOREIGN INTELLIGENCE.

This Day arrived the Mails from Holland *and* Flanders.

STOCKHOLM, AUGUST 25.

THE King has ordered ten thousand measures of meal, of twenty pounds each, to be distributed to the poor.

All the old Senators received their dismission on Saturday last by a note which the King sent to each of them; after which his Majesty nominated some new Counsellors and Senators, declaring at the same time that he kept two in *petto*.

The great change in the Government of this kingdom hath been proclaimed (the same day it was here) at Gothenbourgh, Carlscroon, and many other places; which *proves* that the whole nation unanimously wished for it. Prince Charles has received the homage of the subjects in Scania and Gothia, in the same manner the King has done here; and General Sprengporten is sent into Finland, to receive the oath of fidelity from that province, which is as ready to give it as the others.

The letters of vocation for the new Senators appointed by the King of Sweden were couched, as in the time of Gustavus Adolphus, in these words:

"GUSTAVUS, by the Grace of God, King of Sweden, sends greeting: We let you know by these presents, that in consequence of your fidelity, and the diligent services which you have in every respect rendered to us, and the confidence which we have always placed in your probity and good-will, we have elected you our Counsellor and Senator of this kingdom; and as we have granted you this honour on account of your fidelity, we doubt not that you will accept it with gratitude, and acquit yourself in it as becomes a true Swede, a man of honour, and a faithful Counsellor and Servant, as we expect of you. We grant you the appointments and rank belonging to this dignity, as it now is or shall be distinguished in the State. So God assist you.

From the Castle of Stockholm, Aug. 22, 1772.

GUSTAVUS.

John de Heband."

Paris, Aug. 30. The Count de St. Germain has had reiterated proposals made to him, on the subject of re-entering into the service of Denmark, but he continues to turn a deaf ear to them.

Paris, Sept. 4. The last letters from Aleppo by way of Marseilles, confirm the victory of Ali-Bey over the Kiaja of the new Caimacan of Egypt, and the taking of Beroot with 13 Russian vessels; adding, that the Chick-Daer had taken Damascus, and that Ali-Bey was preparing to reap the fruits of his victory by marching into Egypt.

Hague, Sept. 6. The States of Holland and West-Friezland will assemble on Wednesday next.

Hague, Sept. 8. In a speech which the King of Sweden addressed to the Dyet on the 21st, his Majesty drew the picture of the condition to which the party of the *Caps* had reduced the kingdom [the Swedes were divided into two parties, distinguished by the names of *Hats* and *Caps*] and concluded by saying, that "to put an end to the misfortunes of the country, he proposed to the Dyet to re-establish the antient and true form of Swedish Government, such as it had been from the time of Gustavus Adolphus to that of Charles XI. in 1680; and that he had drawn the plan thereof, &c." which being read by a Secretary, all the members immediately cried out, "*We approve of it.*"

IRELAND.

Dublin, Sept. 5. The following melancholy accident happened near Rathdowny, in the Queen's county, a few days ago: a young man charged a small brass cannon with pebbles, and laid a wager it would carry a mile; he accordingly brought the piece into a field, in order to level at a tree a considerable way off, but unfortunately shot his sweetheart, who was coming over a ditch at the same instant. The girl is since dead of her wounds, and the young man so disordered in his senses that it is thought he will soon follow her.

SCOTLAND.

Edinburgh, Sept. 7. We hear from Newcastle, that last Monday evening an out-house and barn were burnt down at Moesden, near Morpeth, which were set on fire by lightning; and a fine ox killed near Netherwitton; there were no marks on it, save an appearance of hair slightly singed.—Several persons, who were travelling during the storm, say, they never saw such quick successions of lightning, the atmosphere appearing in almost a continual flame for two hours.

Leeds, Sept. 8. At the opening of the subscription for a new navigable canal from Leeds to Selby, at the King's Arms in this town, on Thursday last, the sum of 32,000l. was subscribed in less than two hours. The said subscription is since then increased upwards of 10,000l. and so sanguine are the wishes and expectations of the people in general, in regard to its success, that we are told more money than will be wanted to compleat the scheme, will be raised within the limits of our town and neighbourhood.

From the LONDON GAZETTE, of Saturday, *Sept.* 12.

Stockholm, August 25.

THERE has been a Plenum Plenorum this morning, being the first under the new form of Government. The King's propositions were read to the States, and consist of four points, all relative to the finances and contributions; and his Majesty demands that they should be finished in fourteen days, after which the Dyet is to separate.

As soon as the propositions were read, all the new Senators, who are in town, took the oaths of their office.

BANKRUPTS.

Robert Bell, of Gravesend, in the county of Kent, Mercer and Draper, to surrender the 10th and 26th of September instant, at Nine in the forenoon, and the 24th of October next, at Ten in the forenoon, at Guildhall, London. Attorney, Mr. Coore, in Laurence-Pountney-Lane, London.

Jeremiah Dicks, late of Warminster, in the county of Wilts, Clothier, to surrender the 2d, 3d, and 24th of October next, at Ten in the forenoon, on each of the said days, at the house of Mr. Joseph Boyter, the Three Lions Inn, in the city of New Sarum, in the aforesaid county. Attorney, Mr. Samuel Shaw, at Fordingbridge, in the county of Southampton.

Henry Reeves, late of Burr-Street, in the parish of St. John, Wapping, in the county of Middlesex, Merchant, to surrender the 19th of September instant, at Nine in the forenoon, the 28th at Five in the afternoon, and the 24th of October next, at Ten in the Forenoon, at Guildhall, London. Attorney, Mr. Booth, in Buckingham-Street, York Buildings.

Nicholas Lutyens, of Lime-Street, London, Merchant, to surrender the 23d of September instant, and the 3d and 24th of October next, at Ten in the forenoon, on each of the said days, at Guildhall, London. Attorney, Mr. Totton, in Spital-square.

David Pierce, late of the parish of Eglwisfach, in the county of Denbigh, Clothier, to surrender the 29th September and 24th of October next, at Eleven in the forenoon, on each of the said days, at the house of Mrs. Deborah Bird, the Golden Talbot, in the Eastgate-Street, in the city of Chester. Attorney, Mr. Peter Jackson, of the city of Chester, Timber-Merchant.

James Sykes, of Leeds, in the county of York, Stuff-Merchant, to surrender the 28th and 29th of September instant, and the 24th of October next, at Three in the afternoon, on each of the said days, at the house of Mr. Stephen Northouse, the White Horse, in Leeds. Attorney, Mr. Shepley, in Leeds aforesaid.

Dividends to be made to Creditors.

John Bedford and John Bedford the Younger, both of Leeds, in the county of York, Merchants, and Copartners, the 7th of October next, at Eleven in the forenoon, at the White Horse, in Leeds aforesaid.

James Facer, of the city of London, Grocer, the 17th of October next, at Ten in the forenoon, at Guildhall, London.

Daking Moore, of the city of London, Grocer, the 17th of October next, at Ten in the forenoon, at Guildhall, London.

Trefuses Lovel the Younger, of Plymouth, in the county of Devon, Merchant, the 7th of October next, at Ten in the forenoon, at the London Inn, in Plymouth.

Hannah Beaufoy, late of the city of Coventry, Grocer, the 13th of October next, at Ten in the forenoon, at the White Bear, in Coventry.

Certificates to be allowed.

Brook Samson, of the city of London, Merchant, on or before the 3d of October next.

Simon Dobbs, of the city of London, Warehouseman, on or before the 3d of October next.

Abraham Favenc, late of Brown's-Lane, Spitalfields, in the county of Middlesex, Weaver, on or before the 3d of October next.

Thomas Dennet, late of Cronton, in the county of Lancaster, Mealman, on or before the 3d of October next.

[*Thus far London Gazette.*]

LONDON.

This day a new writ was issued under the Great Seal for the election of a Member for the city of Rochester, in the room of the late John Calcraft, Esq. The election will come on the latter end of the next week.

Joseph Martin, Esq; Member for Gatton, in Surry, who served the office of Sheriff last year, and was lately chosen Alderman of Limestreet Ward, in the room of Sir Robert Kite, has declined the gown, and in a polite letter to the inhabitants recommended somebody else to their choice.

Benjamin Hammet, Esq; is now talked of as a successor to Mr. Martin, or, more properly speaking, to Sir Robert Kite; for as Mr. Martin has never accepted the Aldermanship, he cannot justly be said to have created a vacancy.

The revolt of the Swedish commander *Hellichius* is not a revolt from the Crown but from the People; and this man, who has been mentioned as a patriot in the papers, was only employed by the King as an instrument of enslaving his country. Previous to the late revolution, the Crown could not march a single soldier without a public insurrection or a public enemy. To justify a march of the troops therefore to the capital, he prevailed on Hellichius to mutiny, being thus furnished with a legal pretence he brought the military to Stockholm, and *forced* the people, as an Hibernian would express it into a *voluntary* surrender of their liberties.

The King of Sweden's regard for the sanctity of oaths is very conspicuous; he publicly swears to renounce the sovereignty, at the very moment his proclamations are issued in the stile of Sovereign; and he calls himself only the first citizen of the state, at the instant in which he commands the people to pay an explicit obedience to his authority.

A writer in one of the morning papers confidently asserts, that the late revolution in Sweden is owing to F——ch councils and F——ch money; that some persons here are no strangers to the political roll which the F——ch Envoy at Stockholm has been playing at the Swedish Court; and that, no longer since than last week, the F——ch Resident at Hamburgh publicly declared before the Magistrates of that free and imperial city, "That the Court of Versailles had *now* a FIRM Ally in the North."

Several companies of private adventurers are now busy in purchasing vessels with a view of going out to the Missisippi; the only thing they desire there is protection, as they are intitled to lands immediately on their arrival; and protection they must have in the British dominions, unless the Ministry think fit not only to make the Spaniards a present of our territories in that part of the world, but of our subjects into the bargain.

So exceedingly profitable is the country adjoining to the Missisippi, that the usual way of computing a man's income is to reckon the number of negroes; the produce of their labour is reckoned at 100l. annually per head, and thus a planter, with ten negroes, is set down at 1000l. a year. In this calculation their maintenance and mortality is allowed for, and a healthy negro is valued at 100l.

On Monday they began picking hops about Sevenoaks, Sundridge, Brasted, and Westram, where they turn out very fine; the speculators [illegible] it is thought, will be great losers as they every day fall in price.

Not long since a Gentleman coming into the coffee-house at Southampton, complained, with a volley of oaths, that he had a violent flux; a Quaker over-hearing him said, "Thou seemest to know how to cure thyself, Friend, for *oaths* are said to be *binding*."

Thursday the following prisoners were capitally convicted at the Old Bailey, viz.

John Jones and John Sandiland, alias Sunderland, for burglariously breaking open and entering the dwelling-house of Aaron Franks, Esq; and stealing thereout a quantity of linen, a silver sauce-pan, and other things.

John Browning, for stealing a bundle containing a quantity of linen, the property of Thomas Simkins, in the dwelling-house of George Burt. And Sarah Truebridge, for stealing 7 guineas, the property of William Francis, in his dwelling house in Tottenham court-road.

Friday the five following prisoners were capitally convicted at the Old Bailey, viz.

Edmund Burton and Isaac Poulton, for feloniously assaulting Henry Leigh, Esq; in Gate-street, Lincoln's-inn, robbing him of his hat, and knocking him down with such violence, that the bone of his arm was *fractured* in endeavouring to save his head.

John White, for feloniously and traiterously coining and counterfeiting the current coin of this realm called shillings, in an upper room in Bartlett's Court, Holbourn, where were found upwards of 1400 counterfeit shillings, and several not finished, and a great number of implements proper for that pernicious business; the intrinsic value of each piece appeared to be about four-pence half-penny, they being composed of half silver and half metal, but considerably short of weight, so as to resemble worn money.

Benjamin Johnson and George Kem, for assaulting William Kitchen on the highway, between Marybone turnpike and the Farthing Pye-house, and robbing him of a silver watch and a shilling.

One was cast for transportation for fourteen years, and five for seven years, amongst whom was Arabella Butler, for selling, paying, and putting off counterfeit halfpence for a less sum than their denomination doth import.

Conclusion of Doctor Kelley's Proclamation.

I AM the person of whom my Gracious Lord spake, when he said to the following effect; —"I shall not judge you; but, if ye believe not these things, Moses, in whom ye trusted, shall judge you *in the last day*."

The Commandments were given in a very solemn and awful manner, and were intended to be the chief guide to human conduct; comprehending, either by plain expression, or very natural implication, all the crimes, as well as virtues, mankind has been able to commit; recommending the latter, and forbidding the former. And, as not only Christians were in possession of them, but likewise Jews and Mahometans (for Mahomed preserved the spirit, though not the letter of them) so will the Jews and Turks, as well as Christians, be judged by them; agreeable to the following declaration in my credentials;

The Christian, Jew, Mahometan,
Will all be judg'd on the same plan;
The decalogue they all possess'd:
And will thereby be blam'd or bless'd.
They most should love the Pow'r divine,
On whom the purest light doth shine;
But love without obedience,
Cannot be fair, but foul pretence,
And must not claim præeminence.
Those who the Gospel ne'er receiv'd,
Nor in the Word of God believ'd,
The Law of Nature was their guide,
'Tis that which will their fate decide;
That Heav'n-born maid Benevolence,
Will be to such the best defence.

The judgment by the Commandments will be performed by such plain rules as cannot be mistaken; and by which, neither I, nor my delegates, can shew any partiality. Those who are tried, will be judged by their own confession, for all will be so well aware of the consequences of aiming at an imposition on that Divine Spirit to whom all hearts are open, that they will not make any such attempt: neither must they do themselves injustice, but speak according to the dictates of their consciences; as their virtues and vices will be duly weighed against each other, with ample allowance for temptations to evil. By the above-mentioned rules people will be able to class themselves, though at ever so great a distance from the seat of judgment; and, should they attempt a sensible imposition, by assuming a colour and class, which they know, in their consciences, does not belong to them, they will soon find their mistake in so doing, and feel a perpetual uneasiness, both in body and mind, till they rectify such mistake. Every individual will wear three marks of distinction; first, that colour of his cloathing which belongs to his proper class; secondly, a badge upon his right breast, expressing the rank he bears in such class; and thirdly, a number on his left breast, shewing the number of that rank; as there will be many of the same rank in each class. By these several distinctions, every person will be so readily known, wherever he or she goes, that they not only will be treated with the respect and deference due to their rank and station; but will also be prevented from committing any such irregularities as might disturb the peace, order, and economy of the community; upon which the general happiness will much depend. These restrictions none need complain of, because they will be under no temptation to commit irregularities; as, wherever they go, all that their nature requires will be amply provided for them, free of all expence, for money will soon cease to be current; so that it can only be a vicious principle can induce them to be disorderly, and consequently deserving of punishment. They will likewise find that the rules and orders issued by the Deputy Judge are not his own; but those of the adorable Deity, who is at all times in all places, and immediately sees and knows when, and in what manner, his orders are obeyed:—To whom be glory, honor, might, majesty, and dominion, now and for ever!

N.B. according to the above plan, the judging of one will prove the judgment of millions; and the judgment of the living will prove also the judgment of the dead; who will all be really born again, and come, as little children, into the kingdom of righteousness, and then die no more. They will come into their proper classes thus:

The Good to Good will children be,
The Bad will have like progeny;
And those who were of middle state,
Be born unto a middling fate:

For the children of each class will be kept apart by themselves; and, when arrived at maturity, will be admitted to all the privileges of that class.

My credentials explain why, as well as how, Divine Goodness is able and willing to bring the dead back again into being, in the very same manner as all (except Adam and Eve) were first brought into existence; and yet be the very identical persons they were before, as much as if the flesh, bones, and every particle of matter deposited in the grave, had remained intire, and become reanimated, without suffering a dissolution. The number of the dead to return upon earth will not be so great as might be expected, by reason all that are now living upon the earth have existed upon it several times before; not knowing, or remembering, any thing that had happened to them in a former

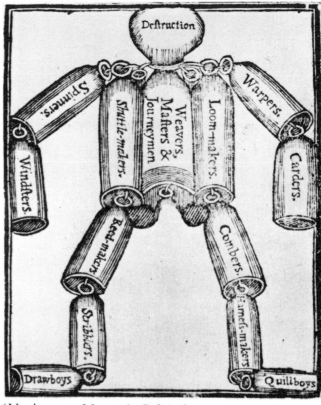

'*Northampton Mercury*' – *Political cartoon 5 December 1720.*
(*Twice life size*)

London to Holyhead, Bristol, Plymouth, Edinburgh, Yarmouth and Dover. This was an additional encouragement to those seeking to establish papers and sell them over as wide an area as possible. Many new weeklies appeared, such as the *Leeds Intelligencer*, begun by Griffith Wright in 1754, and becoming the now familiar *Yorkshire Post* in 1883.

In addition to printing their own papers, many local printers now acted as selling agents for papers from neighbouring towns that did not compete with their own journals. When, as an example, Thomas Boddely established the *Bath Journal* in 1744, Robert Raikes was the agent for it in Gloucester, Benjamin Collins in Salisbury, Harvey Berrow in Worcester and Robert Goadby in Sherborne.

John Linden put out the first issue of the *Hampshire Chronicle* in 1772 to serve the thriving port of Southampton, and its hinterland. In the same year was founded the *Hartford Mercury*. Stephen Austin, its founder, was apprenticed to George Kearsley who, as printer of the offending *North Briton*, was imprisoned with John Wilkes. Austin took charge of the business while his employer was in gaol – and it was possibly Wilkes's knowledge of the Hertford area (I use the modern spelling here) that led Austin to select it as the site of his own newspaper.

Reading through these pages one is quickly attracted to the ebullience of life recorded there. Three samples may serve to illustrate the point – all taken from the *Hartford Mercury* dated Friday, 18 September 1772.

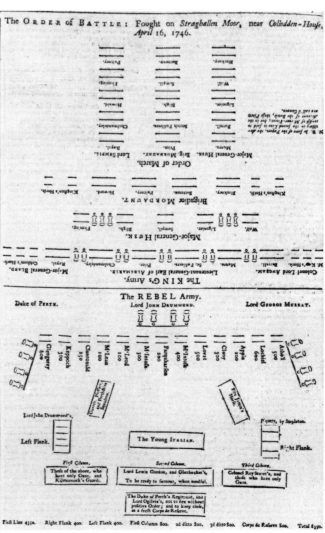

Battle of Culloden – '*Ipswich Journal*' *10 May 1746*

Not long since a Gentleman coming into the coffee-house at Southampton, complained, with a volley of oaths, that he had a violent flux; a Quaker over-hearing him said, 'thou seemest to know how to cure thyself, Friend, for *oaths* are said to be binding.

Bath, September 14. Monday as William Sutton and William Carter were drinking together at the Bear and Castle inn at Marlborough, the latter put eight shillings and six pence into a glass of beer, telling the former he should keep as much of the money as he could swallow with the liquor, whereupon Sutton took up the glass, and with the beer swallowed five shillings and sixpence: He at first complained of great weight in his stomach, but after that left him was easy, and on Thursday morning the money came from him.

The workmen that were repairing the Chamberlain's Office, adjoining to the Court of Common-Pleas, where Mr Fordyce's Commission was sitting, finding that many of the populace had, by means of their ladders and scaffolds, got upon the leads to look in at the windows of the Court, took the opportunity of turning it to account. They first applied to those spectators who had good places (front boxes as they called them) for something to drink, but that proving ineffectual, they cleared them all down, and would let none up again without paying sixpence, which was very readily complied with by several, and the windows were soon crowded again. But what was very mortifying to the spectators, after sweating three hours in the crowd, the fly rogue of a Bricklayer who had let them up his ladder, was gone, and they were obliged to pay sixpence-a-piece to another to let them down again.

SURVIVING PROVINCIAL PAPERS FOUNDED BEFORE
1776

Berrow's *Worcester Journal*	founded 1690 (?)
Lincoln, Rutland and Stamford Mercury	1695 (?)
Kentish Gazette	1717
Mercury and Herald (Northampton)	1720
Gloucester Journal	1722
Berkshire Mercury	1723
Norwich Mercury	1726
Salisbury Journal	1729
Chester Courant	1730
Western Gazette (Somerset)	1736
Cambridge Independent Press and *Chronicle*	1744
Yorkshire Post	1754
Bath Weekly Chonicle	1757
Bath and West Evening Chronicle	1760
Essex Chronicle	1764
Reading Chronicle	1770
Hampshire Chronicle	1772
Hertfordshire Mercury	1772
Shrewsbury Chronicle	1772
Western Times and Gazette	1772
Chester Chronicle	1775

SOMERSET HOUSE STAMP OFFICE.—THE ILLUSTRATED LONDON NEWS PAPER UNLOADING.

Reports of Revolutions

An aphorism commonly quoted is that a nation gets the newspapers it deserves. This has a curiously punitive flavour as if at the behest of some omniscient force some kind of punishment is being matched with some kind of crime. What, however, is certainly true – and may, in fact, be a way of saying the same thing differently – is that newspapers are sensitive barometers of the mood of their time.

This is instantly apparent to anyone who spends time reading eighteenth-century newspapers. During its last quarter the social stability of two major international communities was dismembered in the name of freedom, run through with violence, riddled with bitterness and despair, and revitalised by new growth. The manner in which these tumultuous events were reported in England is in striking contrast. Despite the most enormous practical difficulties hindering the transmission of regular reports, weekly despatches from the first of these events appeared almost unfailingly in papers of every class and place here, and these were read with the deepest attention and discussed at length, with passion, forceful argument and sympathy. The second aroused so little general interest that for almost three years hardly a single mention of it appears.

Reference to just one newspaper in one place is enough to make this point clear. Its relevance is that it sets the scene for the next phase of newspaper growth.

Salisbury, in Wiltshire, is notable for its splendid cathedral standing on the banks of the River Avon. Those who go there, and see on the local news stands copies of the *Salisbury Journal* would hardly suspect that it is but three short of its 250th anniversary. In its offices are file copies that go back to almost its first year. In them, we can discover exactly how the pre-revolutionary events of 1775 in the British American colony were presented to the readers along the Hampshire–Wiltshire border.

The year opened quietly enough. On 2 January, it is reported that

The General Congress in America, before they broke up, adressed a Letter to the inhabitants of Canada, which concludes thus: 'We do not ask you, by this adress, to commence acts of hostility against the government of our common sovereign. We only invite you to consult your own glory and welfare, and not suffer yourselves to be inveigled or intimidated by infamous ministers so far, as to become the instruments of their cruelty and despotism, but to unite with us in one social compact, formed on the generous principles of equal liberty, and cemented by such an exchange of beneficial and endearing offices as to render it perpetual.

One week later, on 9 January, this one of civil resistance is continued by adjacent reports concerning the payment of taxes, which were central to the American dispute with Britain. The first is an extract from the *Massachusett's Gazette* of 10 November 1774, which contains General Gage's proclamation, which exhorts the inhabitants of the Province not to comply with the requisition and resolves of the Provincial Congress, respecting the regulation of the militia, and the electing and appointing a Receiver-General, into whose hands the Provincial Congress ordered the constables and collectors to pay the monies of the Province.

The point of the widely unpopular General's proclamation is made clear in the second item.

The Treasurer of the province, by an address to the Sheriffs, contained in the same paper, calls upon the Sheriffs of the several counties, as they regard their oaths and would avoid the penalties of the law, to bring into the Treasury such public monies as they have in their hands.

But a slightly more militant note is set by one further paragraph in the same issue –

Boston, November 21. We have now eleven regiments in this town, besides the artillery. In the last transports that arrived here came a large quantity of powder, cannon balls, shells, etc...

Two weeks were to follow before a further report appears on 23 January.

The following is a Copy of the Petition of the General Congress Held at Philadelphia in November last to The King. 'Most gracious Sovereign, We your Majesty's faithful subjects of the colonies of North America, etc, in behalf of ourselves and the inhabitants of those colonies who have deputed us to represent them in General Congress, by this our humble petition beg leave to lay our grievances before The Throne.'

Thereafter follows a full statement of the American case against the payment of the increased taxes demanded of them by the British Government.

A further item gives some flavour of the attitude of ordinary American people.

Thursday's Post. America. Boston December 13. People travelling the high roads are seized and obliged to declare themselves Whigs, their name for rebels, and to curse the K——— and the P———t, and to wish the island of Great Britain SUNK in the SEA, before they are permitted to pass. . . .

These being the months of winter, and with more than two thousand miles of ocean to cross, with all the vicissitudes likely to beset sail-driven craft, an interval of two weeks between despatches is not only understandable, but, in keeping with the difficulties of their arrival, is commendable. So it is that on 6 February, the first report was printed in Salisbury of the angry events of the previous 16 December.

Portsmouth – (New Hampshire). We have been in confusion here for two days, on account of an express from Boston, informing that two regiments were coming to take possession of our fort. By beat of drum 200 men immediately assembled, and went to the castle in two gondolas, who on their way were joined by 150 more, and demanded the surrender of the fort, which Captain Cochrane refused, and fired three guns, but no lives were lost; upon which they immediately scaled the walls, disarmed the Captain and his men, took possession of 97 barrels of powder, put it on board the gondolas, brought it up to town, and went off with it to some distance in the country.

Yet, the American colonists were not alone in their fight. Much support for their cause was to be found in England itself, not only among the ordinary readers of Salisbury and similar centres, but in official circles also, as witness, on Monday, 13 February – 'Substance of LORD CH——M's proposed BILL for settling the TROUBLES in AMERICA' – in which is stated two central matters of principle entirely in accord with the American case

... Nevertheless, in order to dispel groundless fears, be it hereby declared, that no military force, however raised, and kept according to law, can ever be lawfully employed to violate and destroy the just rights of the people. Moreover, be it declared, that no tax, or other charge for his Majesty's revenue, shall be levied, from British freemen in America, without common consent by act of Provincial Assembly there, duly convened for that purpose.

With ill-advised zeal, the Lower House, as reported on 20 February, took a more corrective view of the American protest.

The whole House went into committee when Lord North moved for the following augmentation of the Navy: That 2000 additional seamen be employed, including 490 marines, for 1775.

That 4 l. per man, per month be allowed for the said men. Lord North remarked, that the rebellious disposition and motions of the colonies made it necessary to have such a guard upon the coasts of North America ...

The strength of the American case, as reported in this local newspaper provoked the publication of an editorial letter in a prime position on the first news page, in which there is no doubt where the sympathies of the writer lay. 'If a method could be proposed for the Americans to advance a moderate sum yearly towards discharging the national debt, it would be attended with a much happier and beneficial issue to Old England, than imposing on them taxes to support luxury. ... A great change in a little time is the earnest wish of, Un Anglois.' Such a letter indicates the measure of reasoned and reasonable support in the locality, of which the newspaper offers a sensible reflection.

Reasonableness on the American side, too, was not lacking. With a studied avoidance of extreme, improper or violent action, the next American tactic is described on 6 March.

New York. January 30th. This day the following agreement took place in the Committee Chamber. Whereas, by the first article of the association of the late Continental-Congress, held at Philadelphia the 5th day of September 1774, it is agreed that from and after the 1st day of December next, we will not import into British America, from Great Britain or Ireland, any goods, wares or merchandize, as shall have been exported from Great Britain or Ireland.

And whereas by the last clause of the tenth article of the said association it is further agreed, that if any goods or merchandize shall be imported after the 1st day of February 1775, the same ought forthwith to be sent back again, without breaking any of the packages thereof.

Even a letter from a serving officer in the British Army indicates no more than placid irritants as being the daily lot of their life there – Monday, 13 March.

Extract of a letter from Boston, January 6. The fleet and army are very healthy; little or no desertion; things in general very moderate in price, and in great plenty. The country people are muleish, and would wish to distress us, but all those in trade readily part with whatever they can command for money. We have very great plenty of wine, rum, beer, and all other drinkables, at prices much lower than you would imagine; for example, rum at 14d. sterling a gallon, or 4d. by the single quart; good port wine for 10d. a bottle, very good cyder for 1d. half-penny a gallon, and beer very cheap, but scarce anybody will drink it. The great difficulty is to find money, for exchange is become very unfavourable to the drawers; it is extremely hard upon the Officers of the army; they at present lose 7 l. 13s. upon every 100 l. they draw for, and it is expected to be double that discount in less than a month; and were we to come to blows with the Americans, our little army must disband for want of cash to pay them, for there is none, or next to none in the military chest, and in case of hostilities, bills would not procure any, for credit would be at an end.

That the Americans pursued their prohibition on British imports is recorded on 3 April.

Boston. February 16. We are informed, that last Friday the Mayor of New-York, assisted by some Aldermen and civil officers, and a number of Tories, in all about 300, attempted to prevent the return of a Glasgow ship then in the harbour, which ship, arriving after the 1st of February, was, according to the association of the grand American continental Congress, to have returned from whence she came without breaking bulk. The people, to the amount of about 400, insisted on her departure, and a skirmish ensued, in which the Mayor and his party were worsted, and his Worship dragged through the streets. We are further informed that the ship, being furnished with necessaries, was ordered to sail in half an hour. The Captain sailed as far as the Hook, where he and his hands left her, but others being procured, she proceeded on her voyage.

A more ominous tone is set, on 22 May, by which expression seems to be given to the rising antagonism between the indigenous American civilian authorities and the bludgeoning, blustering British military.

Williamsburgh, April 1. At a meeting of Delegates for the counties in the colony of Virginia, at Richmond, on Monday the 20th of March, and the following days, they came to several resolutions, the principal of which are as follows:– That it is recommended to the inhabitants of the several counties of this colony, that they form one or more volunteer companies of infantry and troops of horse, in each county, and to be in constant training and readiness, to act on any great emergency. That each company of infantry consist of 68 rank and file; and each troop of horse of thirty,

34

exclusive of officers; and every man to be provided with proper arms, one pound of gunpowder, and four pounds of ball at least.

The balloon went up on 5 June.

London, Tuesday, May 30. Advices from America. From the ESSEX GAZETTE, published at SALEM, in New-England. Salem, April 25. Last Wednesday, the 19th of April, the troops of his Britannic Majesty commenced hostilities upon the People of this Province, attended with circumstances of cruelty not less brutal than what our venerable ancestors received from the vilest Savages of the wilderness...

Then follows a description of how a detachment of eight or nine hundred men advanced from Boston to Concord. At Lexington they fired on a gathering of local people, were forced to retreat, reinforcements led by Lord Percy brought their numbers up to eighteen hundred; they returned to take Lexington, retreated again to Charlestown. While in Lexington, they pillaged, burnt and destroyed homes, property, and shot down unarmed civilians. 'But the savage barbarity exercised upon the bodies of our unfortunate brethren who fell, is almost incredible; not contented with shooting down the unarmed, aged and infirm, they disregarded the cries of the wounded, killing them without mercy, and mangling their bodies in the most shocking manner.'

Clearly, the objectivity of this report is suspect, even though we can assume that strong feelings were doubtless roused on both sides during this engagement. What is significant, however, is that this direct reprint of a report appearing in a partisan American paper is the version, or a version, of the events that the ordinary reader in Salisbury was prepared to accept as being at least as truthful as any statement put out by the British Government, and probably might be much more honest.

That a strong body of sympathetic opinion existed in England at that time seems to have been recognised as something usefully to be fostered by the American Provincial Congress, for in the same issue there appeared the following announcement which has about it all the flavour of a pre-paid insertion. This was a form of advertising service commonly offered by newspapers to those who had a cause which they wished to ventilate publicly. Doubtless the American statement appeared first in one of the London papers, and was picked up by the Salisbury editor as worthy of reprinting. It reads:

In the Provincial Congress held on the 26th of April last, at Wattertown in New England, the following Adress was agreed to. 'To the Inhabitants of Great-Britain, Friends and Fellow Subjects. Hostilities are at length commenced in this Colony ... To give a particular account of the ravages of the troops, as they retreated from Concord to Charles-town, would be very difficult ... These, Brethren, are marks of Ministerial Vengeance against this Colony, for refusing, with her sister Colonies, a submission to slavery ...

From then on, tempers ran high, and the tide of events rapidly downhill.

Monday, July 3, 1775. Particulars of the taking of TICON-DEROGA by the Provincials. Philadelphia, May 6. The Rage Militaire, as the French call a passion for arms, has taken possession of the whole Continent. The city of Philadelphia has turned out 4000 men, 300 of whom are Quakers. Every county in our province is awakened, and several thousand Riflemen on our frontiers are in readiness to march down to our assistance at a moment's warning if necessary.

A month and a half later, on 14 August, the die, it seemed was finally to be cast. An address from the Provincial Congress of New York was presented on the 26th. ultimo to the Generalissimo of all the forces in the confederated Colonies of America, pledging allegiance and support. His reply read as follows:

Gentlemen, at the same time that with you I deplore the unhappy necessity of such an apointment, as that which I am now honoured, I cannot but feel sentiments of the highest gratitude for this affecting instance of distinction and regard. May your warmest wishes be realized in the success of America, at this important and interesting period; and be assured, that every exertion of my worthy colleagues and myself, will be equally extended to the re-establishment of peace and harmony between the Mother-Country and these colonies; as to the fatal but necessary operations of war, when we assume the soldier, we did not lay aside the citizen, and we shall most sincerely rejoice with you, in that happy hour when the establishment of American liberty, on the most firm and solid foundations, shall enable us to return to our private stations, in the bosom of a free, peaceful, and happy country.

It is signed – 'G. Washington.'

From the length and frequency of these American reports it is clear that these matters were of deep and immediate interest to the Salisbury reader. They touched his patriotism and his pocket. And when the colony fell away from British sovereignty, it was as if a deep disenchantment turned him away from all interest in foreign affairs.

If that is a superficial summary of the change in mood undergone by newspaper readers, it is a fact that, scanning the pages of the Salisbury Journal in the years following the American Declaration of Independence, there is a marked shrinkage in the space devoted to overseas news from all sources. In 1786 a petulant editorial complains that in England inflation is rampant and unemployment rife; that in the world at large the nation's prestige stands at nothing, and that few friends remain on whom she can rely for support and encouragement.

When the first rumbles of that other Revolution began, in 1789, to filter across the Channel from France, the Salisbury editor thought it barely worth a mention. Only two items of sufficient interest to be presented to the Salisbury readership occurred during that entire year, the first a snippet of such extraordinary triviality that the contrast with the American coverage fourteen years earlier is shattering.

Monday, February 23, 1789. The King of France has long lived abstemiously, his chief food being potatoes, turnips, parsnips, etc. He uses no tea, eats meat scarcely more than once a week with which he drinks a glass or two of Burgundy.

Only one brief hint at trouble was printed on 11 May.

Insurrection at Paris. Advice has just been received of a recent insurrection at Paris ... The source of this evil, we hear, was a declaration made by a proprietor of a large manufactury in that city, importing, 'that 15 sous a day were sufficient to support a journeyman and his family, provided that certain taxes were abolished.' This declaration ... was so misconceived ... that they (the workers) surrounded his house with the most hostile intentions. The guards were ordered out to preserve the peace, but the multitude were so enraged that they threw stones at them, and proceeded to such violence as to kill some of the soldiers, in consequence of which a very large party of the military were drawn forth, and a shocking slaughter is said to have ensued, in which more than 600 persons were killed on the spot.

The scene of this dreadful massacre, we understand, was the Fauborg de St. Antoine.

This episode aside, French affairs are briefly noted in the paper as though nothing of any unusual consequence was taking place there. Debates are reported in the Assembly, and the King's round of social and official functions are given the most cursory treatment. Not until three years have passed, in the summer of 1792, does any indication show itself on the bland, comfortable pages, of untoward happenings. Monday, 2 July 1792.

Paris June 25. The King has issued a Proclamation, in which, after noticing that 'a multitude, excited by some factious persons, had come with arms into the habitation of the King; had drawn cannon over into the hall of the guard; had forced the doors of his apartment by hatchets; and there, audaciously abusing the name of the Nation, had endeavoured to obtain by force, the sanction which his Majesty had constitutionally refused to two decrees, etc.' he says, that 'if he can make the sacrifice of his repose, he cannot also make that of his duty. If those who would overthrow his monarchy, require *one further crime*, they may commit it. In the present crisis, he will give to all the constituted authorities an example of that courage and firmness, which alone can save the empire, in consequence he orders all administrative bodies and municipalities to watch over the safety of persons and property.'

Six weeks later, further indications of the growing civil disorder are published. Monday, 13 August.

The terror spread in Paris – the sea coast is full of emigrants; – at Dunkirk not a bed to be had. – Six ladies on Wednesday last came over in an open boat from Calais to Dover for want of accommodation.

The people in Paris are just as gay, as thoughtless, as fantastic, as idle, and as dissipated as if their country was in the highest state of prosperity ... They seem merely to live for the hour, and take no thought for the morrow.

One assumes that word of mouth rumour must have prepared the newspaper reading citizen of Salisbury for the climax; its appearance in the pages of the paper came with all the suddenness of a thunder clap. 'Monday, August 20th. FRANCE. The following particulars respecting the King's Dethronement etc. were brought by Wednesday's mail.'

An untrue rumour was spread that the Mayor of Paris (Mons Pethion) was held prisoner by the King. As a result

Immense crowds ... surrounded the Assembly, venting the most violent language against the King and his Ministers – As daylight appeared, they proceeded from violence of words to violence of actions ... detached parties went off in several directions, and took numerous Courtiers, Guards, and others ... A mock trial ensued, and the unfortunate victims were instantly massacred, and their heads affixed on poles ... By nine in the morning the Tuilleries was surrounded by at least twenty thousand of the mob ... The King became seriously and justly alarmed ... He accordingly quitted the Palace, accompanied by the Queen and Royal Children ...

Now the despatches came flooding in. Monday, 3 September.

M. de la Port, Intendent of the Civil List, was tried by the new Court at Paris on the 22nd, between one and two o'clock. He was condemned to be beheaded, and the sentence was executed the same evening in the Place du Carousal. When sentence was passed upon him, he turned to the spectators, and said, 'Citizens, I solemnly declare to you, that I die innocent.'

Thus was the first mention made, in Salisbury, of the use of the guillotine.

These turbulent grand designs in France cast ripples on these quieter shores. Monday, 24 September.

An immense quantity of wheat is now ready at different parts of the coast of Essex, etc. to be exported, on the first favourable opportunity, to France. The medium price of wheat falling to a certain sum, allows this to be done by law; but should that not happen, it will most assuredly be smuggled away. At a time, like the present, when we are inundated by foreigners, who are likely to continue here for some time, and when every article of provision is above its common price, some speedy and effectual method should be taken to stop this threatened evil; an evil pregnant with so much danger to the very existence of the poor.

As often happens, when emotions have run their course like summer insects, it is the harder judgments of commerce that finally prevail. The year, in the *Salisbury Journal*, closes with two matters of practical concern. Monday, 31 December.

Government have discovered and timely defeated a plan of the French Republic, to buy up all the hemp in this country for the equipment of their navy, having missed the season for such supplies from the Baltic – their hostile disposition towards this country is pretty evident from this circumstance.

But the last word for cynical realism must certainly be reserved for this paragraph in the same issue. 'Policies are now open at Lloyds for five guineas to receive an hundred, if there should be a Governing Monarch in France on Christmas day of the ensuing year.'

The loss of North America hurt both the pride and the purse of the English; the downfall of the French monarchy, although that much closer to home, was merely a circumstance of marginal interest to the generality of readers. Yet, it was into this national mood of little-islandism that John Walter chose to project his new paper.

There had already begun that particular distinction that was later to separate the local from the national press. Local papers forswore allegiance to any cause or faction; in their service to a community all shades of opinion could find expression in their pages. The London metropolitan press, from which the great nationals grew, found their support by particularising their appeal to certain political or commercial ideals. In the first issue of his *Daily Universal Register*, dated Saturday, 1 January 1785, John Walter noted that

... every News-paper published in London is calculated for a particular set of readers only; so that if each set were to change its favourite publication for another, the commutation would produce disgust and dissatisfaction to all ... A News-paper, conducted on the true and natural principles of such a publication, ought to be the Register of the times ...

And, true to that principle, the paper changed its title three years later to *The Times* or *Daily Universal Register*. Today, of course, we know it simply as *The Times*.

With provincial interest turning away from foreign affairs, it is typical of Walter's approach, that he should seek to make a feature of such reports, despite the 'immense' cost of maintaining foreign correspondents. Most papers took their reports directly from the pages of foreign newspapers to which they subscribed. This information was augmented in a casual manner by letters that came in from businessmen, soldiers and British officials who happened to be in, or have had direct experience of, particular places of interest. Walter set out to place his own men in key places, so that they should provide him with informed and exclusive despatches. Doubtless to augment the Head Office back-up to such a system, the following announcement was printed in his advertisement columns on 27 August 1792.

Wanted immediately, A Gentleman who is capable of translating the French language. In order to prevent trouble, he must be a perfect Master of the English Language, have some knowledge of the Political State of Europe and be thoroughly capable of the situation he undertakes: His employment will be permanent and take up a considerable share of his attention; for which a handsome salary will be allowed.

Walter had already announced, on 21 May, that

we have established a new correspondence both at Brussels and Paris, which we trust will furnish us with the most regular and early intelligence ... Our communications will not be confined to the ordinary conveyance by the foreign Mails only, as we have taken such measures as will enable us to receive Letters from abroad on those days when the Foreign Mails do not become due.

It seems that these arrangements worked well for a time.

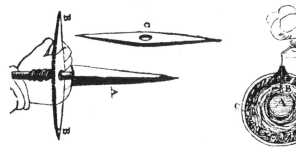

SECTION OF DAGGER, OR PIKE BLADE.   SECTION OF GRENADE.

First illustrated crime story – 'The Observer', 1820

We have some reason to be proud of our Foreign Correspondence in this Day's paper ... The Brussels Gazette has been stopped from being printed since the French troops entered Flanders. From this disappointment we are led to believe that none of the other Morning Papers of this Day will have any news from Flanders.

One up to *The Times*! But with the political position in Paris rapidly declining from harangue to slaughter, and with the allied armies of Austria and Prussia, under the command of the Duke of Brunswick posing an immediate threat, Walter's network broke down.

It is a matter of great vexation to us, that the plans we had laid for obtaining the most early correspondence from Paris and Bruxelles should have been so frequently obstructed by the interruption of letters in the Post-Offices abroad. We had taken the most certain measures to procure a Daily Correspondence from both these places, by having Agents at the Out-ports to forward our letters; but from the circuitous channels which they must now pass through, and from the frequent stoppage of all kind of correspondence from France, which is not tinctured with the spirit of rebellion, we have been subject to daily disappointments.

However, these were problems to be overcome. In spite of the declaration of war against Britain in 1793, Walter was able to crow, a year later that '... on Monday night, though it was a late hour, we received all the Newspapers printed at Brussels on *Saturday* last; and we had a letter from Ostend, dated on *Sunday afternoon*. We do not contend for any greater expedition!'

Six years after *The Times*, in 1791, there fluttered onto the London streets the first issue of yet another long survivor, named then as it has since remained *The Observer*. Patrick O'Donovan, in a brief history, says: 'No great paper had a more casual or a more squalid beginning than *The Observer*. The paper was born by Greed out of Amateur Incompetence. It was the child of a nasty time and it reflected its time.'

As ever, its editorial aspirations were proposed in the most lofty tones – 'To every rank and order will The Observer ... breathe invariably, the spirit of enlightened freedom, decent toleration, and universal benevolence.' A later masthead proclaims that the paper is – 'Unbiassed by Prejudice – Uninfluenced by Party, Whose Principle is Independence, whose Object is Truth and Dissemination of every Species of Knowledge that may conduce to the Happiness of Society, will be dispatched from London early on Sunday Morning, and delivered in every Part of Great Britain with the utmost Expedition.'

The editor's idea of what exactly might 'conduce to the Happiness of Society' proved a curious one, finding expression substantially in the reporting of 'rick-fires, stage-coach accidents, rapes and abductions'. Indeed, O'Donovan claims for the paper the distinction of having invented the crime story. To anyone familiar with the paper's present sobriety, these revelations must ring most curiously indeed.

Elsewhere in England during these years other papers had been started, at Bury St. Edmunds, Doncaster, Wolverhampton, York, Canterbury and Portsmouth, all of which were to survive to the present day.

But it was in the nineteenth century that the English newspaper was to have its fullest and richest flowering.

SURVIVING ENGLISH PAPERS FOUNDED BETWEEN 1776 AND 1800

Bury Free Press	founded 1782
The Times	1785
Doncaster Gazette	1786
Wolverhampton Chronicle	1789
Yorkshire Gazette and Herald	1790
The Observer	1791
Kent Herald	1792
Morning Advertiser (London)	1794
Hampshire Telegraph (Portsmouth)	1799
Newsman Herald (Chelmsford)	1800

Threats from Within and Without

The turn of the nineteenth century was a good time for English newspapers, despite a punitive Stamp Tax that raised prices to 6½d and 7d per copy – roughly, the equivalent of two pounds sterling now. But disasters abounded, disruption was at every hand. Europe was in turmoil. Discontent ran riot at home. Costs were rising: wages falling. Unemployment and inflation undermined stability. The loss of the North American colonies had left biting wounds. National confidence was low. The French Revolution, followed by Napoleon's rampage, presaged similar possibilities here. There was plenty of material to fill the papers.

The trouble, for the papers, was getting it. War and entrenched interests barred their way equally. These difficulties particularly afflicted *The Times*, which made such a feature of its foreign news. Despatches from Europe foundered on many rocks. Commanders of packets carrying mail had orders, if they were challenged by French ships, to run while they could, fight when they could no longer run, and to throw the mails overboard when they could no longer fight.

A further hindrance was a self-imposed regulation within the Post Office that, on arrival in London, foreign mail for Cabinet Ministers and Foreign Ambassadors was to be given priority. Often, urgent despatches for papers from their correspondents lay about the postal offices for hours until the priority traffic had been dealt with. Papers tried to bribe postal clerks to expedite their despatches, or to have their mail addressed to somebody on the priority list. A further hold-up arose from the translation rights. Postal clerks had a monopoly in the translation of foreign-language papers and reports for which a fee was charged. This also held up delivery.

Eventually, in an attempt to tidy up a messy situation, the postal authorities combined the priority payments and translation fees into a fixed charge to newspapers for handling their foreign mail. When *The Times* refused to make this payment, its mail was held back.

The papers fought back. In an odd way, the continental disorders helped them. Because of the coastal blockade of Holland and France, smugglers were employed to bring news despatches across. This was one way of by-passing the official post. In addition, elaborate codes were contrived whereby reports from particular correspondents were sent to priority addresses, such as merchant bankers. In time, these arrangements became so efficient that *The Times* had earlier news of events than the Foreign Office.

This ding-dong between the papers and Government continued unabated during the early years of the century. When the mail packet service was transferred from the Post Office to the Admiralty in 1815, the Secretary of the Admiralty became responsible for censorship, obstruction and deprivation. At home, after the Peterloo massacre, there were increased restrictions of press freedom.

Whilst most national metropolitan papers had a clearly defined political character, in the provinces a distinction was beginning to be drawn between papers supporting any faction, and those of a neutral style serving every interest in a locality. In practice, however, neutral papers were thought to be traditionalist, and therefore in support of the Tory Government, while factional papers supported Reformist movements of one kind or another.

Thomas Flindell of Helford in Cornwall was a neutral Tory. Born in 1767, at the age of 23 he was editing the *Doncaster Gazette*. Eight years later, he went back to his native county to start a printing business. Shortage of capital dogged him for many years. But when influential people in Truro supplied him with that, he published, on 2 July 1803, *The Royal Cornwall Gazette and Falmouth Packet*. The paper seemed sure of success. By a subscription of fifty guineas, it enjoyed the Royal patronage of the Prince of Wales, as Duke of Cornwall. Because Falmouth was a first port of call, news of the British army in the Peninsula War was received two days ahead of London. *The Royal Cornwall Gazette* scooped all the London papers with the news of Nelson's victory and death at Trafalgar in 1805.

But, the paper had an Achilles heel – its political style. Bribery and corruption in local affairs was widespread. Only a minority qualified, under the property laws, for voting rights. These were openly sold to the highest bidder. Often they were sold twice. Sometimes people contrived to get their names on two voting registers, thus having two votes to sell. The going rate was five guineas per vote (about five hundred pounds sterling by today's values) and political agents would set up shop in local inns, jangling great bags of golden guineas.

The Royal Cornwall Gazette tried to by-pass these issues, and by many readers was found wanting. The time had come to promote a Reform newspaper. And so *The West Briton* was founded on Friday, 20 July 1810.

If further calamities were necessary to guarantee the success of the paper, these were supplied by the rapidly deteriorating financial position – the run on the London banks, with nine of them having to stop payment, and bankruptcies rising to the unprecedented level of over a thousand a month.

An editorial battle waged between Flindell of the *Gazette* and Edward Budd of the *West Briton*. In the end Budd won, as the Stamp Duty figures of 1854 confirm: *The West Briton* 161,000 copies, *Royal Cornwall Gazette* 70,000 copies.

In these years, other papers were being started in other places for very similar reasons. One such rivalry was between the *Leicester Herald* and the *Leicester Chronicle*, both, as it happens, anti-government organs, and competing for the reformist readership. Against the strongly entrenched traditionalist *Leicester Journal* neither had much of a chance: by splitting their support they had no chance at all, then. Both succumbed to official pressure, to arise later. The point of noting this sad little story here is to record the prosecution mounted against the *Herald* by Spencer Perceval who was to achieve notoriety by becoming Prime Minister, and in that office, as an expression of that larger resentment grumbling in the shires, was assassinated.

A full report of the event is to be found in *The Morning Post* of Tuesday, 12 May 1812.

A few minutes after five o'clock yesterday afternoon, MR PERCEVAL proceeded on foot and alone from his residence in Downing Street to the House of Commons. – On entering the lobby, a man, who had been some time there, fired, and shot him through the left breast, near his heart. MR PERCEVAL walked forward for three or four yards, as if nothing had happened, and had reached the midway between the door of the lobby and the immediate door of the House, when he staggered, and sank on his knees, exclaiming in a faint voice, 'I am murdered, murdered!' LORD FRANCIS OSBORNE, and MR RIDLEY COLBOURNE, who were passing from the House at the time, and MR FRANCIS PHILLIPS, a gentleman from the neighbourhood of Manchester, who happened to be in the lobby, instantly rushed forwards, raised, and supported him. MR PERCEVAL groaned twice very deeply, and was carried into the Speaker's Secretary's room, (the door leading to which is between the fire place in the lobby, and the vote office) where he bled profusely, both from the wound and from his mouth, and in about five minutes, without uttering a single word, expired in the arms of MR PHILLIPS. The lobby was very thin, not above twenty persons being in it. The assassin, as soon as he had perpetrated this diabolical act, made no attempt whatever to escape, but retreated to a bench near the fire place in the lobby. A Gentleman of the name of JERDAN, who had followed MR PERCEVAL into the lobby immediately seized him, and never quitted his grasp until he was taken into the House of Commons. While held securely on the bench, MR BURGESS, the Solicitor of Curzon-street, Mayfair (who was also in the lobby), wrenched the pistol which he had just discharged, and which was yet warm, from the right hand of the assassin.

Thence follows two further columns of this model of carefully detailed reportage.

One innovation, improvement, modification, rationalisation – call it what you will – very much to the taste of the modern reader, was introduced at this time. Between Salisbury, in the 1770s, and Windsor in 1812, printers gradually discarded the long 'f', used in place of the 's'. And, just as in Salisbury, so in Windsor, events of national and international drama rubbed shoulders with items of a more parochial nature. When, 25 miles to the west of London, there was published, on Saturday, 1 August of that year, the first issue of *The Windsor and Eton Express* (of the Counties of Berks, Bucks, Middlesex, Surry, Herts, Oxon, Hants and Wilts. Published at Windsor on Saturday Evening; and distributed with a circuit of Thirty Miles, early on Sunday morning) every general interest was thought to be catered for. This was to be one of the neutralist, conformist papers.

The very numerous and respectable population of the Counties in the vicinity of Windsor, their Agricultural and Commercial Property, have not unreasonably suggested, that *a Weekly Newspaper, uniting the merits of an important and original source of general and local information, with the publication of Advertisements essential to the immediate business of the neighbourhood*, might expect a due portion of public favour.

In fact, a paper of comfortable, and comforting, middle-class commercial appeal. Which, oddly, it still is. There is a very decent decorousness about the paper's offices today – and its pages are, it would seem, as determinedly undeterred by the unsettling events now, as they were in those early years of the nineteenth century. Except that now its coverage confines itself almost entirely to events of the locality. When that larger outer world intrudes, it is, perhaps, because just across the road stands Windsor Castle, where the Queen often resides.

News, in that first issue, began with a War Department despatch (dated 27 July), about the Peninsula War in Spain; an Admiralty Office despatch (dated 28 July) reporting a naval engagement in the Channel with a French Lugger, the *Ville de Caen*; the Anholt Mail from Warsaw (dated 30 June) describes the position of Russian and Polish forces facing Napoleon's allies, the Austrians; via Gottenburgh (18 July) comes a Supplement to the *St. Petersburgh Gazette* (3 July) in which is published an announcement from the Russian Headquarters (29 June) to the effect that a state of war must now be considered to exist between Russia and France as a consequence of the French invasion and attack on Russian forces at KOWNE. Riga is declared to be a city in a state of siege.

Then follows one of the most curious incidents ever to find its way into print: a declaration of war between two major world powers, in which the war is concluded virtually within the space of one issue of the newspaper, without a shot being fired. There is printed a formal – 'Declaration of War between the United Kingdom of Great Britain and Ireland, and their Dependencies thereof, and the United States of America, and their Territories', dated 18 June 1812, and signed – James Madison. Just a few lines further on, in an editorial comment, the annulment of this outbreak is anticipated –

... it will be one of the most singular events that ever occurred in history, that a war should have been begun and ended by the subtraction of that which was the chief subject of contention, (ie., the detaining of American ships by British Naval Forces) in so short a time, that, in fact, the chief excuse of the war should have been abolished at the moment when the declaration of it was issued.

The following week's issue of the paper reports that –

A respectable morning paper says, that

a letter from Liverpool states the arrival at that port, at a late hour on Tuesday evening, of a vessel from North America, with intelligence, 'that the Proclamation repealing the Orders in Council [i.e., annulling the orders to arrest American ships], had been received in America, with acclamations of joy in every quarter where it was made known, and that Mr President Madison had been constrained to issue a Proclamation declaring America and Great Britain to be at Peace. War was also immediately declared against France ...'

It can hardly be said that nineteenth-century events moved slowly! And that instant swing from war with Britain to war with France has an ironic ring in the light of another event reported in that first issue.

An American vessel, with a number of passengers on board, had been detained by the French in Calais for a year and a half. When, in July of 1812, they were released, Napoleon's creaking public relations machinery went ponderously into action. Each of the passengers was handed a circular letter from the District Prefect, which read –

Gentlemen – You are leaving France to return to your country – into the bosom of a nation allied to ours. The French Government, penetrated with the motives which distinguish its triumphant career, only wishes that you may repeat to your countrymen the exact recital of what you have seen. I am charged by my Government to inform you, that it will endeavour to protect those who keep within the bounds of reason, in proportion as it will punish those, who, carried away by unruly passions, partake of the rage of our enemies, – spreading alarming reports of France – and by false conjectures engender animosity. The eyes of France are turned to the new world as well as to this, and the hero who governs her knows well how to distinguish the friends of peace and concord, from her enemies. If any one among you has cause to complain of any rigorous treatment, he must not attribute it to an unjust motive, but to the impossibility under which a Government, surrounded by enemies, has of guarding against her attacks, without exercising such rigorous measures, but our friendship for the United States is sincere.

An example of those 'alarming reports' and 'false conjectures' is presented on the same page.

By a vessel lately from Bordeaux, with a cargo of wine, information has been received that the distress of that city, and of the neighbouring districts, are almost as great as during any period of the revolution. Bread was at ten sous, or 5d. a pound: formerly it was reckoned dear at four sous. The people crowded to the bakers' shops, en queue, as during Robespierre's time, and many went away disappointed. The peasants fed on beans and Indian corn, and were reduced to skeletons. Yet the terror of the military despotism kept every thing quiet, and likely to continue so. The vine growers had in some degree, been relieved unexpectedly by the produce of last year's vintage which had sold well and readily, owing to speculation from this country. The present vintage was also promising. By a recent decree, Buonaparte has shut up all private schools, and even prohibited the use of private tutors at home. All the boys or young men, wishing for education, must go to the Lyceums, there to imbibe military habits and servile obedience.

Meanwhile, with a calm and distant aplomb, the House of Lords, on Monday 27 July, read for the third time, and passed, The Religious Worship Bill, 'for better securing the Jurisdiction of the Church of England.' While in the House of Commons the following day there was debated the general measures for the suppression of violence arising from 'the troubled state of the nation and the many justified grievances to be remedied'.

Spy plots, and counter-spy plots, were very much in evidence.

On Saturday evening the following persons were apprehended at Rye and Winchelsea, who were presumed to be principally concerned in aiding General Philippon in his escape from this country to France, viz. – Hughes, the landlord of the Lion Inn at Rye, and the post-master of that town. Robinson, the person who, it is said, accompanied the French General from Oswestry (where he had been imprisoned), and who went with him in the boat to the French shore. Hutter and Turner, the two smugglers who carried the General over. The track of Philippon was traced to Rye, by the vigilance and activity of Vickery and Peakes of the Bow-Street Office. The offenders underwent a private examination yesterday at the Bow-Street Office, and were remanded to prison for a further examination.

It has appeared from evidence of one of those men, that a scheme had been laid for entrapping General Sarrazin, who was to have been invited to an entertainment, and then seized and gagged, and carried to the coast, in order to be transported to the French shore. The perpetrators were to have had a reward of £5000 sterling, for this base business ...

However, amid all these heady matters, more sober, civil considerations were not neglected, as witness the activities of the Association for the Relief of the Manufacturing and Labouring Poor.

The augmentation of our stock of animal food, from the inexaustible resources of the ocean, appears to be regarded as a most important branch of exertion by this Society. They have lately contracted for an early supply of 200 tons of salted cod. This contract will have the effect of engaging a number of fishermen, who are now usually quite unemployed; and about 450,000 lb. of acceptable and nutritious animal food will be thus added to the general quantity of diet, which, but for the establishment of this association, the community would not have possessed.

A Summary of Politics outlined the general position in Europe, and reported with astonishing brevity that 'The Treaty of Peace between England and Sweden has been officially announced'.

And on 30 July –

This day was committed to the county gaol of Reading, by Edward Parker, Esq., Mayor of Windsor, under a sentence of fourteen days hard labour, Thomas Higgs, a post boy in the employ of the postmaster of this town, for suffering a man of the name of Henry Styles, to ride on the horse with the bag of letters which he was conveying to Staines, on the evening of the 24th inst. contrary to the statute.

Disturbances, both foreign and domestic, notwithstanding – the Theatre Royal at Windsor opened for its summer season. 'On Monday evening, August 3, their Majesties Servants (from the Theatres Royal, London) will perform the celebrated Comedy of WILD OATS, or The Strolling Gentleman . . .'

No event for many years had quite caught the English attention so completely as the Battle of Waterloo, as it was to be dubbed. It was a clash of giants. The heroic, unflappable Wellington against the heroic, unpredictable Buonaparte.

The little Corsican's rampage across Europe had posed a threat against which the English had fought for more than a decade. Not even the most extreme of the Reformers was willing to accept the European parade as a token for future possibilities at home. Despite ravagements in political and economic affairs, English national identity remained intact and able effectively to defend itself. Now, that issue, at last was to be put to the test. Napoleon's escape from Elba had placed these matters in the scales of chance once more. In this mood, the nation faced the prelude, the overture to the main event.

For two papers Wellington's victory could hardly have been more opportune. Number One of *The Patriot*, or *Carlisle and Cumberland Advertiser*, was dated Saturday, 3 June 1815. On the front page, an excerpt from the *London Gazette* reads:

A letter received by the Duchess of Wellington on Monday last from the Duke, gave reasons to expect that a great battle would soon be fought by the army under his Grace's command. Advices brought by Mr Hunter, the messenger who arrived on Saturday, repeat the same expectations. Whether the British were to be attacked, or to be the assailants, is not specified, but in either case we trust that the event will be fortune and glorious for our country's arms.

Sixteen days later, on a Sunday evening in mid-June, Napoleon's career ended in blood-stained ruins.

But perhaps no editor could have been more grateful for the neat timing of the British victory than James Amphlett of Lichfield. News of the successful outcome of the battle reached him just in time for his first issue. Almost the whole of the back page of the *Lichfield Mercury* dated Friday, 7 July 1815, is given over to a full report of the triumph. Three full columns cover eyewitness accounts of the fight, from both the British and French points of view. There is a summary of reports put out in the French papers. And the announcement of Napoleon's abdication –

Frenchmen! In commencing war for maintaining the national independence, I relied on the union of all efforts, of all wills, and the concurrence of all the national authorities. I had reason to hope for success, and I braved all the declarations of the Powers against me. Circumstances appear to me changed. I offer myself as a sacrifice to the hatred of the enemies of France. May they prove sincere in their declarations, and have really directed them only against my powers! My political life is terminated, and I proclaim my son under the title of Napoleon the II Emperor of the French. The present Ministers will provisionally form the Council of the Government. The interest which I take in my son induces me to invite the Chambers to form without delay the Regency by law. Unite all for the public safety, in order to remain an independent nation.

(Signed) Napoleon.

Commercial pressures and the need to expand brought fresh problems to a craft industry in which technical innovation had hardly made any impact. A typical response was amalgamation with a view to rationalising printing and distribution. In 1838, one such resulted in the *Essex, Herts and Kent Mercury* serving an ungainly territory split in two by the bulk of London, and the broad span of the River Thames. The editor saddled with this awkward offspring was J. B. Harvey, who, in his memoirs, described how he tackled the problem. To ensure that Kent and Herts readers had their copies on Wednesday, part of the paper had to be printed in London.

The four outside pages were printed in Colchester, and on Saturday afternoons these half-printed sheets were packed in two large boxes, and suspended under a carriage or machine constructed for the purpose, and as night traveling was compulsory, the body of the vehicle was fitted up as a sleeping apartment, furnished with accommodation for reading and writing, and amply lighted. Besides the indispensable hammock, it also contained sufficient warlike stores, consisting of a musket (with bayonet fixed), a shot belt, powder flask and life preserver. Thus equipped, the weekly transit of the editor from Colchester to the Metropolis was thought to be sufficiently assured, while the precious cargo of broadsheets had a sure safe-guard for the fatal disaster of capture.

This editorial coach left Colchester each Saturday afternoon at five. At Kelvedon it met the opposite Colchester coach coming from London. On board this were reports from Kent and Herts. These the editor prepared for the printers, as his coach lurched through the night along the rough highway, completing the task by midnight, when he was due to arrive at Chelmsford. There, he had supper and changed horses. Pushing on into the darkness, London was reached by nine on the Sunday morning, where the partly-printed sheets and the edited reports were handed over to the printers. Printing completed, and the pages proofread, the editor headed back on Monday night, arriving again at Colchester at noon on Tuesday. And this was a weekly routine!

In the forefront of the political papers, there now came the *Manchester Guardian* (now *The Guardian*). Born of a socially conscious, religious-backed movement, it was founded by John Edward Taylor in 1821, to serve

the classes to whom, more especially, Advertisements are addressed . . . It will zealously enforce the principles of civil and religious liberty . . . it will warmly advocate the cause of Reform; it will endeavour to assist in the diffusion of just principles of Political Economy; and support without

THE LICHFIELD MERCURY;
AND MIDLAND CHRONICLE.

No. 1. Vol. 1.　　　　LICHFIELD, FRIDAY, JULY 7, 1815.　　　　Price Sixpence Halfpenny.

PRINTED BY JAMES AMPHLETT, AT THE OFFICE, IN BOAR STREET, LICHFIELD.

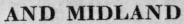

CITY OF LICHFIELD.

NOTICE is hereby given, that the next GENERAL GAOL DELIVERY, for the City and County of the City of Lichfield, will be held at the Guildhall in the said City, on Monday the seventh day of August next, at ten o'clock in the forenoon.

STEPHEN SIMPSON,
Town Clerk.

FARM AT SHENSTONE.

To be Sold by Auction,

On Wednesday the 12th day of July next, at the Bull's Head, at Shenstone, in the county of Stafford, at four o'clock in the afternoon:—

PARTICULARS
OF A VALUABLE
FREEHOLD ESTATE;

CONSISTING of the MANOR of FULFIN, with good Farm House and Buildings, and 219a. 2r. 30p. of excellent Arable, Meadow, and Pasture LAND, most desirably situated within one mile and a half of the City of Lichfield. Also, a large commodious FAMILY HOUSE, at the east entrance of the City of Lichfield; which will be

SOLD BY AUCTION,
By WILLIAM HARRIS,

PROSPECTUS
OF THE
LICHFIELD MERCURY.

TO THE PUBLIC.

The advantages of a PUBLIC JOURNAL, to a district which had been deprived of any medium of publicity of its own, and, which, in all its communications with the public, was obliged to avail itself of the partial and irregular circulation of many different Provincial Journals, are such, that it does not require any laboured illustration to make them felt and appreciated.

J. LEONARD,
AGENT FOR
The Lichfield Mercury,

MOST respectfully begs leave to return his grateful and sincere thanks to the Nobility, Gentry, and Inhabitants of RUGELEY and its vicinity.

Circulating Library,

A GENERAL ASSORTMENT OF
STATIONERY,

A GREAT VARIETY OF
BOOKS,
IN PLAIN AND ELEGANT BINDINGS.

BOOKBINDING,

MUSIC AND MUSICAL INSTRUMENTS
MILITARY BANDS SUPPLIED.
GENUINE PATENT MEDICINES

Perfumery of the very best quality.

reference to the party from which they emanate, all serviceable measures.

These included the replacement of 'antiquated and despotic Governments ... by institutions conformable to the increased intelligence of the ages'.

In a leading article for the first issue Taylor wrote that he would avoid scurrility and slander, and that the paper would express opinions on public matters in a manner 'that even our political opponents shall admit the propriety of the spirit in which they are written, however fundamentally they may *differ* from their *own* principles and views'.

That all was not well in England is amply confirmed in Issue One of the *Brighton Gazette*, of Thursday, 22 February 1821.

At the present crisis, when the breath of faction, blasphemy and sedition, is spreading its baneful influence over the mind, threatening destruction to those institutions which can alone preserve the happiness and welfare of the country – when opinions injurious to the best interests of the nation, and principles undermining the order and regulations of society, are disseminated by designing and discontented men, it becomes necessary that every means should be used to oppose their progress, and to prevent the blow which is meditated against our lives, and liberties, and our property. With this view, in opposition to those doctrines tending to excite and inflame the public mind, to protect our civil and religious rights from invasion, and for the preservation of our ancient Constitution, as an auxiliary, politically, the BRIGHTON GAZETTE is established.

That such firm middle-class sentiments should prevail in Brighton is hardly surprising. A fashionable retreat for Royalty, it had long attracted the wealthy and idle of London. No less than 48 stage coaches a day covered the run from London to Brighton, and a further 26 daily services ran into the town on other routes. Nor were these conveyances as slow as we might presume. In 1830 the Red Rover coach did the run in four hours.

Those same signs of disaffection that had provoked the Brighton editor were equally current in London, and showed themselves on the first pages of the *Sunday Times*.

Sunday, 20 October 1822 –

If we turn from the contemplation of this disgusting scene (Europe) to the internal state of our country, an endless and unvarying succession of almost general distress presents itself to our view. Bankruptcy, beggary, and calamity, with giant strides, stalk through this once-smiling and flourishing country; while the weight of taxation, and an obstinate adherence on the part of Ministers to the same profligate waste of the national resources, and the same corrupt system to which are to be attributed all our reverses, precludes all rational hope of returning prosperity.

The similarity of these editorial utterances to those now in circulation is striking, and confirms the view that all phases of a nation's life run in cycles. As evidence –

Does Ireland present a more favourable scene? If the evils that overwhelm this country, and have been enumerated until the tongue of complaint has become weary of its task, exhibit the most frightful omens for the future, is there any better prospect in the present condition of the sister Kingdom? Have not the privations and miseries, the penury and oppressions of the lesser island, grown out of the political evils and cruel neglect of the greater? What Englishman, who does not prefer the suggestions of chimerical hope to the informing light of his understanding, can even fancy that he sees the dawn of better days?

The present state of England (consequent to that of America and Europe) is truly deplorable and inauspicious. Unhappily the worst part of her prospect is its termination. The appalling scene closes with the gloomy sky and barren land. Should, however (from some most improbable and unexpected cause), the clouds break, and the soil improve, we will be the first to hail the change with hearts as gladdened, as our minds will be surprised.

However, no such negative thoughts apparently disturbed the mind of James Lomax when he set himself the task of composing a dedication to the first publication of the *Stockport Advertiser*. Friday, 29 March 1822 – he wrote '... we profess ourselves the honest and loyal supporters of our Gracious King, the devoted servants of the laws; the affectionate friends of our fellow-countrymen...'

The Stockport paper, like most provincial papers, was still in 1822, set by hand and printed on a hand press. Two men were employed in the operation, one inking the type and placing the paper on the type, while the other ran the type under the press to secure the impression on the paper. When one side of the paper was printed, the process was repeated for the other side. The output was about 200 copies an hour.

Contrast this with the first installation of a steam press by *The Times* in 1814. The first use of it was made on 29 November.

Our Journal of this day presents to the public the practical result of the greatest improvement connected with printing since the discovery of the art itself. The reader of this paragraph now holds in his hand one of the many thousand impressions of *The Times* newspaper, which were taken off last night by a mechanical apparatus.

The apparatus in question was the First Steam Printing Machine built by two Germans, Frederick Koenig and Andrew Bauer, capable of printing 1,100 sheets an hour. After more than four centuries of printing, with barely a change from the original techniques of Caxton, the age of technology was about to bite deeply to the heart of the craft world of the English newspaper.

That bite came with astonishing speed. The old Stanhope hand press had a maximum capacity of 250 sheets an hour. The Koenig press pushed that up to 1,100, and then with modifications raised this to 1,800, i.e., 900 sheets on both sides. In 1818 William Cowper, in partnership with his brother-in-law Ambrose Applegath, had perfected a new printing machine capable of print-

The Sunday Times.

ed upon your minds, let it be instilled into your children, that the LIBERTY OF THE PRESS is the PALLADIUM of all the Civil, Political and RELIGIOUS RIGHTS of an ENGLISHMAN.

LONDON: SUNDAY, OCTOBER 20, 1822.

On Saturday, April 27th, 1822, was published, No. 1. of

THE MUSEUM; or, Record of Literature, Fine Arts, Science, Antiquities, the Drama, &c., &c.— This work is devoted to, 1st, General Literature, including Reviews of Books, and Essays on Men and Manners; 2d, the Belles Lettres and Fine Arts; 3d, Science and Philosophy; 4th, Antiquities and Biography; 5th, Varieties and Facetiæ, including Poetry, &c.

THE MUSEUM is neatly printed on the largest sized sheet, in quarto, containing 16 pages, or 48 columns, and delivered early on Saturday, price 6d. in London and its Environs; or 1s. if sent FREE by Post, on Saturday evening into the country.—Book Clubs, Reading Societies, and persons who are not particularly desirous of having the work on the day of publication, may receive the numbers weekly, at 5d. each, or monthly, with the Reviews and Magazines, by giving a particular order to their respective Booksellers or Agents.—Country Subscribers, wishing to plete their sets, may purchase the numbers unstamped through their Booksellers.—THE MUSEUM is also made up into QUARTERLY PARTS, for the use of the colonies, or for persons travelling.

ORIGINAL STRICTURES.

TO OUR READERS.

We this day submit to the public a new, and, we hope, attractive and useful publication, the principal object of which is to instil an invigorating spirit, suitable to the character and exigencies of the times in which we live. It is not for us to boast of our own merit, but we may allow ourselves to hope, that in the execution of our design, we shall be found not wholly to have failed. In explaining the motive of our undertaking—the feelings by which we have been urged—we shall be permitted to expatiate, with decent confidence, on the patriotism we profess, and the mode we have adopted for its display, and beneficial operation.

entitled to be free! Convinced ourselves of the eternal political truth, that where the public press shrinks from its bounden duty, liberty is in the direst danger; and that, if annihilated or invaded, the same press is the only remaining means of its recovery, the only surviving hope of the people—we determined, instead of being discouraged and laying upon our oars, to apply our utmost strength with that renovated and glowing ardour, worthy of the cause so near and dear to our hearts; and to have nothing more to wish or hope for, in aid of our earnest and ardent exertions, than the favouring and auspicious gale of public encouragement.

Our motive, then, for instituting THE SUNDAY TIMES is explained. Of the merit of the *particulars*

Masthead of the first issue of 'The Sunday Times'. William Corder, who was convicted of the Red Barn Murder, advertised for a wife in the columns of that paper

The Stanhope Press

ing 2,400 (1,200 on both sides) in an hour. This machine, the Cowper Stereotype was soon replaced by another, designed by the same two men, that printed a staggering 4,000 sheets on both sides. This was their 'multiple' machine of 1827, with four cylinders, beneath which the forme, or frame of type, passed, fed with paper by four boys.

The basis of the new machine was the replacement of the old flat plates, with plates cast from curved moulds made of papier mâché – a method which is only now being replaced in Fleet Street by photo offset.

The Cowper Stereotype Press

The Koenig Steam Press

SURVIVING NEWSPAPERS FOUNDED BETWEEN 1801
AND 1825

Warwick Advertiser	founded 1806
The Western Sunday Independent (Plymouth)	1808
Berwick Advertiser	1808
Cheltenham Chronicle and Gloucester Graphic	1809
Suffolk Mercury	1810
Leicester Chronicle	1810
The West Briton and Royal Cornwall Gazette	1810
Macclesfield Express	1811
Windsor, Slough and Eton Express	1812
Evening Gazette (Colchester)	1814
Durham Advertiser	1814
Cumberland News	1815
Lichfield Mercury	1815
Mid-Kent Gazette	1815
Wiltshire Gazette and Herald	1816
Westmoreland Gazette	1818
The Guardian (Manchester and London)	1821
Brighton and Hove Gazette	1821
Sunday Times	1822
Stockport Advertiser	1822
North Devon Journal-Herald	1824
Journal of Commerce (Liverpool)	1825

Published by C. Baldwin

The Standard.

Signifer statue Signum:
HIC OPTIME MANEBIMUS.

Plant here THE STANDARD:
Here we shall best remain.

MONDAY, MAY 21, 1827.

but all their efforts proving unavailing against the increasing rush of the water, they were forced to retreat towards the shaft. The instant the accident occurred, a general consternation prevailed amongst the workmen, and they simultaneously rushed towards the shaft—*sauve qui peut* was the universal sentiment, and in their hurry several ludicrous accidents took place. It is with pleasure we announce, that no life was lost on the occasion, though the engineers, and particularly Tallatt, narrowly escaped drowning. It appears that at a quarter before seven o'clock, the 12 shields, or frame-works, were in the act of being propelled forward at the end of the tunnel, to enable the workmen to excavate more securely ; and at that time the tunnel extended 580 feet under the Thames. The workmen employed in propelling No. 11 and 12 shields, observed the soil to give way between these shields, and in a few seconds afterwards the water poured in through an aperture about six inches in diameter. Tallatt, the engineer, screwed up three door-ways as he retreated towards the shaft, and he was obliged to swim a considerable distance. A workman named Gutis was also in the water for some time. Tallatt being a good swimmer, remained at the top of the water, about ten feet below the top of the shaft, till Messrs. Brunel, junior, and Gravatt, came to his assistance. Mr. Brunel, junior, plunged into the water, and affixed a rope round Tallatt, and he was drawn up in a state of exhaustion to the top of the shaft. From the time the water first broke in, till the tunnel and shaft were filled to the level of the river, twelve minutes elapsed. The engineers are quite confident that they shall be able to repair the injury, and that the only consequence which will arise from it, will be the retarding of the work for about a fortnight. This day Mr. Brunel will descend in a diving bell, to ascertain the extent of the injury, and to adopt means of stopping the aperture caused by the influx of the water. Should the means proposed to be used be successful, the water in the tunnel will be drawn up, by means of steam engines in a few days.

The following is a letter, from the principal engineer, on the above subject :—

" Mr. Editor—I feel it a duty incumbent on me to make known to the public an accident which occurred this evening to the tunnel, by the water from the Thames overpowering the exertions which, at the time, could be opposed to it. Although this circumstance will retard

Victoriana and the Great Exhibition

The second quarter of the nineteenth century was a period of upsurge in English national morale. After the disasters and uncertainties of the preceding years, the country was getting its second wind. Such, certainly, is the impression gained from reading papers of the period. Gone are the anguished, breast-beating editorials: gone the shrill bewailing of adverse fate: gone the nervous brooding on an unclear future. Discord remained, of course. But social inter-class discord is a perennial theme in English society. One suspects that, properly applied, it is the source of much national vitality and regeneration. Competition in the 'we'll-show-them' mood supplies the stimulus for innovation and new activity.

A powerful sub-theme at that time was anti-Catholicism. It led in 1827 to the founding of *The Standard* as a London daily devoted to the anti-Catholic cause. Thirty years later, it was being published in morning and evening editions, the latter being the commercially successful one. People got into the habit of asking for "the evening edition of *The Standard*'. In 1860 the inevitable and obvious course was accepted. The morning edition was ended, and the paper continued as The *Evening Standard*.

Its title, rather unexpectly, derived from the latin tag used at its masthead:

> Signifer Statue Signum,
> Hic Optime Manebimus.
> Plant here the Standard,
> Here we shall best remain.

The span of events across which the paper's pages extend illustrates well the tide of circumstance on which English buoyancy rose:

28 August 1833	Abolition of Slavery in British Colonies
28 June 1838	Coronation of Queen Victoria
1839	Discovery of gold in Australia
1840	First Penny Post
25 March 1843	Opening of the First Tunnel beneath the Thames
1848	Discovery of gold in America
1851	The Great Exhibition
25 October 1854	Charge of the Light Brigade
5 November 1854	Battle of Inkerman
1857	The Indian Mutiny
1861	American Civil War
4 April 1865	Assassination of Lincoln
1867	Opening of Suez Canal
1870	Siege of Paris
23 October 1871	Meeting of Stanley and Livingstone
28 December 1879	Tay Bridge Disaster
2 July 1881	Shooting of President Garfield
3 September 1882	Battle of Tel-el-Kebir
1890	Opening of Tower Bridge
10 October 1899	Boer War
17 May 1900	Relief of Mafeking.

Characteristic of the paper's early style is a certain bluntness in the reporting that, by today's standards, is refreshing. Straw remains straw; no bricks are made from it:

23 May, 1827. City 1 pm. The transactions this morning have been scarcely worth noticing.
Court of Chancery. The proceedings this morning in the Court of Chancery were entirely devoid of interest.
Court of King's Bench. This being the last day of Term the Court was occupied until 11 o'clock in hearing motions from Junior Counsel at the Bar of no public interest.
25 May 1827. Smithfield. Prime Scots this morning are quoted at 5/2d to 5/4d. a stone: Best mutton 5/- to 5/6d a stone. In lamb there is nothing to notice.

With matching bluntness, the *Bucks Herald* (1832) dealt in its issue of 11 January 1851, with the prevailing corruption in local elections:

A Candidate! What calculations of golden advantages does the name excite. He is regarded as a rich booty and prize, to be made the most of. His pockets are pulled at by his 'friends' from all sides. He sees burdensome debts contracted daily against him. But he mustn't breathe a complaint 'it is the custom, and he must expect it' – 'he is in the hands of his committee'. They, for the time are lords of his substance. And in a right regal manner do they dispose of it. At their nod daily feasts are spread for a whole month at this publichouse, and streams of gratuitous brandy and water are set flowing in that. Troops of musicians and flag men, and placard bearers innumerable, are called into action ... The Candidate pays for all. Yes, and a cruel extortion it is to him, unless he be a wealthy or well-supplied and woefully unscrupulous competitor for Parliamentary honours.

Thus spoke the voice of moderate independence against the financially entrenched interests in the Aylesbury Election of December 1850. An eye-witness account in the same issue completes the picture:

The publichouses were open as usual. Dinners, suppers, toddy and tea as plentiful as ever. People were drunk on Monday, Tuesday, Wednesday, Thursday, Friday, Saturday and Sunday morning – gloriously drunk. We saw them in publichouses drunk, rolling through the streets drunk, carried home by their wives drunk. And they were drunk not at their own expense. The publicans boast it was the best Election they ever saw, for, say they, the money was paid down beforehand. We must also add that persons wearing the cloth of gentlemen were drunk – not drunk as pigs are drunk, for pigs have more sense, but as far gone as ever men were who degrade themselves to a position lower than the lowest brute.

Avowedly independent, the paper began its career fighting to find a place between an established Whig organ, *The Bucks Gazette*, and an equally powerful Tory paper, *The Buckinghamshire, Bedfordshire and Hertfordshire Chronicle.* Understandably, therefore, its rare stand on a political matter was in an arena favourable to, and manipulated by, the major parties. Elsewhere, the paper reserved its spleen for non-political issues – opposition to the London–Birmingham Railway:

We oppose it (the proposed railway) on local and general and political grounds. Locally, because we believe it will prejudice the interests in Bucks and its adjacent counties very materially ... Generally, it will ruin all the masters, canal proprietors and carriers. It will destroy the breeding of horses and the growth of corn and fodder. Politically, should this scheme be carried into effect the example will be followed throughout the country and render England a mass of smoke and iron-work – rurality would be utterly destroyed, privacy completely annihilated.

(That was in 1832; twenty-eight years later, the paper supported the building of new railways.)

And, the sale of wives:

On Monday week a fellow exhibited his wife for sale, with a halter round her waist, in Melksham Market, Wiltshire, and she was purchased by a neighbour for 2/6. On Friday week a man named Stradling offered his wife for sale in Bath Market. The lady, it appeared, had been sold for 2/6 on Monday, at Lansdown Fair, but the bargain was not considered legal, first because the sale was not held in a public market place, and, secondly, because the purchaser had a wife already. The lady was dashingly attired, and had a halter, covered with silk, round her neck. The biddings mounted at last to five shillings, at which sum it was understood she was bought in. We had some satisfaction in adding that the husband was taken up and committed for causing a disturbance.

Also, the singing of hymns in Church, a custom then being introduced: 'It is my intention (said the then Vicar of Aylesbury) to have a hymn sung during our services in this church on Sundays. Hymns are now used in all churches, with very few exceptions, and we shall be amongst the last to adopt them.'

The loyalty of a readership to a paper is probably more an emotional than an intellectual attachment. This is particularly so with local papers. And while that emotional appeal may be based on some editorial theme, such as a class or financial interest, or a political philosophy, attachment to place offers, from a publishing point of view, a more effective long-term stratagem. The risk that a politically neutral paper might be identified with traditionalist Tory concepts could be dispelled, editors found, by declaring their overall allegiance to their place of publication. Again and again, introductory editorials contain a forthright declaration of the freedom of their pages to all opinions expressed locally. And while the distinction between political local papers and 'place' papers did not generally end during the last years of the century, the possibility of being neutral and non-establishment became increasingly viable. Having said that, it is curious how, in these last years of the twentieth century, local papers, for so long politically neutral, and indeed, politically naive in their editorial attitudes, are now, under extensive programmes of amalgamation into publishing groups under centralised control, evolving stronger political manifestations that, to a degree, ape those of the London-based national press.

Lincolnshire had a politically Conservative paper in 1830. It failed. Two years later, local members of the legal profession met to 'take into consideration the expediency of establishing a new county newspaper'. The feeling of the meeting was in favour of the enterprise. Six thousand pounds were subscribed in twenty-five pound shares. Benjamin Smith, a well-known Stamford solicitor was voted Chairman of the founding company.

The paper, while nominally 'based upon those Sound Constitutional Principles by which the King is secured in the exercise of his just Prerogatives' was also edited 'without regard to party or local politics'. Some inkling of this editorial flavour can be gleaned from a celebratory poem, written by a gentleman subscriber in Caistor, and published in the second issue of the *Lincolnshire Chronicle*, dated 11 January 1833.

THE 'CHRONICLE'S' WELCOME

Bon jour, Monsieur 'Chronicle', comment vous pertez vous?
I've waited long in anxious hope to have a peep at you.
Your portly limbs and body sleek; your head so long and wise;
Tho' but an infant, born this week, you're sure to give surprise.
Thy face intelligent declares what most men wish to learn;
And who can thy good natured smiles uncourteously return?
Thou tell'st of Fairs, Donations, Deaths, of Marriages and Crimes,
And greets us on the new born year with 'Oddity's' happy rhymes;
Our morals, too, thou wilt o'erlook – our vices wilt reprove,
And by thy genial influence, gain our esteem and love.
The head defenceless thou wilt shield – nor give to virtue pain,
We ne'er will force thee from the field – our hearts thou soon will gain;
O! may'st thou Freedom's weapons wield – and long – long be thy reign!

The year 1837 marked the appearance of yet another Conservative local paper – *The Wilts and Gloucestershire Standard.* Under pressure from the Reformists, traditionalists were reacting hard. The year is significant, looking back. William the Fourth died in September. The *Bucks Herald* in its obituary notice, referred to 'The good and kind-hearted William the Fourth has become a 'clod of the valley' ... Benevolent, well-intentioned, this monarch was ever anxious for the well-being of this land over which he ruled...'

But good intentions lack that power of attraction and concentration necessary to a national figurehead. And,

THE WILTS AND GLOUCESTERSHIRE
Standard.

PRO REGE, LEGE, ARIS ET FOCIS.

VOL. I.—No. 1.   SATURDAY, JANUARY 28, 1837.   PRICE 5D.

for whatever reason, the nation's restoring energies had to have a fresh focus, which they found in the image of Victoria, the new, young Queen.

That almost essential class fight had to have its potential destructiveness contained by new targets. The danger is well enough defined in the first prospectus of *The Wilts and Gloucestershire Standard* (Saturday, 28 January 1837)

Will the men of Wilts and Gloucester be backward in the defence of that Constitution which they are bound to preserve as the most precious inheritance of their children, and transmit to them entire and uninjured as they received it from their ancestors? Will they allow the fierce spirit of a licentious Democracy...to acquire such fearful ascendancy, as to threaten every point of the social edifice with destruction...

And the first editorial continues this partisan attack:

Men of Wilts and Gloucester – The Constitution of Great Britain, by securing to you the blessings of a good Government and rational freedom, has enabled you to apply your industry, husband your wealth, and extend your commerce, until your country has become mistress of the seas, the storehouse of the world, rich in all the varied products of the earth, the arbiter of nations, feared, honoured, and envied by every other country on the face of the globe.

In what condition is the ... Commons' House of Parliament...that which was once the theatre of all that was intelligent, wise and eloquent, has become the scene of violence, abuse, and empty declamation.

In what state is the Church? ... The same anti-Christian and infidel faction, has attacked the venerable edifice ... the people have been seduced from their faith ... and measures introduced which, by doing away with the necessity of making the solemnization of marriage a religious sanction, and reducing it to a Civil contract, have struck at the very root of religion, and the morality of England.

What is the present state of England? ... Have not the Ministers ... supported the democratic principles throughout Europe? Have they not made themselves parties to the internecine strife of Spain and Portugal, assisted France in her grasping views, and opposed themselves to legitimate authority throughout the Continent; and have they not rendered Holland and Russia, and Prussia, and Austria, and Germany inimical to English interests ...

What is the state of agriculture? Has not the fundamental interest of the country been neglected and abused by men unacquainted with the soil or its products; and have not associations been formed by the same faction for the purpose of opposing the interests of the farmer, reducing him to a level with the miserable continental producer?

What is the state of Ireland? Absolutely without law, without government; the people physically in a wretched condition ... and the whole country under the control of ... the Papist, incendiary, and agitator, who ... by reducing Ireland to a complete state of anarchy and revolution ... may rejoice among the ruins, and feed upon the spoil.

Parliament is approaching, the Session is about to open. What are the measures which with unblushing effrontery are proposed by these men as being necessary to their scheme of government. First, the *Ballot* is declared to be the groundwork, next *Annual Parliaments* then *Universal Suffrage*, an un-

controlled *Press*, the *severence* of Church and State, the *extinction* of the House of Lords, and the paramount *supremacy* of the House of Commons.

A crisis is approaching, and the country is preparing to strike the blow, and Monarchy or Anarchy, Government or mob-violence, Conservatism or spoilation, are the only alternatives. It only requires one universal effort – a pull, a strong pull, and a pull altogether – and the day is ours.

It rings oddly now to see principles which are generally revered today, denounced in such uncompromising terms. But this full-blooded style of writing was a long-standing tradition in English editorial writing, and the rest of the paper takes a much more moderate tone. In the immediately adjacent column to the fire-brand flames, we read 'In aid too of the general spirit of advancement we hail with pleasure the projection and adoption of the various new lines of rail-road...' And on the subject of Russo-American relations 'Russia forgives democracy in America on account of its slaves, as America forgives despotism in Russia in consideration of her serfs.'

Victorian papers, in their headlong race for survival, explored many ingenious formulae for success. The first 'give-away' papers date from this time – papers in which all the revenue comes from the advertising – the paper is distributed to its readers free of charge. *The Lynn Advertiser* of 1841 was one such. The *Leicester Advertiser* which came out the year following, started as an auc-

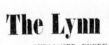

The Southport Visiter

AND GENERAL ADVERTISER.

NO. 1. VOL. I.   SATURDAY, MAY 4TH, 1844.   PRICE THREEPENCE.

TRINITY CHURCH, SOUTHPORT.

ON SUNDAY next, May 5th, 1844, TWO SERMONS will be preached in the above Church, and Collections made towards defraying the existing debt, and the current Church Expenses.

The Morning Service will commence at half-past Ten, and the Afternoon Service at Three.

VICTORIA HOUSE, LORDS'-STREET.

MRS. and Miss HOUGHTON return their sincere thanks to the Ladies and Visiters of Southport for the very liberal support they have received since they commenced business as above, and beg respectfully to intimate that they have in stock an assortment of FASHIONABLE MILLINERY, Tuscan and Straw Bonnets, Brazilian Hats, Ribbons, Laces, Flowers, and other Fancy Goods, the whole of which are now ready for inspection.

COMMERCIAL HOUSE, SOUTHPORT.

LINEN AND WOOLLEN DRAPERY, HOSIERY,
Hats, Caps, Bonnets, &c.

RICHARD RIMMER,

EVER grateful for favors conferred, begs to inform his numerous customers that he has in stock an immense variety of goods in the above branches of business, which have been carefully selected from the first Manufacturers, and are such that he can confidently recommend to his friends for their durability and cheapness. They may be *equalled by some, but surpassed by none.*

R. R. Is weekly receiving additions to his present stock.

Best XX DUBLIN PORTER, Bottled and Draught ; Pale India Burton Ale, &c., constantly on sale.

MILLINERY,
BABY LINEN, LACE, AND FANCY WAREHOUSE.

FAMILY MOURNING.

MRS. AND MISS SHUFFLEBOTHAM

GRATEFULLY return their warmest thanks to their friends for past favors, and respectfully beg to inform the Ladies and Visiters of Southport and its vicinity, that Miss S. has returned from London, with an entire new selection of fashionable Millinery, Bonnets, Caps, Collars, Ribbons, Children's Dresses, Coats, Blouses, and other fancy goods ; and, agreeably to the wish of many of their friends, they have entered into the Straw business ; the stock, which is entirely new, consists of Ladies' and Children's Bonnets, in great variety, Gentlemen's and Youth's Hats ; the whole of which is now ready for inspection.

Orders in each department of the business particularly attended to.

May 3rd, 1844.

FASHIONABLE DRESSMAKING AND MILLINERY.
4, WALKER'S TERRACE.

E. LEWIS having commenced the above business, respectfully solicits the patronage of the Ladies and Visiters of Southport.

STAY AND CORSET ESTABLISHMENT.

C. EVANS,
STAY AND CORSET MAKER,
Grove Cottage, Lords'-street,

BEGS to return her most sincere thanks to the Ladies and Visiters of Southport, for the very liberal patronage and support with which she has been favored since she commenced the above business, and hopes, by strict attention to all commands, to merit a continuance of their favors.

Southport, May 1st, 1844.

Apartments, &c.

CHARLTON'S
CLAREMONT PRIVATE FAMILY HOTEL,
(With or without Board,)
ON THE VICTORIA PROMENADE,
Fronting to the Sea.

M. CHARLTON, in tendering his most grateful acknowledgments for the very liberal encouragement he has met with since opening the above establishment, begs to assure his friends and the visiters generally to this most healthy and delightful watering-place, that it shall be, as it ever has been, his constant study to afford them all the quiet, comfort, and convenience of home.

Good Post Horses, very handsome Carriage, and steady Drivers.

N.B.—Agent for the sale of Bass & Co.'s celebrated India PALE ALE, in Casks and Bottles.

MISS MORLEY

RESPECTFULLY informs her Friends and the Visiters of Southport that she has taken and furnished a comfortable Cottage, in Sea Bank-road, near the Bold Arms Hotel, for the accommodation of Lodgers.

MRS. SMITH,
No. 8, UNION-TERRACE, SOUTHPORT,
(Late Rose-Hill,)
LODGINGS.

SCARISBRICK ARMS AND COMMERCIAL HOTEL, SOUTHPORT.

JAMES HUNT, proprietor of the above establishment, (which is situated near the centre of the village,) takes this opportunity of presenting to his numerous friends, and the visiters to this most attractive watering-place, his unfeigned acknowledgments for the very handsome and particularly liberal encouragement hitherto conferred upon him ; and in soliciting the favor of their future patronage, he embraces the present opportunity of assuring them that his utmost endeavours shall at all times be exerted for their comfort and convenience.

Families can be accommodated with private Apartments on the usual terms.

Board at the Public Ordinaries, 5s. per day. Do. privately 6s. per day.

Coaches to and from the Railway Station at Euxton ; from thence persons may proceed to all parts of the kingdom.

Patent-safety Omnibus (built by Cowburn, of Manchester), and other Conveyances, to meet the Packet-Boat to and from Manchester daily.

Open and close Carriages, with very superior Horses, and steady drivers.

Livery Stables, and Lock-up Coach-houses ; with every other requisite for such a large and commodious establishment.

VICTORIA BATHS, SOUTHPORT.

WILLIAM BALL begs to inform the Visiters of Southport, and the public in general, that he has taken and entered upon the above named Baths, and trusts, by due attention to all (especially invalids) who may favor him with their support, to prove himself worthy of their confidence and patronage.

Cards of terms may be had on application at the Baths.

Subscribers of one pound per annum will be entitled to use the Baths at the usual reduced terms.

N.B.—No person with an offensive ailment will be allowed to bathe in these Baths.

THOMAS STALEY,

DISPENSING CHEMIST, AND DEALER IN TEAS, COFFEE, &c.,

RETURNS his sincere thanks to the Inhabitants and Visiters of Southport, for the long-continued and increasing share of their confidence and support.

He desires to inform his friends and the public, that having made extensive alterations in his Shop and premises, with a view of entering more fully into the GROCERY BUSINESS, he is now prepared to execute their orders for every article of superior Grocery, at such prices, consistent with quality, as he flatters himself will give entire satisfaction.

He has just returned from the Potteries, with a choice selection of superb ORNAMENTS, suitable for the Drawing-room or Toilette, and will be obliged by a call to inspect this department of his business.

Personal attention is invariably paid to the Dispensing of Prescriptions and Family Recipes.

Schweppe's and Thompson's Ærated Waters.   Cigars and Snuffs.

REMOVED FROM CORONATION-WALK.

GEORGE MERCER,
FASHIONABLE BOOT AND SHOEMAKER,
LORDS'-STREET.

MOST respectfully announces to the Inhabitants and Visiters of Southport, that he has *removed* from the Shop in Coronation-walk to the premises next to Mr. Tyrer's, Grocer, where he carries on the business in all its departments : he, therefore, takes the opportunity, through the medium of this journal, of thanking them for all past favors, with a hope to share in their future support, which will ever be esteemed with gratitude. He also begs to state that it is his intention to keep a choice and well-selected stock of the most fashionable goods, of the best make and quality, constantly on hand, so that Ladies may have an opportunity of being fitted to their entire satisfaction, and at the same time may rely with confidence on the quality of the article.

May 3rd, 1844.

WATERLOO HOUSE,
EAST BANK-STREET, SOUTHPORT.

THOMAS DEAN,
LINEN AND WOOLLEN DRAPER, HOSIER,
Glover, Haberdasher, and Laceman,

BEGS most respectfully to tender his sincere thanks for the very liberal encouragement he has met with since he commenced business, and to inform his many kind friends that he has made arrangements with some of the first houses in the trade to supply him with every description of goods suitable for the present and forthcoming season, and hopes by strict attention to business, to merit a continuance of their favors.

T. D. Further intimates, that he has now a well-selected stock of Boys' and Men's London and French Hats, Cloth Caps, Broad and Narrow West of England Cloths, Fancy Trowserings, and Vests, in every variety ; which will be found well worthy of inspection.

Family Mourning and Funerals furnished.

tioneer's sheet. Yet, a further curious concept is typified by the *Southport Visiter* of 1884. As the name might suggest, the prime reason for publishing the journal was to list, in order of hotel, boarding house and cottage, all those pleasure-seekers staying in the town. Advertisements, local news and entertainment fill the bulk of the remaining pages, of which the following is characteristic:

A fop sitting by a beautiful woman in a ball room, began to praise, and at once exclaim, 'That beautiful neck! – oh, that I could place my hand upon that soft bosom!' 'Sir, (says the lady), give me your hand, and I will place it in a much softer place.' He gave his hand with a delightful simper, and the lady took it and placed it upon his own head.

The first issue of *The Bedford Times* (1845) gives no indication of political allegiance, except as a promoter of railway expansion. By contrast with the inhibiting attitude of *The Bucks Gazette* a few years earlier, these pages are crammed with the prospectuses of Railway companies, and news of their growth. The Great Leeds and London Direct Railway announces a proposal to build a 120-mile link with the Eastern Counties Railway at Bedford. The Tring, Cambridge and Newmarket Railway Company invites investment, as does the Eastern Counties Extension and Cambridge and Worcester Direct Railway. In a brief box advertisement, the Northampton, Bedford and Cambridge Railway advises that – 'NOTICE IS HEREBY GIVEN, That in consequence of an important arrangement being in progress

with another Company, the Parliamentary Contract and Subscriber's Agreement will not be ready for execution, and the scrip for shares will not be issued for a few days.'

In fact, Saturday, 18 October 1845, seems to have an entirely different mood to that of eight years before. Now, the editors are confident enough of public approval to devote almost their whole editorial to the subject of

Railway Communication ... The voice of popular outcry and agitation is drowned by the louder sounds which arise from the steam-leviathans that are ceaselessly threading their way through our towns and fields; while in the distance there booms upon the expectant ear, with scarce less distinctness the voices of myriads of mammoths that are waiting impatiently to pass through, by, and round, our habitations in every direction. Ours, if not, in the allegorical sense, the *iron* age, is at least the age of veritable iron. Railroads are the passion of the day, and engross alike, the capital, the energies, and the mind of the country.

Engineers, and workers in iron, are doing more for the world *now*, than the efforts of philanthropists have been able to accomplish for centuries. They are bringing men and places into intimate connection; and, by producing perfect intercommunication, are enabling nations to understand each other, and thus eradicating prejudices which have endured for ages. Distinctions of race can avail nothing against the progress of such a power.

When men know that their interests are identical, they must look with a favourable and fraternal feeling on each other, and the differences which have been engendered by distance. Intimate commercial relations must necessarily, under such a system, exist between the nations of Europe. One will exchange its peculiar products for those of another, with the utmost facility; and thus each will be taught to rely on those pursuits for success, in which it is fitted by climate and natural resources, rather than to aim at rivalry in pursuits for which it has no fitness, and no adequate resources. There will be, nationally and universally, an adaptation of skill and labour to local circumstances; the principle of the division of labour will be carried out to its fullest extent, and thus the world's means will be economised, and the world's prosperity promoted.

In such high-flown terms did the arrival of the railway presage European union, and it is perhaps a part of the human tragedy that these hopes had, for more than a century, to be deferred.

The joint themes of thriving expansion and social unrest were secured on equally firm foundations. As *The Derbyshire Advertiser* of 7 January 1846 expressed it – 'Present situation of England – railroad mad on one hand, and short of food on the other ...' Investment money was readily available for every kind of technical innovation. Yet, taxation laws kept the cost of food high. General wage levels had barely moved for a century and many working families had to exist on the same few shillings a week that their grand parents had earned. As a result, England lived a familiar paradox – prosperity fed on poverty. Crime rates rose, and, as the same paper reported on 25 February of the same year – 'dur-

ing the last five years crime has increased nearly 35 per cent., that nearly half of all the criminals convicted have been under 20 years of age, and that half of them had been under 16 years of age!' Shades of our own times when society has still barely begun to examine disruptive phenomena for cause and effect.

But, as we have seen, bad times are good times for papers. Conformists and reformists both desired to see their respective opinions confirmed in print. Circulations rose, and the introduction of the electric telegraph accelerated the distribution of news reports. (The *South Shields Gazette* published its first Telegraphic News Edition on 1 May 1851.)

These conflicting strains of the early Victorian era rose to a national climax in 1851 with the celebration of the Great Exhibition in which every class of society, emotionally at least, joined hands.

A balanced perspective can, perhaps, be gained from the vantage of one popular national paper whose editorial base is broad enough to encompass a variety of views. For this I have chosen the *News of the World*, first published on Sunday, 1 October 1843, and continued today, as then, a popular Sunday paper.

It declared its editorial intentions in its first page – 'To give to the poorer classes of society a paper that would suit their means, and to the middle, as well as the rich, a journal, which from its immense circulation, should command their attention, have been the influencing motives that have caused the appearance of "THE NEWS OF THE WORLD".'

A characteristic irreverence towards 'Royals' was established in that first issue with this jokey piece titled – 'Effects of Foreign Travels on the Queen.'

As going abroad is generally considered to 'finish the education', we may presume that something has been added by her foreign trip to that perfection which it was always customary to find in Queen Victoria. A trip to the Continent, which is supposed to give polish to the lawyer's clerk, and add brilliancy to the bagman, must have rendered her Majesty – dazzling as she was before – something almost too bright to contemplate. We understand that the Queen had learnt, from the price of provisions in France and Belgium, a few lessons that will have their effect upon the mode in which the next speech from the Throne will deal with the question of the Corn Laws. It is said, that, at dinner one day with her uncle, King Leopold, Victoria, giving an arch look towards the children, and then at their parents, remarked that Brussels sprouts were the only article the people of Belgium were obliged to pay very dearly for. We can fancy her Majesty marketing at home, with the recollection fresh upon her of prices abroad – for economy is the order of the day in the household. We should not wonder if an inspection of the Windsor Castle butcher's bill may not induce her Majesty to put up with tariff beef, of which she has had a taste during her recent trip to the Continent. Perhaps the homely habits of her fellow-sovereigns, who frequently go into shops and cheapen goods – as Louis Phillipe once did a cotton umbrella – may induce her Majesty to follow their example; and as Leopold gave an impetus to commerce by buying a few shirt-buttons in one of the arcades, Victoria may make her purchases in the Burlington or Lowther. What will she say to magic lanterns at half-a-crown, when she has seen the very same thing for a couple of francs – one-and-eight – on the other side of the water?

No Sunday paper, of course, is complete without its domestic pages, of which these two samples bear the true flavour.

Beech Leaves. The leaves of this tree are often used as a substitute for feathers in a bed. Evelyn says, that being gathered about the fall, and somewhat before they are much frost-bitten, they form the best and easiest mattrasses in the world, instead of straw; because, besides their tenderness and loose lying together, they continue sweet for seven or eight years, long before which time straw becomes musty and hard.

The *Academie d'Industrie* states that a girdle worn round the body above the bowels – that is over the epigastrum – will prevent sea sickness. It is said to operate by keeping the intestines from pressing upwards against the diaphragm when the ship descends from the top of a wave. The upward motion of the vessel does not cause the sensation of sea sickness, but affords an instantaneous relief.

The realities of life, however, are not far away. Prisoners, it is reported, in her Majesty's prisons, are dying of starvation. No official provision is made for them to be fed, and those who lack money, or, after long periods in prison, run short, are left to die. Further on down the page, there is a confession by a nine-year-old boy to the crime of murdering his six-year-old companion by throwing him in the Regent's Canal in London.

Sport (Horse Racing and Cricket), Theatre reviews and Fashions are followed by what would now be regarded as typical *News of the World* stories. Extraordinary Charge of Drugging and Violation (A chemist accused of drugging a female servant, raping her, and then dumping her in the Thames). A Woman Poisoned by Endeavouring to Procure a Miscarriage. Sudden Death of a Gentleman of Fortune. Death in a Birmingham Railway Train. Disease and Mortality Amongst the Cattle. Suicide at Blackfriar's Bridge. Book Reviews and the Fine Arts are followed by – 'Extortionate Demands at Public Edifices' –

Whatever simple ruralists imagine, the gryphons here have claws ... they are orthodox folk, who love full-sized loaves and fishes, like their betters, and would accept but two groats less than a crown, current coin of the realm, from St. Paul himself, if he come by chance to visit his own temple ... to see St Paul's ... would cost what we have stated ... about one day's wages of a verger, or respectable cathedral servant ... We give the authorised tariff of expenses ... else it might make a reader think we are romancing.

To View the Monuments and Body of the Church	2d.
To the Whispering Gallery and the two outside Galleries	6d.
To the Ball	1s. 6d.
To the Library, Great Bell, Geometrical Staircase and Model Room	1s. 0d.
Clock	2d.
Crypt or Vaults	1s. 0d.
	4s. 4d.

News from Scotland includes 'Serious Riot at Roskeen' and 'Deforcement of the Presbytery of Tain'. And 'Perth – A Luscious Bath'.

As several porters were engaged loading two puncheons of molasses at the shore on a cart, one of them was subjected to an inundation of the contents of one of the casks, that for a while created apprehensions in the minds of those about him, as to whether he would not really lose his life. He was fastening an end of rope at the back of the cart, when the puncheon suddenly burst and the whole of the luscious contents in a mass descended upon him, with a violence that laid him prostrate, 'buried in sweets'. He remained for some time entirely invisible, buried beneath the treacle, which from its nature, he could not shake off, while those about him, disliking the idea of getting themselves similarly besmeared, made no effort to assist him. The liquid at length gradually rolled off, and the deplorable subject of the immersion endeavoured to rise, but he dropped again. This he did so often, that his companions at length, fearing that he might be suffocated, went to his assistance. On being raised to his feet, he was very much exhausted, and from his exhaustion, as well as the state of his clothes, he was unable to walk until he had got a drop to revive him.

'Predictions of the Weather for the Week' came – not from the Meteorological Office – but, from 'A Correspondent' –

October. This month will record fearful storms and earthquakes, especially the middle of the month, from the 11th to the 18th; principally on the 17th, when there are many and complex aspects in the celestial machinery. These earthquakes and storms will occur in India, near the River Indus, Greece, and Mexico. The West Indies are again devoted to the elements, as well as those parts of South America near Quito and Lima. During this month many valuable lives will be lost, and much property destroyed.

    1st – Cloudy – showers at noon.
    2nd – Rainy; cloudy.
    3rd – Windy; cloudy.
    4th – Drizzle; overcast; clearer at night.
    5th – Warmer; windy.
    6th – Chiefly fine.
    7th – Probably small rain; windy.

This general style, capitalising on the experience of over two centuries of journalism, was the carefully chosen basis for the *News of the World*'s commercial success. An average circulation of 60,000 copies per edition was claimed. Generally three versions of the paper were printed each week, the layout being updated in the modern manner to bring in new stories or reports, dropping old ones, or relegating them to inner or back pages.

Popular journalism now (i.e., the same paper and its daily and weekly contemporaries – *The Sun, The Mirror*, etc) is based on impact, crisp, vivid writing, speed and variety. Reporting the Festival Exhibition of 1951, the popular press generally and the public they served could not sustain a detailed interest in that event for a long period of time. Consequently, press coverage rose and fell like a tide – at times the Festival seemed almost out of sight.

Not so in 1851. If the Festival Exhibition was designed as a national morale booster after twelve grey years of war and post-war austerity, its Great predecessor a century before was presented as a confirmation, for all the world to see, of a powerful morale boost already achieved.

The readership was hungry for news of it. No item was too small to escape their attention. From the first visit of the Society of Arts to the Crystal Palace building site, through detailed descriptions of the use of Cornish granite, the Musical Instruments to appear, and baiting items about a musical bed as a cure for insomnia, they demanded – and got – every morsel of information. Not the American Revolution, not the French, not even Napoleon had held such public sway. The Great Exhibition was given a density of attention never previously accorded to any single event. Page after page, column upon column. It is a tribute to readership stamina and journalistic craft that the interest could be sustained for so many months. For the editors of the *News of the World* it must have been an important testing ground. It was a test of their popular style, a test of their ability to discover fresh ideas, to explore every possible connection likely to prove of interest.

Logically, they began, on 5 January, with a scene-setting 'Chronological Record of the Principal Events of the Year 1850'. Followed by an examination of the means whereby foreign visitors were to arrive in England.

American visitors to the Great Exhibition are about to be conveyed to our shores at a very commodious and economical rate. Merchants vessels, which have accommodation for 60 passengers, are to take them the entire journey, from America and back, with first-class accommodation while on board, for £20, allowing them six weeks to remain in England.

That the Exhibition should be held at all was a matter not entirely free of comment.

Sunday, January 12. We seldom feel it to be our duty to dissent from the political and social doctrines, promulgated by the *Times*, and never willingly do so, except when we find, one of the occasional writers of that journal adopting a course which is likely to lead it in a wrong direction, or to convey an inaccurate view of affairs in this country, or abroad.

One of the few occasions on which we are bound openly to express our dissent from the *Times* is, when it endeavours, as in a sentence like the following, to give expression to a sentiment, as if it were one that could be universally approved of. The sentence to which we object so especially is to be found in an article published on Monday last, in the *Times*.

'Upon the whole,' says the *Times*, January 6, 1851, 'the moment at which we now stand, at this opening of the second half of the nineteenth century, may claim, as far at least as *this country and its offshoots are concerned*, to be the MOST PROSPEROUS – perhaps, we may say the *most imposing* EPOCH in our natural history.'

In the opinion of *some classes* of the community this may be *the most prosperous* epoch in the history of England; but in the estimation of the great body of the working, the productive, the industrial, the poorer classes, it is undeserving the name of 'prosperous'.

Having thus identified and served its non-*Times* reading audience, the paper's editors then go on to prove themselves substantially wrong, by confirming with the material they choose to print, their readers' genuine attachment to the idea of the Exhibition, whether as a confirmation or otherwise of prosperity.

No journalist can resist the opportunity to warn of future dangers.

January 19. Is the great metropolitan river (The Thames) to remain nothing more than a common sewer in 1851? The distressing accounts which the last West Indian mail has brought of the frightful ravages of the cholera in the island of Jamaica, are well calculated to direct the attention of the authorities and of the public at home to the contingency of a similar visitation falling upon London in the ensuing spring.

Story after story, headlines and titles, nothing is omitted. Should admission be free? Visit of Prince Albert – New Iron Railings – Coming Doom of the Trees. Exhibition opening confirmed as 1 May. Working Men's Associations organising cheap excursions to the Exhibition. France will be the largest Foreign Exhibitor, followed by The Zollverein, Austria, Belgium, Russia, Turkey, Switzerland, Holland. Temporary Augmentation of the Police Force. A rustic lootable has been constructed by Thomas Bates, a labourer of St. Albans. A 16-pounder howitzer is coming from the Government of Spain.

'American Contributions – The Secretary of the United States Navy has given notice that the frigate St. Lawrence will be in readiness to sail for London on the 1st of February with articles for the world's fair.'

Invasions of England. There will be in London this summer, hordes of Anglo-Saxons from the West, children of the rebels against his late Majesty George the Third, of Republicans from France, of Republican-Absolutists from Germany, of Swedes, Turks, South Americans, Hindoos – of races agreeing in nothing, perhaps, except hatred to perfidious Albion …!

On 23 February is reported the Queen's Visit to the unfinished Exhibition Building. Testing the Strength of the Galleries. 'Contributions from China – But few articles will be sent from China. The 8,250 dolls. collected in Canton is to be returned to the respective subscribers. Some of whom, however, intend the transmission of a few packages. At Shanghai the merchants appear to be as apathetic on the matter as in Hong Kong.'

2 March. The Russian Emperor intends to spend 10,000 silver roubles at the Exhibition. Trinidad is sending specimens of wood – Bois d'orange or fustic, the Sapadilla, Green Poui, the Copai. Arrival of the First Man of War with Works of Art and Vertu. Arrival of the French Commissioners and Staff. A costly marble

table is coming from Malta. 15 cases of articles from Greece. An Albanian dress worth 2,000 dollars on which 50 persons worked for 3 months in the making. Another visit from the Queen. Contributions from Jersey. Articles from Hamburg. Contributions from Syria.

16 March. More testing of the Galleries. More Foreign Arrivals. The Official Exhibition Catalogue will appear in four editions – English, French, German, and a special illustrated edition. 20 tons of type specially cast – 26 million letters.

23 March. France needs more Exhibition space. Some articles withheld from the Exhibition because of the organisers' refusal to insure them against loss by piracy. A Specimen of Rock Salt weighing 2 tons from Northwich. A Contribution from Queen Pomara – but details not known.

30 March. More arrivals. Wet weather. Arrival from Austria. Everywhere extraordinary activity.

6 April. Leakage in the Roof. A Piece of Wire A Mile Long (for the electric telegraph). Destruction of a Work of Art – a glass exhibit blown over by a gust of wind.

13 April. A Visit to the Crystal Palace. Additional Church Services during the Exhibition. Trespassers in the Glass Building arrested by the police. Removal of trees in the building. Renaming London streets with direction signs to aid foreign visitors. Shoeblacks appointed to the Exhibition. Prince Albert receives Foreign Commissioners at Buckingham Palace.

And then, on 27 April, the climax –

Within a few hours, it may be said, after the publication of this paper, the Crystal Palace – that marvel of human ingenuity – will have its gates opened to the public, and the civilised world invited within its pellucid walls, to behold the most extraordinary combination of the productions of human skill and ingenuity that has ever been witnessed since the formation of the globe.

So it continues for three quarters of a column, followed by the Inauguration of the Crystal Palace by the Queen, which takes up two more columns.

But, even at this high-point, an ingrained journalistic instinct will not allow the paper to forget its original seed of dissent. May 4 –

England is, at this moment, presenting to the civilised world two exhibitions as unparalleled each in its character as they are dissimilar in their kind. For the one exhibition the nations of mankind are indebted to the genius, the talent, the judgment and the discrimination of Prince Albert; and for the other it may be thankful to the labours, the zeal, the Christian charity, and the philanthropic dauntless energy of the Rev. Sidney Godolphin Osborne.

This is a reference to a report published by Sidney Osborne on the number of deaths by sheer neglect occurring in Irish Work Houses. 'I have now good proofs that the deaths in the Kilrush Union for the twelve months ending March 25th, 1851, will exceed eighteen hundred.' (Letter from S. G. Osborne in *The Times*, 30 April 1848.)

Yet, it would take more than that brief acid touch

to hold back THE GREAT EXHIBITION. Preparations for Her Majesty's Reception. Clearing Out the Building. The Opening. The Royal Procession. Interior of the Crystal Palace. Arrival of the Queen. Commissioners' Report. Archbishop's Blessing. Return of the Queen to Buckingham Palace. Contributions of the Royal Family to the Great Exhibition. Guide for Visitors. Arrival of the Turkish Frigate Feiza Baari. Funds for Erecting the Crystal Palace. Catalogues. Military Preparations. Police Arrangements. Arrival of Visitors.

Then, on 11 May, there begins to be published a detailed description of every stand, every item. The Koh-i-Nor. Electric Clocks. Artificial Illumination. Electric Light. Pianofortes. Lace Gassing Machinery. Silks and Velvets. Irish Manufactures. Model of a Colliery. Needle Making. Exhibitions of Glass. Articles of Plate. Alphabets of the Whole Globe. Textiles – Cotton. Sculpture. Another Visit from the Queen.

18 May. Receipts to date £12,937–10–0d. Department of Precious Metals. Working Machinery. Show of Carriages. Display of Carpets. Exhibition of Hardware. Gorgeous Furniture. More than 30,000 visitors daily.

On 25 May, an American criticism that the English were making too much profit from the Exhibition. Estimated costs – £196,000. Estimated receipts – £690,000.

Every week, for the remainder of the Exhibition and beyond, the paper carried a similar torrent of print. And, this was but one paper of many, an interest reflected many times over through the rest of the country.

Between three and four columns every week amounted to a remarkable wordage. In its way, although predating the era of mass circulation, it was a journalistic peak.

SURVIVING NEWSPAPERS FOUNDED BETWEEN 1826 AND 1850

News of the World (London)	1843
Kentish Independent	1843
Fleetwood Chronicle	1843
Weston Mercury and Somerset Herald	1843
Southport Visiter	1844
West Lancashire Visitor	1844
Bedfordshire Times	1845
Isle of Ely and Wisbech Advertiser	1845
Blackpool Herald	1845
Poole and Dorset Herald	1846
Rugby Advertiser	1846
Derbyshire Advertiser	1846
Darlington and Stockport Times	1847
Harrogate Herald	1847
Lincolnshire Free Press	1847
Oswestry and Border Counties Advertiser	1849
Shields Gazette	1849
Sidmouth Herald and Directory	1849
Dartmouth Chronicle	1850

Daily Telegraph & Courier.

No. 1.]   LONDON, FRIDAY, JUNE 29, 1855.   [TWOPENCE.

The Sporting Life,

PUBLISHED EVERY WEDNESDAY AND SATURDAY.]   [IN TIME FOR THE EARLY MORNING TRAINS.

VOL. I.—No. 12.   LONDON, SATURDAY, APRIL 30, 1859.   ONE PENNY.

NOTICE.

Our Journal is this week published under a fresh title, according to the decision of Vice-Chancellor Sir John Stuart. The Paper will, however, undergo no other alteration.

The Penny Press

In the quarter century from 1851, there was an explosion – an eruption of newspapers. It was not yet a torrent. The age of mass circulation had not yet come. But the groundwork was being laid. The evidence is still with us. At this present time, in 1976, of all the papers still being printed and published, no less than 260 of them originated in those years. It was one of the best of all times for starting a paper, and many took the plunge. If that number have survived, it can be imagined the much greater number that began and failed.

There were many reasons for the surge. Already mounting commercial pressures and increased circulations had brought about a steady decrease in the price at which papers could be sold, from 7d down to 3d. The ending of the advertisement tax in 1853, the Stamp Duty tax in 1855, and the duty payable on raw paper a few years later, further lowered prices, down to 2d, and then 1d. The rise of a lower middle class in society, literate and with money to spend, provided a wider audience for popular papers to aim at.

As towns expanded, and new suburbs were built up around the old town centres, more and more local papers were called into being. Again and again, in a pattern that had almost become a tradition of the trade, the combination of jobbing printer, book seller and stationer, led to the creation of a township or district newspaper, from which an additional income could be derived by the sale of patent medicines, advertised in its pages. Further, the ownership of a newspaper proved likely to afford the ambitious or socially-minded a new route, an open-sesame, to a place of influence in local affairs.

Political, and even religious influence, was not absent from editorial counsels – *The Whitehaven News* (1852) was started by William Alsop, the head of a devout Quaker family. His son, also William, was apparently not of that faith. When the father retired, the son took over, and purely commercial considerations replaced Quaker zeal.

John Tasker, who founded *The Craven Herald* (1853), was a Methodist; also, in conformity with tradition, a printer, bookseller, stationer and, unexpectedly, an agent for Horniman's teas. The paper was then a monthly, a formula commonly used for a preliminary test of the market. It was discontinued when James, John's son, was appointed Post-Master of Skipton – a post that required his removal from the other enterprise to avoid a conflict of interest in the public service. When John retired in 1874, the stationery business was sold to the Skipton Conservative Newspaper Company who revived the paper as a penny weekly, and gave it a political slant.

Typical of the proliferation of newspapers in the new suburbs spreading around London is *The Surrey Comet*. Typically, it was started by a printer, Thomas Philpott, in 1854. Russell Knapp bought the paper and the associated printing and stationery business. When he died, editorship of the paper was taken over by William Drewett, previously employed as a reporter. Later, the Knapps and the Drewetts came together in ownership of *The Surrey Comet*, the former owning the paper, the latter, the printing works.

Family connections of this kind tend still to run through these local paper businesses. The Knapps and Drewetts still publish the *Comet*. Benjamin Lansdown started the *Wiltshire Times* in 1855. Michael Lansdown, a great grandson, is still a director, and editor of the local division, although the paper itself has come under group ownership. The Holmes family continue to own and run the *Andover Advertiser* (1857) despite many overtures from bigger business. The Thomason's management of the *Middlesex Chronicle* (1858) maintains an unbroken link, again, within the framework of group ownership.

Printing technology has altered but slowly. The Albion press made way for the Wharfedale, which, in turn was followed by the American Hoe press, and the Cossar. Gas engines gradually replaced steam.

By contrast with this spate of provincial journalism, only one London national daily stems from this period. London's growth had, in one sense, already happened. National distribution of papers from the capital had largely been accomplished with the advent of the railways from the 1840s onwards. In another sense, London's greatest growth was yet to come. The ½d paper (although the distinction of being the first English paper to sell for a ½d had already been achieved by *The Shields Gazette* in 1864) selling nationally would still have to wait another quarter century.

The one London paper to date from this time – *The Daily Telegraph* – did, however, represent a significant step towards this. First published under the name – *Daily Telegraph and Courier*, its first issues show a clear attempt to identify a new newspaper audience. Its style is crisper and emotive in style. It deals with national issues, and national dramas, in a popular, more readable way, that is in contrast with the painstakingly thorough, but more stodgy presentation of the earlier *News of the World*.

In its first issue, the conflict with the older newspaper hierarchy is made clear.

Friday, June 29, 1855. . . . That a legislative enactment (i.e., repeal of the Stamp Act) which tends to the more general diffusion of sound knowledge, can be unwise, is indeed to assert that which is simply ridiculous. It was all very well for our older contemporaries of the Morning Press to presage all manner of evil from the moment of the passing of the Newspaper Stamp Bill – that was quite natural. We cannot be angry with the monopolist for not joyfully welcoming the intruder . . .

The editorial in the same issue takes up the matter of a 'Cheap Press' and makes an interesting comparison with the United States – '. . . that glorious off-shoot of the Anglo-Saxon stock . . .'

'As an evidence of the more general diffusion of knowledge in the trans-Atlantic Republic, we find there are 2,800 newspapers in existence, of which number 424 are published in the New England States amongst the descendents of the Pilgrim Fathers, 876 in the middle States, 716 in the Southern or *Slave* States, and 784 in the Western States bordering upon the mighty waters of the Ohio – the Mississippi, the Missouri, and Arkansas. Thus the wild trapper of the far west, and the rough and ready woodsman of the Atlantic States, alike enjoy the luxury of a Free Press.

To further analyze the statistics of the American Press, it appears that there is one journal for every 7,261 inhabitants; and these journals are sub-divided into 350 Dailies, 150 Tri-weeklies, 125 semi-weeklies, and 2,000 Weeklies. The amount of paper consumed in the United States to supply this great demand, is equal to 130,000 tons, or $13\frac{1}{2}$ lbs. per head; and that for a population of 23,000,000; while in the United Kingdom, with a population of 28,000,000, we only consume 80,000 tons of paper per annum. or $4\frac{3}{4}$ lbs. per head, and in France with its 35,000,000, inhabitants, 70,000 tons, or 4 lbs per head is only consumed . . .

How far then, are we behind hand in the progress and diffusion of healthy and useful knowledge in comparison with our Anglo-American brothers . . . ?

An almost narrative style is used for the introduction of thematic arguments in the editorial columns. The 30 June edition of that same year contains a lengthy critique of the Army's recruiting programme.

If anyone will take the trouble, soon after sunrise, to skirt the precincts of St. James's Palace, make his exit by Buckingham Gate, and past the Royal Stables, he will have an ample opportunity afforded him to study the physical appearance of the existing substitute for our splendid regiments of Guards who have been despatched to the Crimea. Either by night or day, at early dawn, or in the blaze of noon, the contrast is sufficiently striking to him who notes it, between those who were and those who are our soldiers. Nothing, save actual experience in the Crimea tells the tale of England's losses more vividly than this. A race of giants is gone from amongst us . . . The Guards are gone; and in their place are substituted what appears to be at first sight a set of toy-box soldiers . . . We do not wish to dampen the ardour of these champions of puberty. They may be 'as valiant as the wrathful dove or most magnanimous mouse.' . . . Still it must be admitted that after a year's war, our soldiers cut a poor figure in martial appearance. The tall ungainly policemen overshadow these little fellows in their ridiculous tunics. Girls laugh at them and urchins mimic their awkward motions.

This discursive, but very readable, introduction leads on to a complaint against the activities of Government Emigration Commissioners who are, it is said, sending able-bodied emigrants to Australia at a time when the army is starved of men. To make up the deficit, attempts are being made to recruit Jews in the USA, Dutchmen from Heligoland, tempting them and others by 'contemplating the offer of grants of land in Canada to anyone who will come to our aid, provided he be a foreigner'.

This is a clever editorial choice of subject. It is broadly based enough to have an immediate appeal across the country, and yet it is strong enough to have a poignant translation in any district or locality.

A similarly apt choice is found on Monday, 2 July 1855.

The energies of Englishmen are inexhaustible, and their industry dauntless. For long they have carried weight against all the world; but it is time to remove all these artificial checks and hindrances, unless they be prepared to see other countries outstrip them. We have no hesitation in saying that, during the past twenty years, the progress of America has been much greater, in proportion, than that of this country. Their laws are wiser, because they avoid the evil of restriction and over legislation.

This is the preamble to a report on the 'Great Demonstration in Hyde Park On the Sunday Trading Bill' by which it was proposed to make it illegal for various kinds of establishment, including pubs, to stay open on Sunday. 'Why, then, in England, should the bad spirit of discontent be let loose through the unwise interference of a few over-sensitive religionists?'

This emotive exploitation of a 'national' issue continues:

The savage and unnecessary assaults committed by the police in Hyde Park on Sunday, upon an unoffending people, deserve our strongest reprehensions. We have no doubt but that the authorities will feel the greatest concern and annoyance at what has taken place, and that they will issue instructions to prevent such scenes in future . . . We have condemned the meeting in Hyde Park with the same impartial justice that we condemned its occasion; but the way to deal with such excitement was to let it alone . . . The misconduct of the police on Sunday is the growth of a despotic and brutal authority long exercised by the myrmidions of the law . . . On Sunday well-dressed females were not exempted from the truncheon argument . . . The 'Force' employed were indignant at the extra work cut out for them by the authorities, and frequently made no distinction of sex, age or person . . . A truncheon aimed by a practised hand at the back of the neck, after rabbit-killing fashion, is about as deadly an accolade as an unoffending citizen can receive.'

And referring again to the brutal constabulary, the opinion is expressed that 'the majority of this body should be sent off to the Crimea, and that fresh and uncorrupted men should be substituted'.

All good, strong, vibrant stuff with a nicely judged readership appeal. But the difficulty – as editors discover today – of finding such themes is a constant one. The solution is often to chase hares in foreign parts, as, for example, when America made its first bid for total prohibition.

In consequence of the interference of the Legislature in passing a prohibitory liquor law, we are informed that the State of Maine, in America, is becoming most drunken and dissipated. In proportion to its population, it is said now to be the most tippling State in the Union ... If a stranger ask for a glass of lemonade, he is treated to whiskey and water ... You are constantly misunderstood if you ask for any mild beverage such as milk or chocolate – silence is interpreted by rum, a nod by peach brandy, and the act of shaking hands by corn whiskey. A remark concerning the weather is a request for mint-julep, and an inquiry after a friend's health means brandy cocktail, or brandy smash. If you look at a man, he motions you round a corner and inquires into the nature of your vanity; if you gaze at a woman she rummages in a basket for a bottle labelled, 'Daffy's Elixir'. The merchant gets elevated in his country house, the parson in his study, and every one else where he can.

Clearly, much of this is intended to be taken with some grains of salt, as similarly an item appearing in the general debate for and against Sunday Trading – '... a number of little girls are made to petition Parliament to put an end to shaving on Sunday ...'

Nevertheless, the liquor question had opened up a fruitful vein of material for editorial ventilation, and on 10 July 1855, we find refreshment of the matter in the guise of a plea for the reduction of Wine Duty.

The first thing that strikes a foreigner on his arrival in London, is the absence of places of refreshment. As soon as his mind has recovered from the overpowering impression of magnitude which this modern Babylon creates, he looks round in vain for his wonted haunts. He finds no counterpart to the cafe of Paris, the pleasure-gardens of Holland, the vine-clad arbours of Germany. Upon inquiry he is shown to the gin-palace of the neighbourhood with its plate-glass windows and its flaunting gaslights – its dingy bar and hard wooden seats ... He will probably witness more of the excessive use of intoxicating liquors in one night than he would during a week in the public resorts of his native town ...

Upon the Continent the labourer or mechanic is enabled to procure wine of a very fair quality at a far less price than that at which he could obtain liquors of a more intoxicating quality. From the nature of the drink, he is satisfied with a quantity much too small to produce any baneful effect. This we take to be the real cause of the comparative absence of drunkenness in the wine-growing districts of France, Germany and Italy.

This argument leads to a recommendation for the reduction of Wine Duty, so that wine could be available to the ordinary drinker, and so reduce drunkenness – '... to outbid the beer shop and spirit stores by more innocent attractions ...'

The poor showing of the British Army in the Crimean war continued to attract much attention, and a powerfully written editorial, on 17 July 1855, went further than any modern editor might go, in attacking the Military.

The English Church is a sale of livings – the British Army a sale of lives. We do not mean by the latter assertion the legitimate homicide which war occasions, and which we regard as we do the law of storms and other purifying processes for the ultimate benefit of mankind; but we refer to the army before Sebastopol; murdered by folly so inconceivable, by incapacity so atrocious, that the whole assumes the shape of a method, and we have no name to express either the deed or our abhorrence of it. 'Poor Lord Raglan' is about to be buried with pomp at Bristol, and PRINCE ALBERT will attend his funeral, in that Field Marshall's uniform in which he continues 'to look so exceedingly well'. Poor Lord Raglan was Commander-in-Chief of our army in the Crimea, and weathered last winter in snug quarters exceedingly well, unconscious of the work of death that was going on in his neighbourhood, and breakfasting with courteous aides-de-camp, whilst a frost-bitten, ragged host – the gaunt piquets in that gloomy burial-yard – were melting away around him far beyond bugle call ... Let us transport our readers to the trenches before Sebastopol, where we listen to a corporal whom we shall select as guide. 'Here is where we lost a lot of our men the other night because they could not fire a second shot with the new-fangled Enfield rifle, sent out by the Ordnance. You see, gentlemen, this weapon has a stock of green wood – a contractor's job – and when it is wet our fellows can't load.' ... Who was Master-General of the Ordnance? ... and we remember that post was still held by Lord Raglan.'

These deliberate attempts to involve ordinary readers in the supposed issues of the day seem to have been strikingly successful. They certainly laid the groundwork for many themes that constantly recur in today's papers. One was the reporting of real, or partly real, dangers to health arising from medical practice, mal-practice or poor legislation. Over the years this has proved a rich lodestone of editorial themes. One of the earliest appeared on 19 July 1855.

The recent disclosures published in The Lancet have excited the alarm of the public ... Few reasonable persons can now doubt that, both in town and country, gross and habitual adulteration is daily practised on every article that we either eat or drink ... Arrowroot, the favourite diet prescribed for the sick, is constantly composed of the inferior articles of sago and tapioca. Anchovies, which are employed to restore the palled appetite are, for the most part, small fish from the Dutch and French seas, painted red, to delight the eye of the epicure at the expense of his palate. Bread, the very staff of life, contains a small proportion of wheat to a large share of mashed potatoes, mixed up with alum. Coffee is another name for chicory, or even bad flour, and bones ground into dust. Chicory itself, the arch-adulterator, owes its flavour to Venetian red, Curry-powder, – that panacea of an English nobleman for popular starvation, is contaminated with the plebian presence of ground rice and red lead; gin, teetotallists will be glad to learn, is too often water flavoured with cayenne; preserves are suspected of a too-familiar acquaintance with salt of copper ... Tea is subject to such a variety of insidious arts, that the only wonder is that it should ever escape unharmed. There is first the practice of substituting re-dried tea leaves for the original and virgin specimens. In 1843 there are stated to have been eight manufactories for the purpose of re-drying tea-leaves in London alone. The exhausted leaves were purchased at hotels and coffee-houses, and elsewhere, at the rate of twopence or three pence per pound, taken to factories, mixed with gum, and re-dried. Even this secondhand flavour of tea is not always to be obtained. Willow, horse-chestnut, and sloe-leaves are made to do duty for the Chinese article – a fact which visitors at country inns can readily testify to from bitter experience ... substances of a most deleterious character – black lead, Prussian blue, Verdigris, – are employed to give a natural appearance to the re-dried or fictitious leaves.

Traffic congestion was another topic of general interest – Arthur Young, the farmer-come-travel writer, was complaining of bad roads and road making more than a century earlier. London had a particular appeal for readers everywhere else in the country, and what afflicted London could be thought to afflict the nation. And so, on 31 July that year, a brisk leader writer's pen reported, that

Every morning throughout most of the year – there are thousands of persons who daily come to the City from the West End of London. They are all men of business – men in whose case the proverb is strictly applicable, that time is money. It is a matter of extreme importance that the transit to and fro should be managed with the utmost rapidity and facility – as long as you can keep within the bounds of the City you have no great case for complaint; the moment, however, you cross the line your troubles begin. In the first place there is Temple Bar, which bars up the entrance into Fleet Street – there is barely room for two carriages to pass abreast beneath it. Supposing ... the horses of your vehicle escape falling on the slippery paving-stones of Fleet-Street, you are next brought to a dead-stop by a long line of carts going along Farringdon-street. Here there is generally a scene of inextricable confusion, rendered still more confounded by the contradictory commands of some member of the civic constabulary ...

The real triumph of internal mismanagement, is Cheapside, on a crowded morning. On each side there are two endless rows of carriages, straggling zig-zag across the street; cabs and omnibuses, private broughams and brewer's drays, hand-trucks and butcher's carts, are mixed together in the wildest medley; carts are unloading at the street doors a yard or more from the curb-stone; long teams are wending their way from the side streets right across the main thoroughfare, horses are kicking, carriages backing, and drivers swearing. It is a sort of London Balaklava transit, repeated every morning from nine to eleven and from three to five in the evening ... For the last two years Threadneedle-street has been in a state of chronic blockade, and at present there is little prospect of its termination. It has taken the Corporation of London much longer to widen a single street of half a furlong's length than the Emperor NAPOLEON has employed in carrying the gigantic Rue Rivoli right through the whole length of Paris.

The present Women's Liberation movement – a modern journalistic triumph – is echoed in these nineteenth-century pages by a kind of Male Liberation equivalent, it being remembered that the majority of newspaper buyers then were men.

Wednesday, August 1, 1855. At present men are employed behind the counter of almost every retail shop in town or country. At grocers, haberdashers and hosiers, men, and men alone are kept as assistants. The number engaged in these occupations is almost incredible. We suspect we should not be far wrong in asserting, that in London alone two hundred thousand men and youths are daily employed upon duties which might be better performed by women. You have but to walk up Regent Street or Piccadilly any summer afternoon ... Behind each counter you will see rows of able-bodied young men engaged in measuring yards of ribbon, discussing, with simpering language, the respective merits of rival bonnets ... From eight in the morning till ten or eleven at night, men, with bodies fitted for hard labour, and minds that might be trained to intellectual pursuits, are occupied upon this fiddle-faddle work ...

On Monday, 20 August 1855, the *Courier* in the title was dropped, and the paper became simply the *Daily Telegraph* which is how it remains today.

Thursday, 24 March 1859 saw the first issue of *The Penny Bell's Life and Sporting News*. This is interesting on two counts. Firstly, there was already a successful paper being published under the name *Bell's Life*. When the older paper took the newer one to Court, it was argued that to limit the name to just one paper was to diminish the public's range of choice. Further, this was the '*Penny*' *Bell's Life*, the other costing two pence. Also, clearly, this was a sporting paper. The Judge ruled in favour of the established paper, and on 30 April 1859, the upstart took the new title of *The Sporting Life*, which it still retains. The paper is interesting for a second reason. It was, and is, devoted exclusively to sporting matters, and presented reports under the headings: Racing Record, Cricketing Record, Aquatic Record (i.e., Sailing and Rowing), Coursing Record, Record of the Ring (i.e., Boxing), Shooting Record, Pedestrian Record (i.e., Running). This sporting base was another formula for attracting a broadly-based, national readership, and it built its appeal on the use of a kind of inbred jargon that only regular, and therefore, knowledgable, readers would understand.

Betting was, of course, the basis for these sporting interests, and the report of a Boxing Match, which appeared in the first issue of 24 March 1859 will illustrate the point.

HOLDEN'S BLACK, AND T. CREW. The day named for this match, to fight at catch weight for £10 a side, was Monday week, at Barron's Bridge, not far from Birmingham; but the police interfered, and other places having been attempted without avail, the men entered into an agreement to meet last Monday at Holly, near Walsall. The Black, from the effects of rheumatism, was not altogether the thing; but still he was the favourite in the betting. First blood was declared in his favour, and continued so for some time, when Crew took the lead, his opponent becoming rather weak, and as the Black got weaker, Crew heavily punished his man most vigorously; and after one hour and forty-five minutes contention, in which time seventy-five rounds were fought, the friends of the Black threw up the sponge in token of defeat.

Editors, as we have discovered, are concerned with two primary issues: how to fill their pages, and what

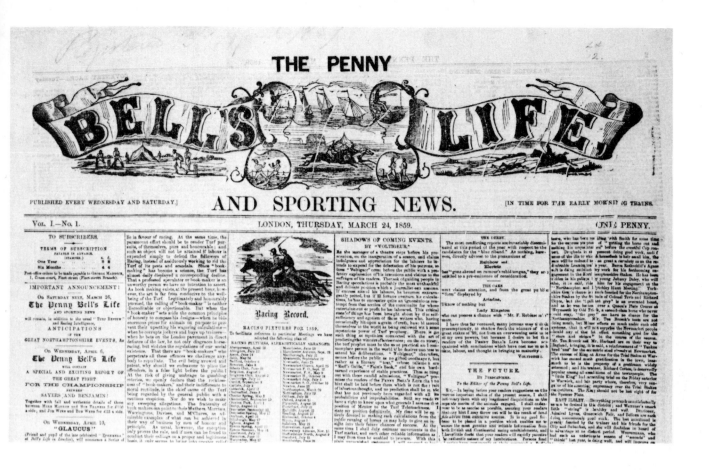

material will be of acceptable interest to their designated readership. In earlier times, these judgments were made crudely, in haste, and with limited market data. Papers were edited by guess and by Gutenberg. From haphazardly gathered selections of London and major foreign papers, spontaneous gleanings of items were reprinted with scant regard for authenticity. Sometimes these were amplified by privately written (and unpaid) letters submitted by correspondents. By the mid-nineteenth century, journalistic techniques had become more astute, more alert, more professional. News hard won by paid employees of papers was not to be casually reprinted by whoever chose to do so. Copyright law was more tightly drawn and observed. Furthermore, the economics of production were bearing more heavily on the smaller papers. Profits were there to be made by those whose decisions were sound. It was still possible, despite the relief from taxation, for badly run papers to go to the wall.

To serve local papers, a form of syndication came into being. Based in London were printers who supplied pages pre-printed with national and international news on one side. These were supplied, simultaneously, to many town papers – delivered by rail weekly, for the local proprietor to fill the blank pages with his own local news. Sometimes, these syndicated pages would also include an editorial.

The start of a new pattern can be seen emerging. The rising national dailies were seeking a national audience.

To attract this support, there was a shift of editorial focus toward national themes. Local papers were still, for the most part, weeklies. The railways had made national daily distribution from London possible and profitable. Local editors, therefore, increasingly had to accept that a significant part of their readership would be buying two papers, a national daily and a local weekly. They had to adapt to fit a new slot in the market. Part of the answer had already been found. The trend away from sectional-interest local papers towards a neutrality that served all interests in a well-defined locality had already helped many papers through a difficult transition. But, their pages still held scope for other items. While the dailies centred on national popular themes, the local weeklies bracketed them – contracting on the one hand to the general appeal of local items, and expanding on the other to include more international material that could be expected to have a general appeal based on national identity. In such a manner was news of the American Civil War presented to readers of the *Andover Advertiser* (1857). As the weeks of 1861 sped by, they read of an unfolding drama in which English interests were to become involved, and a conflict in which England might, reluctantly, become embroiled.

'Friday, January 11, 1861. A telegram arrived in London in the early part of the week to the effect that South Carolina seceded from the American Union on the 19th of December by an unanimous vote of 169 members.

65

The news created great excitement in the House of Representatives.'

And a week later

The Secession Movement in America. The advices this week from America are of the same serious tenor as those previously to hand; and it is hard to tell what will be the upshot of all. A Southern confederation seems to be the probable end of the mania; but the Southerners themselves are in a dilemma how to break off their fiscal relations with the Federal Government without occasioning difficulties which might be at first ruinous to both. The next step, we presume, will be the despatching of Southern representatives to England, and the question of their reception by our Government will not be less important than was the recognition of Louis Napoleon's *coup d'etat* by Lord Palmerston.

The people of Charleston continue their belligerent demonstrations. The arsenal, containing thousands of stands of arms belonging to the Government, has been formally taken possession of by the State troops, and the muskets appropriated to their use...

According to a letter from Boston dated December 20th, (1860), preparations for war are being made in Massachusetts and New Hampshire. The writer says: 'There is no disguising the fact that Massachusetts is ready to respond promptly to any demand made upon her for troops to sustain the Union and the laws...'

Considerable excitement also exists in consequence of the reports that the muskets removed from the Springfield Armoury have been distributed over the South.

Four weeks later –

Friday, February 8, 1861. We learn from America that Colonel Hayne, commanding the States forces in Florida, had telegraphed to President Buchanan that he would not attack Fort Pickens, and that the Southern States would avoid a collision, in the hope of an amicable adjustment and from a desire to preserve peace. The Senators from Florida, Alabama and Mississippi had withdrawn from the Senate. It having been rumoured in New York that the Navy yard would be attacked, Marines were ordered under arms, but no attack took place. Georgia had signed a secession *ordinance*.

Friday, May 17, 1861. The American telegram ... instead of bringing news of a battle, as some expected, announces that the prospects of an immediate collision have diminished. Washington was now considered safe, it being defended by a force of 18,000 men, and telegraphic communication restored between that city and New York...

A syndicated editorial in the same issue – no indication is given as to the identity of the author – draws the threads of the story together.

The unhappy quarrel and fratricidal bloodshed in America have aroused in this country the utmost horror and disgust: especially at the conduct of the Southern States. But besides the horror we feel at this internecine war, there has been a feeling of alarm lest Great Britain might in any way be dragged into the war, in consequence of a close connection with the country, in language, interests, commerce and religion. We are glad, therefore, to see that a royal proclamation has been issued by this country announcing that all persons enlisting, or fitting out ships for foreign service, render themselves liable to fine and imprisonment.

But, just two weeks after these disarming sentiments –

Friday, May 31, 1861. Another Gold Find. The approaching conflict between the Northern and Southern States has so filled the public mind that ordinary topics of American and Canadian news have been almost disregarded of late. Notwithstanding, however, the anxieties and difficulties occasioned by the American complications, the keenest curiosity and interest has been excited by the accounts received from Nova Scotia of the success which has attended the search after gold in that province.

The Secessionists have threatened Fort Monroe, but were compelled to retire. An attack on a large scale is, however, anticipated. Ammunition and heavy ordnance continue to arrive at Harper's Ferry from the South...

In the midst of these preoccupations, the repeal of the duty payable on raw paper, obliged the *Andover Advertiser* to consider its own future.

One of the most hotly debated measures of the present session has been the Repeal of the Duty on paper, and one of the first results of its anticipated repeal is the increased and, we trust, improved form in which the Andover Advertiser is this week published.

Five years ago, it was considered impossible to maintain a weekly newspaper in the Town of Andover; but we thought that a *monthly* journal ... would be better than none.

A few months trial, however, served to elicit the fact, that ... a weekly publication would meet public approval, and the result was, that January 1858, saw the first weekly Andover paper. Since that time our motto has been 'onward' and our circulation has gone on increasing from 300 to nearly 1300 a week, whilst our advertisements have increased from about two columns, to an average of seven columns weekly.

This – 'has had the result of diminishing the local news by encroaching gradually, but surely, on the space allotted to it.'

We have met this – 'by increasing, very considerably, both the space for local news and that for advertisements ... at no small additional expense to ourselves.'

So, there!

Meanwhile, back in America.

June 7, 1861. Two grand camps are about to be formed, where volunteers will be received and drilled. One camp will be on Staten Island, from whence troops will be transported to the Atlantic States, and the other at Gettysburg, Pennsylvania, for the supply of the service in this direction and in the South-West.

June 28, 1861. New York, June 15. Harper's Ferry has been evacuated by the Confederates in great haste. They attempted to destroy the railway bridge, but failed.

The Confederates have abandoned the whole line of the Potomac, with the intention of concentrating their forces at Manassas Junction.

Ordinary concerns return with a piece on 18 October, titled 'How Towns Spring Up in the American Prairies'. *The Times'* correspondent gives the following animated description of one of those places which spring up in the Prairies of America, and grow with a rapidity of which we, in the Old World, can scarcely form a conception. The letter is dated from Racine, in the State of Wisconsin.

The place from which this letter is dated is one of the wonderful creations of the grain harvests and immigration in the vast prairie tracts which lie on the western shores of the Michigan inland sea. It looks like a Russian settlement – not unlike; indeed, to the suburbs of Kherson, with a view of wide, muddy streets, plank footpaths, wooden houses, shady trees by the roadside, spires and metalled domes, and well-built houses of brick, rising above the dead level of the edifices of timber. Here, too, are to be seen the omnipresent German beer saloon, and the well-known names and trades followed by the Teutons in Russland as in the United States...

By the end of the year, urgent and sombre concerns had returned to dog the American question.

Friday, December 13, 1861. One subject above all others continues to pervade the public mind – the probabilities of war with America ... the national mind is unsettled, and 'Shall we go to war?' is the question on every lip.

Whatever may be the natural pride of the Washington Cabinet ... we may rest assured that the great mass of the American people will have no desire for actual war.

England's Ultimatum. We believe it will be found that the terms demanded from the Americans by the British Government in reference to the outrage committed on the British flag by the officers of the San Jacinto are – first, an unconditional apology, and, secondly, the immediate release of Messrs. Slidell and Mason, the Confederate Commissioners delegated to the Governments of Great Britain and France.

After this brief confrontation, the *Andover* paper seems to have taken a more distant and reserved interest in the American war.

Friday, April 18, 1862. An American Guerilla. The name of the mysterious marauder, John Morgan, is on the lips of everyone, for his daring coolness and disregard of fear has become a by-word even among our own army. (says a New York Paper). This Colonel John Morgan, for so he styles himself, is said to be native of Lexington, Ky, whose father was a respectable manufacturer of jeans.

Now, there are events closer to home demanding coverage, such as the possibility of a French invasion, against which danger there was to be formed a Volunteer Rifle Corps. But men so engaged could not be in two places at once. They could not, for example, be also on the cricket pitch.

While, however, we wish the Rifle Corps every success, we cannot help feeling that they are doing much to abolish the manly English game ... We do not think that the great county and district clubs are on the wane, but we know that in many small towns the rifle corps has utterly destroyed the cricket club...

The validity of this comment can be judged from an announcement that appeared each week. '13th Hants Rifle Volunteer Corps. Company drill Wednesday morning and Thursday evening at 7 o'clock. Musketry

drill Monday, Tuesday and Thursday mornings, and Monday and Tuesday evenings at 7 o'clock.'

The Liberty of the Press was the subject of a syndicated editorial to appear on 6 June 1862. – 'Unfavourable comparison of France.'

In the bright little Island of which we glory to be natives, the press, as a rule, and even the penny press ... is well conducted and dignified ... and expresses its opinions of men and things in the most unreserved way possible ... Contrast this with the French press ... the Emperor of France is the press ... (it) says only just what he thinks fit, and if an unfortunate newspaper proprietor ventures to have an opinion of his own ... any fine morning the paper may be suppressed ...

Three years later, the paper's syndicated editorial was reflecting the influence of the national dailies. Its choice of subject on 18 August 1865 was as much a national as a local issue.

The Murder Mania. It is hardly safe for a nervous person to take up a daily paper. The murder mania has reached such a pitch that scarcely a week or even a day is allowed to pass without the perpetration of a revolting murder in some part of the United Kingdom ... The punishment of death is also totally misplaced ... (criminals) know that hanging causes almost instantaneous death, and therefore they do not dread the detection of their crimes, because they look upon the punishment as momentary.

During the summer of that year, American interest had sunk to such a low profile that, on 28 April, under the heading 'Topics of the Week' the paper was able to inform its readers –

The *sensations* of the past week have been melodramatic enough to satisfy the most morbid imagination. From America, the news of the surrender of Lee, with all his army was sufficiently startling, but it was nothing compared with what was to follow. The next thing was the voluntary surrender of Miss Constance Kent, and her confession of the murder of her infant brother. While *all* England was aghast at this terrible *dénouement*, another telegram came from the American mail ship Nova Scotia, with the astounding news that the President of the United States was assassinated...

By the end of the year, these American events had sunk into some remote editorial limbo. 'December 29, 1865. Although the past year can scarcely be described as an eventful one...

Limitation of space prevents more than a summary of the large number of papers surviving from this period. A list follows in date order. It is an interesting exercise to plot these geographically. The very large number of suburban London papers is of considerable significance. They demonstrate the appeal of the local paper, even when it has to compete with the much larger London national dailies.

SURVIVING PAPERS FOUNDED BETWEEN 1851
AND 1875

Wells Journal	1851	East Kent Gazette	1855
Burnley Express	1852	Suffolk Free Press	1855
Leigh Reporter	1852	Isle of Wight Mercury	1855
Wakefield Express	1852	Islington Gazette	1856
Whitehaven News	1852	Beverley Guardian	1856
West Sussex Gazette	1853	Eastbourne Gazette	1856
Buckingham Advertiser	1853	Gravesend Reporter	1856
Goole Times	1853	Bucks Free Press	1856
Hastings Observer (and St. Leonards)	1853	Cornish Post	1856
Ormskirk Advertiser	1853	Market Rasen Monitor	1856
St. Helen's News and Advertiser	1853	Rochdale Observer	1856
Craven Herald	1853	Thame Gazette	1856
News and Advertiser (Yorkshire)	1853	City Press (London)	1857
Warrington Guardian	1853	Chelsea News	1857
Wigan Observer	1853	Marylebone Mercury	1857
Surrey Comet	1854	St. Pancras Chronicle	1857
Northumberland Gazette	1854	Westminster and Pimlico News	1857
Teesdale Mercury	1854	Andover Advertiser	1857
Bideford Advertiser	1854	Birmingham Post	1857
Bridgnorth Journal	1854	Hull Times	1857
Cheshire Observer	1854	Lincolnshire Times	1857
Derbyshire Times	1854	Cornish Times	1857
Grantham Journal	1854	Tavistock Gazette	1857
Kingsbridge Gazette	1854	Wetherby News	1857
Market Harborough Advertiser	1854	Pulman's Weekly News (Somerset)	1857
Morpeth Herald	1854	Middlesex Chronicle	1858
Newark Advertiser	1854	Stratford and Newham Express	1858
Newport Advertiser	1854	Barnsley Chronicle	1858
Oldham Chronicle	1854	Bournemouth Times	1858
Peterborough Express and Advertiser	1854	Western Daily Express (Bristol)	1858
Staffordshire Western Sentinel	1854	Dewsbury Reporter	1858
Mid-Wales Journal	1854	Dover Express	1858
North and South Shropshire Journals	1854	Exmouth Journal	1858
Wiltshire Times	1854	Hemel Hempstead Gazette	1858
Shepton Mallet Journal	1854	South York Advertiser	1858
Whitby Gazette	1854	Tiverton Gazette	1858
Daily Telegraph (London)	1855	The Sporting Life (London)	1859
Harrow Observer	1855	Barnet Press	1859
Wembley Observer	1855	Enfield Gazette and Observer	1859
West London Observer	1855	Kent Messenger	1859
Kentish Express	1855	Bridlington Free Press	1859
Ashton-under-Lyne Reporter	1855	Chatham News	1859
Blackburn Times	1855	Surrey Mail	1859
Bridgwater Mercury	1855	Glossop Chronicle	1859
Bridport News	1855	Hitchin Gazette	1859
Bury Times	1855	Marlborough Times	1859
Chatham Standard	1855	Melton Mowbray Times	1859
Christchurch Times	1855	Bucks Standard	1859
Congleton Chronicle	1855	Prescott Reporter	1859
Falmouth Packet	1855	Redditch Indicator	1859
Gainsborough News	1855	Wednesbury Boro News	1859
Guildford Times	1855	Woodbridge Reporter	1859
Halesworth Times	1855	Hampstead and Highgate Express	1860
Heywood Advertiser	1855	Bromsgrove Messenger	1860
Liverpool Post	1855	North Somerset Mercury	1860
Ludlow Advertiser	1855	Driffield Times	1860
Luton News	1855	Evesham Journal	1860
Malvern Gazette	1855	Faversham Times	1860
Thomson's Weekly News (Lancashire)	1855	Knutsford Guardian	1860
Herts Reporter	1855	Northwich Guardian	1860
Herts Advertiser	1855	Cumberland Herald	1860
Scarborough Mercury	1855	Western Morning News (Devon)	1860
Morning Telegraph (Yorkshire)	1855	Salisbury Times	1860

Selby Times	1860	South Kensington News	1869
Stratford-on-Avon Herald	1860	Sutton and Cheam Advertiser	1869
Totnes Times	1860	Dartford Chronicle	1869
Wellington Weekly News	1860	West Sussex County Times (Horsham)	1869
West Somerset Free Press	1860	Hunts Post	1869
Edmonton Weekly Herald	1861	Maidenhead Advertiser	1869
Southgate and Palmer's Green Weekly Herald	1861	Retford Times	1869
Tottenham Weekly Herald	1861	Evening Gazette (York)	1869
Wood Green Weekly Herald	1861	Tenbury Wells Advertiser	1869
Herts Observer	1861	Waltham Forest Times	1870
Ilkley Gazette	1861	Birmingham Evening Mail	1870
Kidderminster Times	1861	Erdington News	1870
Beds Observer	1861	Northern Echo (Durham)	1870
Central Somerset Gazette	1861	Folkestone Herald	1870
Witney Gazette	1861	Kidderminster Shuttle	1870
Altrincham Guardian	1862	Isle of Thanet Gazette	1870
Essex Weekly News	1862	Eastern Daily Press	1870
Keighley News	1862	Oxford University Gazette	1870
Oxford Times	1862	Pudsey News	1870
Runcorn Guardian	1862	Bolton Journal	1871
Middlesex County Times and West Middlesex Gazette	1863	Chorley Guardian	1871
Cheshunt Telegraph	1863	Crediton Gazette	1871
Knaresboro Post	1863	Crowle Advertiser	1871
Mid-Devon Advertiser	1863	Huddersfield Daily Express	1871
Pateley Bridge Herald	1863	Lydney Observer	1871
West Herts Observer	1863	Coop News (Lancashire)	1871
Hackney Gazette and North London Advertiser	1864	Morley Observer	1871
Burnham-on-Sea Gazette	1864	Sydenham Gazette	1872
Diss Express	1864	Bognor Regis Observer	1872
Express and Echo (Exter)	1864	Chatteris Advertiser	1872
Surrey Advertiser (Guildford)	1864	Ely Standard	1872
Hexham Courant	1864	Epworth Bells	1872
Ossett Observer	1864	Cambridgeshire Times	1872
Whitstable Times	1864	Newmarket Journal	1872
Clapham and Lambeth News	1865	Peterboro Standard	1872
South London Press	1865	South Molton Gazette	1872
East Kent Mercury	1865	Kent Courier	1872
Dunstable Gazette	1865	Richmond and Twickenham Times	1873
St. Helen's Reporter	1865	Gloucester Echo	1873
East London Advertiser	1866	Farnworth Journal	1873
Accrington Observer and Times	1866	Leigh Journal	1873
Dudley Herald	1866	Southend Standard	1873
East Kent Times	1866	Evening Sentinel (Staffordshire)	1873
Isle of Wight Chronicle	1866	Echo (Durham)	1873
Bexley and Welling Observer	1867	Devon and Somerset News	1873
Erith and Crayford Observer	1867	Bedford Record	1874
North Berks Herald	1867	Blyth News	1874
Bolton Evening News	1867	Chard News	1874
Newbury Weekly News	1867	Dean Forest Guardian	1874
Ross Gazette	1867	Coleshill Chronicle	1874
Spenborough Guardian	1867	Colne Times	1874
County Express (Worcester)	1867	Crewe Chronicle	1874
Acton Gazette and West London Post	1868	Eccles Journal	1874
Kilburn Times	1868	East Anglian Daily Times	1874
Streatham News	1868	Leicester Mercury	1874
Telegraph and Argus (Bradford)	1868	The Visitor (Morecambe, Heysham and Lancaster)	1874
Macclesfield Advertiser	1868	Warley News Telephone	1874
Manchester Evening News	1868	Alderley Advertiser	1874
Sheerness Times	1868	Express and Star (Stafford)	1874
Tamworth Herald	1868	West Cumberland Times	1874
Croydon Advertiser	1869	Hendon Times	1875
Holborn Guardian	1869	High Peak Reporter (Derby)	1875
Kensington News and Post	1869	Swinton Journal	1875

Youth,
an Illustrated Journal

WITH WHICH IS INCORPORATED

"THE BOYS' NEWSPAPER" AND "THE BOYS' ILLUSTRATED NEWS."

VOL. I.—No. 1.   *Registered as a Newspaper*   WEDNESDAY, AUGUST 2, 1882.   *for Transmission Abroad.*   PRICE TWOPENCE.

HALFORD OF DUNSTAN'S.
A STORY OF OXFORD LIFE.

BY C. G. THOMPSON,

CHAPTER I.
FIRST IMPRESSIONS.

"SIALF PAST seven, sir! Breakfast in or out, sir? In, sir? Alone, sir? *Very* good, sir."

The speaker —a short, stout, middle aged man, with a rosy face and a bottle nose, who had suddenly appeared at the foot of Austin Halford's bed on the first morning of his first term at "Dunstan's," looked solemnly into the freshman's only partially opened eyes, drew a long sigh, and vanished. Hurriedly collecting his drowsy thoughts, Halford sprang out of bed and commenced his toilette. At a quarter to eight the chapel bell sounded out upon the college, and in ten minutes more, after carefully arraying himself in his cap and gown before the looking-glass, he descended the staircase and proceeded, a little nervously, it must be confessed, across the "quad." At the chapel door stood a gentleman in a more pretentious gown than that with which he, as a commoner, had been furnished on the preceding day. Thinking he was someone in authority, and wishing to ingratiate himself with the dons from the first, Austin raised his hat. The man placed his hand upon his mouth to conceal a smile, and referred to a piece of paper.

"What name?" he asked.

"Austin Halford."

"Thanks." The gentleman marked the paper with a pencil and turned his face another way. The freshman passed on into the chapel, and, finding himself the cynosure of several pairs of eyes, blushed modestly, hesitated, and slipped into the first seat that appeared unoccupied. For the next few there was a stream of men passing into the seats; then the bell ceased; the Rev. Samuel Bloggs, the sub-dean, instantly rose and, in a stentorian voice, began, "When the wicked man"—but paused abruptly as a small man shuffled up the aisle in a pair of slippers a size too large for him and very much worn down at the heels. This man's gown was slit up the back; the college cap, which he carried in one hand, was broken and battered; and in his other hand was a formidable volume bearing the inscription "Common Prayer." With this book clasped to his breast with one hand, and with the other both holding his gown at the shoulder and carrying his cap, the small man bore down upon the seat which Halford had taken, regarded him gravely for a moment, and then crossed and took a vacant place opposite to him. The service recommenced. The small man looked up, caught the eye of one of Halford's neighbours, drew in his lips as if checking a convulsion of laughter and chuckled audibly. There was a titter; the Rev. Samuel Bloggs dropped a word; and the small man opened his volume and was lost to sight for a few moments. Then the men sitting on the other side of the chapel saw a slipperless foot stealing out in search of its rightful complement, which had been unhappily dropped a yard or two from the seat, and the ineffectual attempts of this foot to describe a semi-circle in space so as to include the slipper provoked another titter amongst the irreverent. The small man placed a warning finger to his lips and disappeared again. In a few seconds, however, the foot stole forth once more, this time furnished with a lasso constructed of one of the strings which hang from the shoulders of a commoner's gown, tied to the ankle, and thus the slipper was triumphantly circumvented. Thenceforth the small man was seen no more, and the service proceeded without any further unseemly incident.

I have given this trifling, and not very creditable, piece of byplay the post of honour in this story, because it is Austin Halford's earliest lively reminiscence of his Oxford days. It serves, also, to introduce him to my readers as he first appeared to the men of his college; and it moreover embraces the person of the man who, from the very first, made a forcible impression upon the freshman's mind, and who, in the future, was destined to exercise a remarkable influence upon his career. This man was Simon Short, named also, by a very natural association of ideas, the "Pieman." His slippers and his Book of Common Prayer—alas! a whited sepulchre, the outward frame being merely a cloak for Rolleston's "Forms of Animal Life"—are firmly imprinted upon the tablets of the minds of many men; his cap and gown are a treasured tradition of "Dunstan's"; and his diminutive stature, careless manner of dressing, and imperturbable gravity in the most comic of his own generation of Oxford men to the present.

I am writing of a Michaelmas term seven or eight years ago. Since then there has been a Royal Commission, halls have been established for the "sweet girl graduates," new "schools" have been opened; yet, between the Oxford of this story and the Oxford of to-day no material difference will be found, and no distinction drawn. To all intents and purposes Halford of Dunstan's might be Halford of Balliol, Brazenose, "Univ.," or any other college, and might have matriculated at the beginning of the ensuing term. Let it be understood, however, that Saint Dunstan's has not been disestablished, and that you who will matriculate next October will find it in exactly the same position as Austin Halford found it, and as it has been found any time during the last four centuries; that the men may not bear the same names, but they will bear the same characters, and, it may also be added, the same faces; that you who are ambitious may read here of the trials and triumphs, the hopes, the despairs, the troubles and amenities of an undergraduate's life; and that the light and the shade, the grave and the gay, will be so intermingled, that the picture, whatever its defects may be, may at least possess the negative merit of being faultily true. So much by way of preface. The story opens with Austin Halford as he presented himself to "Dunstan's" men on his first appearance in chapel.

First of all, Slider, the captain of the S.D.C.B.C., saw in the freshman a man with long arms, who, despite a despicable habit of poking forward his head and rounding his shoulders, might be got into shape and made an oar. Slinger, the captain of the S.D.C.C.C., tried to picture the latest arrival at the wicket, and thought the stoop betrayed a trained eye ever on the alert for a possible ball. Sprinter, the president of the S.D.C.A.C., would not have been surprised to hear that the "fresher" could run like a hare; and each of these three gentlemen resolved that it would be as well to call upon him. Now, Slider, Slinger, and Sprinter represented the opinion of physical or athletic "Dunstans," and the college was celebrated for its exploits on the river and in the field. Intellectual Dunstans, as represented by the president of the College Debating Society, the young gentleman who "was going "in for the Newdigate, the "smugs" and the "cultured" Ruskinites and Paterites, considered the broad brow and deep-set, thoughtful eyes of the freshman indicative of latent gifts, but feared that there was more gross

Press Explosion

The question of style was to prove critical in the development of a popular press. All the ground work had otherwise been laid. Printing techniques had improved to the point where the mass production of papers was practicable. The introduction of the telegraph and telephone accelerated the arrival of news reports. Transport systems, both on sea and land, were available to distribute daily papers on a mass basis. Education had made a majority of the population literate. A century and a half earlier the application of advertising revenue had shown how to lower the selling price and so increase circulation. What was now needed was some stylistic innovation to create mass demand, some twist of words and presentation that would attract the money of a mass public.

The innovation came. Credit for it is generally given to Alfred Harmsworth, later to be Lord Northcliffe. Yet, as with other new ideas, like the moving film and theory of evolution, one man sweeps the credit, while many do the work.

Born Alfred Charles William Harmsworth at Chapelizod, near Dublin, on 15 July 1865, he was the son of an indigent English barrister, Alfred Harmsworth. He did not attend school until he was eight, and proved an indifferent scholar. When the family returned to London, living on the edge of Hampstead Heath, Harmsworth went to school in nearby St John's Wood where he edited the magazine of his small, private day school.

George Samuel Jealous had started the Hampstead and Highgate Express in 1860. Near neighbours of his were the Harmsworth family, and young Alfred was allowed in the composing room on press days. Jealous gave the boy a printing press for a birthday present, and later gave him the chance to do small reporting jobs during the school holidays. His first full-time engagement was as assistant-editor of *Youth* – an illustrated paper for boys, produced by the *Illustrated London News*.

The first issue, dated Wednesday 2 August 1882, gives a firm indication of the upper middle class readership at which it was aimed.

On the first page appears 'Helford of Dunstan's – A Story of Oxford Life', by C. G. Thomson. This is followed on the inner pages by 'News from Schools', of which the most prominent are Eton College, Harrow School and Marlborough College. Then, 'A Trip to the Tasman Glaciers', by a Settler in the Towns. More fiction – 'Don Diego' – An Adventure in the Pyrenees', by Henry Hollier. An Illustrated page – 'The Australian Cricketers'. 'The Bombardment of Alexandria', by a Midshipman. 'Golden Youth', by Keppel Brierly.

It would be conveniently agreeable to be able to point to the *Exchange and Mart* page as having been originated by the young Harmsworth. Despite having his touch, there is no evidence for this. It is presented under such headings as 'Animals, Birds, etc., Athletics, Bicycles, Books, etc., Jewellery, Miscellaneous, Music and Stamps'. Then follows Acrostics and Puzzles, Chess, and an Illustrated Supplement 'New Wars and Old Warriors'.

An interest he seems to have retained all his life was in cycling. Whether this predates 1886, or began then, is not clear. For it was in that year that he went to Coventry to edit the *Bicycling News* for Edward Iliffe, later to be one of his competitors in publishing. Two years later, at the age of 23, with modest savings, he took an office at 26, Paternoster Square, London, and from there, on 2 June 1888, began his career as a publisher with the first issue of a modest weekly called *Answers to Correspondents*. Based on George Newnes's already successful *Tit-Bits*, the contents of its first issue give an indication of the popular approach forming in his mind. In particular, it is informative to compare his list of titles for his items with the writing of headlines, which he later evolved.

At the top of the front page are the words 'Interesting – Extraordinary – Amusing'. The paper announces itself as 'Answers to Correspondents on Every Subject Under the Sun'. Of course, as the editor cannily points out in an introduction titled 'How Do You Do', for the first issue there could not be any correspondents. He was, therefore, obliged to choose topics that he judged his readers might want to know about. This is his list:

Ass drawing water
A Living Clock
Silk Stockings
Hair Powder
Origin of Grog
Eccentric Character
Then and Now
Death from Imagination
Forests Under the Sea
Richard Whittington
Elwes the Miser
Vails to Servants
The Earl of Leicester
Ancient London
A Fortnight in Brighton
Fossil Bacon
A terrible time with a Cobra
Artificial Memory
Stones from the Heavens
Charles Fox as a Gamester
About horse racing
Queen Caroline,
Living on Nothing a Year
Right and Left Boots
George III at Home

Where he hid it
An experimental dinner
Jokes

The paper sold for 1d – its title was later shortened to *Answers*. In a later issue, Harmsworth, as editor, complained of the large number of bogus questions sent in, such as 'Why are no bus conductors bald?' He declares the editorial policy – every question sent in is answered (if it can be): those of general interest are published, the others are dealt with by post. Medical Questions are handled by 'A Doctor and a qualified lady'. Legal Questions are sent to a Barrister and solicitor. For questions of Employment, he has 'Two acknowledged authorities'. Personal matters are not encouraged, but receive attention. Household Questions are answered by 'an experienced lady'. Literary and Other Questions go to competent authorities.

As *Answers* found a good market, Alfred was joined by his brother Harold, who henceforth handled all financial matters, leaving Alfred a clear hand to concentrate on the editorial side. As a result, in 1890, they entered the children's comic market with *Comic Cuts* (Amusing Without Being Vulgar), *Chips* – and the women's magazine field with *Forget-Me-Nots*.

The *London Evening News*, in 1894, was almost bankrupt. Alfred Harmsworth took it over, and transformed it into a popular paper with short crisp news stories, striking headlines, a daily story, a column for women, and other modern features. Within the year, circulation had risen to 160,000 and the profits were enormous. As a result the Harmsworth brothers conceived the idea of a national chain of halfpenny morning papers throughout the major provincial cities. They bought two papers in Glasgow, merging them into the *Glasgow Daily Record*, and others in Leeds.

The *Evening News* was for Harmsworth a key enterprise, and it is worth examining in some detail. The first issue for which he was wholly responsible was that of 2 July 1894. The front page had a seven-column layout, typical of the period. From left to right, the first three columns contained nothing but box advertisements. Column Four was headed – 'All the World Day By Day'. Each item is accorded a single paragraph. These are headed – 'British Officer Killed in the Straits Settlements. Remarkable Love Tragedy in Brussels. Cable Brevities. Advice Gratis – Queries Answered for Impecunious Clients by Our Legal Editor'. In this last item, Harmsworth can be seen harking back to the experience of *Answers*. The brief samples have none of the crisp and vivid quality with which his name, and that of popular journalism, has become associated.

In Column Five is reported Cycling and Athletic Notes. Column Six has Cricket Chronicle. Not until Column Seven is there any 'news' – Fatal Fire at Clapham, Terrible Family Tragedy, Boating Fatality at Blackfriars, Murder and Mutilation. Today's Weather.

On Saturday, 21 July there was added to this rather unattractive mixture 'Voice of the People' – a column

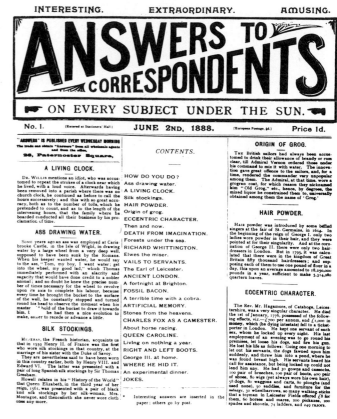

of correspondence. That same issue also contained very brief illustrations of Chess and Draughts Games, the first slight use of illustrative material having taken place on 11 July, when the score cards of the contestants at the Bisley Meeting between the Volunteers and Regulars were reproduced.

However, Harmsworth's delicate editorial censors were at work. For, on Friday, 31 August, a new front page format appeared. The advertisements were reduced to a single column on the left. Six columns of news were headed in something approaching the crisper style. Column Two – Fun in St Pancras, Another Battersea Scandal, Killed by a Grindstone, Was It Suicide Or Apoplexy? Sending Round the Hat. Column Three – Bones in Bishopsgate, Blue Jackets Fired Upon, The Registration Courts, The Irish Mails, Miles of Forest Fires, Burglary at Wood Green. Column Four – Cab Runner Nuisance, Leicester Votes, Not True About Aird, For the Soul of the Earl, Message from the Sea, Trades Congress Delegate in Trouble, Killed in the Pit. Column Five – Shelling Samoan Rebels, The Boiler Burst (Passengers Blown to Atoms by a Locomotive Explosion), Servant's Body in a Box, Who Will be the New Judge? What is a Boot Club? Revolt against Political 'Bosses'. Column Six – Butcher's Breach (Amusing Love Letters), The Ways of Guardians, Dutch Bombarding MATARAM. Column Seven – Rescued to Die, Fire on the Canton, The Small-Pox Epidemic, The Borough Outrage, Burned to Death, Collision on Herne Hill, Hypnotism and Lunacy, The Clergyman's Big D——.

This is quite exciting stuff. One's attention is being caught – even at an ephemeral level – and one is being invited to read, to find out. Further ideas come, pumping fresh life into the paper – a Saturday Sports edition, the increasing use of illustrations.

By Tuesday, 25 September, the Actual Sale of the paper – as announced in a proud and boastful box, was 110,000. 'More than any other London halfpenny paper. Not one day's sale, nor a week's, but daily for three months.'

Features begin to appear, illustrated on the front page. Among the first, on Saturday, 6 October was No. One of 'Men Who Have Earned Success' – a series which Harmsworth was later to carry across to the *Daily Mail*. *Woman's World* started here.

The narrative style of headline first came on Friday, 26 October, above an interview in prison given by a man awaiting trial on a charge of murder.

Friday, 26 October 1894.
Read Interviewed in Gaol
Description of his Life and Doings in Prison at Chelmsford
Fiction his Favourite Reading
Elaborate Preparations For His Defence at the Trial Next Week.

And, again on Friday, 2 November.
'Death of the Czar' followed by illustrations showing 'The Palace at Livada Where the Czar Died. The Kremlin, Moscow, Where the Late Czar was Crowned. Winter Palace, St. Petersburg, The Czar Aged 20/38/46/49. The New Czar.'

A Special Edition on 16 November announced that the *Evening News* had broken the world's record with the unprecedented total sale of 394,447 copies. 'Had we been able to supply the demand it would have amounted to over half a million.' During those days, with the enormous demand created by an illustrated report of Read's trial, Harmsworth made desperate attempts to increase his print runs, trying to buy time on the presses of other papers. His actual sales during the four days – Monday to Thursday – of that week amounted to over a million copies.

A curious editorial theme came into the columns during the run up to Christmas in that first year. It began on Monday, 17 December.

8000 Anarchists in London. Where These Enemies of Society Live in this Great Metropolis. Some Startling Finds. Accompanied by Illustrations from Secret Anarchist Prints – (1) RAVACHOL, The Patron Saint (As He Is Represented in Anarchist Prints), (2) How to Deal With a Capitalist.

This theme was continued on 18 December, with a print sub-titled 'This Picture Now Being Extensively Circulated Represents The Anarchist Watching the Dawn of the New Year Which is Represented by a Blood-Red Sun'.

On 20 December – 'Murder and Pillage. The Motto of an Anarchist Journal Printed in London. The Question of Bomb Throwing. Some Interesting Facts Con-cerning Methods of Propaganda.' Friday, 21 December – 'Morality and Marriage. The Inner Views of the Professed Enemies of Society. Some Notable Women. Facts About the Anarchist Criminals and Bomb Carrying.'

Clearly, a great influx of new ideas transformed the pages of the *Evening News* under Harmsworth's direction. But it is fair to ask what the source of those ideas might have been. This question can best be answered by an examination of the first national daily Harmsworth began himself. This was the *Daily Mail*, whose first issue is ostensibly dated Monday, 4 May 1896.

I say ostensibly because registration copies of the paper were first published on Monday, 19 February in that same year. In these, Harmsworth, with the experience of the *Evening News* behind him seems to have been exploring further editorial ideas. One of these was the use of the banner headline. That first issue, for example, across the top of the front page carries – 'The Boers Are Building New Forts And Getting New Guns!' There was no link with any story on the front page. Indeed, the reader has to make a careful search of pages two and three to find any reference to the subject at all.

Other typical headlines are:

February 19 – 'What the Little Englanders Would Like to Do With Dr. Jim'[1]

[1] i.e., Dr Jameson.

The "Evening News" has the Largest Sale of any Evening Paper in London.

February 20 – 'Troubles Don't Come Singly to Johannesburg.'

February 25 – 'Query:– Shall We Lose South Africa? See Article on this Page.'

Here for the first time in these registration issues was a direct front page link between the headline and the text which continued beneath it – 'Shall We Lose South Africa? Will Germany Get It? – A Sober Warning.'

This front page link is abandoned as soon as introduced. Instead, a textual reference is made to where the connecting piece is to be found:

February 26 – 'The Extraordinary Demonstration at Bow St. – See Page 2.'

February 28 – 'The Need For a Strong Navy – See Page 2.'

But, one senses that the editor's use of the device is uncertain. This is confirmed on Wednesday, 4 March, when the headline simply states: 'Four Columns of Advertisements Are Held Over To-day.' Again, on the next day, the headline reads – 'This is the 400th Birthday of the British Empire.' Ten days later, ideas are flowing again. 'There is Going To Be Big Trouble in the Soudan' says the headline, with a cascade of supporting headings. 'War Cloud in the Soudan. Troops Are to Advance At Once and Occupy Dongola. The Fall of Kassala Imminent And a Dervish Descent upon Egypt

May Be Anticipated At Any Moment.' All this supported by a map illustrating 'Where the Trouble Is'.

Something goes sadly wrong on Saturday, 21 March. The front page headline reads – 'Will Manitoba Secede To The United States?' Thereafter, there is not a single further reference to the story anywhere in the paper. Indeed, it is as if the editor has lost faith in the idea as

an attention grabber. By the end of that month, it had degenerated to a kind of instant advertisement for the paper itself. 30 March – 'Tomorrow's Short Story on Page 1 Will Be Of Enthralling Interest'. Perhaps it was. The headline certainly was not.

A genuine news use was tried again on 17 April. 'A Quiet Budget With No New Taxes'. But, by 23 April, there was a return to the advertising use. 'Do You Want A Bright Morning Newspaper? The "Daily Mail" Will Be Ready on May 4th.' 24 April – 'Have You Ordered Your Newsagent To Get You A Copy of the "Daily Mail"?'

News again on 25 April. 'President Kruger Has Replied, And Says He Won't Come to England'.

28 April – 'You Must Wait Till May 4 For the "Daily Mail"'.

30 April – 'A £1000 Note Would Not Purchase A Copy of the "Daily Mail" Today'.

Then, on 4 May, the first issue of the paper in its proper format appears. All the experimentation has been cast aside, rejected. The paper is a conventional 8 page paper, with 7 columns per page. There are no headlines – a marked absence of front page illustration. The formal layout is a visual replica of those established papers with which Harmsworth seems to have decided he must now compete. It might almost be the conventional story of the successful new boy having finally, and purely for his own satisfaction, decided to take on and beat the establishment on its own terms.

Yet, one sees Harmsworth's problem. He had already achieved a popular success with the *Evening News*. The *Daily Mail* was his own paper, the one he had nurtured, fought for, created. Much of his money was tied up in it. It had to be successful.

The necessity to publish three months of registration numbers to protect his title gave him the opportunity to play with ideas. It gave him also the chance to play games with his competitors. For, although his major triumphs were yet to come, Harmsworth was already enough of a force for the sensitive war horses of Fleet Street to have brought their battle sights to bear on him.

Perhaps, too, Harmsworth had already set his own sights on that hessian-backed accolade of the Street, *The Times*, that time and fortune were to bring under his control in 1906.

But, we are still ten years before that time. And there they were, the establishment of Fleet Street. And Harmsworth had to beat them at their own game if for no other reason than to prove himself in his own eyes.

In the event, the *Daily Mail* proved to be a remarkably sophisticated product. Its sober, conventional appearance could lead to it being confused with the *Telegraph* at twenty paces. In that sense, it was truly, as it claimed, 'The Penny Paper for One Halfpenny'. That achievement was not wholly Alfred's. The other half belonged to the genius of his brother Harold in attracting advertising revenue to offset the cost of production and so keep the selling price down.

The *Daily Mail's* other self-given title was 'The busy man's daily journal'. Perhaps its ultimate triumph was that, not only could that claim be justified, but the paper was also just as much that of the busy man's wife. Its news stories were well informed, crisply written, and lavishly headlined so that a summary of the day's events could be gathered just by scanning the page headings. In addition, there were illustrated feature articles for information and entertainment, articles of interest to women, political and social gossip, serials and short stories, and on Saturdays, lavish sports reports. In these, Harmsworth's old interest – cycling – always had a prominent place.

The paper was quick success – rather more of a *succès d'estime* to begin with than an outright commercial block-buster. On 4 June, it claimed a daily sale of 171,121, which was well up in the league tables. But, it did not break the record levels already chalked up by the *Evening News* for some little while. It did eventually establish a world record for sales which it never lost while its founder was alive.

Since those days, radio and television have arisen to challenge the supremacy of the newspaper. Group ownership has modified the pattern of local papers. Printing by photographic methods, with computer-controlled layouts are being introduced. Yet, while some national papers are struggling, many local papers thrive. Some of these have reverted to a former style, abandoning their calculated neutrality for a strong, locally-based, political stance.

Even now, despite the problems and competition, there are still those worthy stalwarts, ready and willing today, to found new newspapers.

To protect their interests, The Newspaper Society continues. Founded in 1836, and representing then a mere eighteen Provincial papers, it now has 290 members who publish between them 81 evening papers, 26 morning papers and about 1,200 weeklies and bi-weeklies. This is the regional strength. The Newspaper Publishers' Association serves the interests of the National London-based papers.

Economic, technical and social problems threaten the life of some nationals, although most local papers still do well. Some question whether newspapers can survive. Technical innovation is making the industry capital intensive. Which, in a sense, is what it was to begin with. For, at rock-bottom, a paper is something produced by a man and a boy in a room – or whatever the modern equivalent may be.

Rather like radio.

SURVIVING PAPERS FOUNDED BETWEEN 1876
AND 1900

Beckenham Journal	1876
Bootle Times	1876
Gloucester Citizen	1876
Scarborough Evening News	1876
Shipley Times and Express	1876
Widnes Weekly News	1876
South Yorkshire Times	1877
Winsford Guardian	1877
The News (Portsmouth)	1877
Bedworth Observer	1877
Nuneaton Observer	1877
Middleton Guardian	1877
Heckmondwike Herald	1877
Harwich and Dovercourt Standard	1877
Mail, Hartlepool	1877
Birkenhead News	1877
Willesden and Brent Chronicle	1877
Balham and Tooting News	1878
Sutton and Cheam Herald	1878
Basingstoke Weekend Gazette	1878
Cannock Advertiser	1878
Gloucestershire Gazette	1878
Evening Post (Nottingham)	1878
Sale Guardian	1879
Surrey Mirror	1879
Liverpool Echo	1879
Derby Evening Telegraph	1879
Bicester Advertiser	1879
Batley News	1879
Hornsey Journal	1879
Lake District Herald	1880
Newton Reporter and Guardian	1880
Evening Argus (Brighton)	1880
Dean Forest Mercury	1880
Leominster and Bromyard News	1880
Chronicle and Echo (Northampton)	1880
Evening Chronicle (Oldham)	1880
Wharfedale and Airedale Observer	1880
Pontefract and Castleford Express	1880
Sevenoaks Chronicle	1880
Spalding Guardian	1880
Thetford Times	1880
Worcester Evening News	1880
Yarmouth Mercury	1880
Warminster Journal	1881
Tunbridge Wells and Tonbridge Advertiser	1881
Teignmouth Post and Gazette	1881
Mirfield Reporter	1881
Ilkeston Advertiser	1881
Hebden Bridge Times	1881
Mid-Sussex Times	1881
East Grinstead Observer	1881
Barrow News	1881
Sidcup Times	1881
Paddington Mercury	1881
Orpington Times	1881
Eltham Times	1881
Chislehurst Times	1881
Bromley Times	1881
Sunday People	1881
Evening News	1881

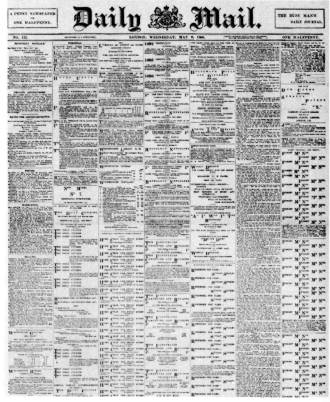

Contrast between the illustrated and headlined registration issue of *The Daily Mail* (above) and the formal final version (below).

Finchley Press	1882	Folkestone Herald	1891
Long Eaton Advertiser	1882	Coventry Evening Telegraph	1891
Midhurst and Petworth Observer	1882	Biggleswade Chronicle	1891
Eastern Evening News (Norwich)	1882	Ampthill News and Flitwick Record	1892
Soham Advertiser	1882	Surrey Herald (Chertsey)	1892
Southport Journal Visiter	1882	Coalville Times	1892
Uttoxeter Advertiser	1882	Easingwold Advertiser	1892
Yorkshire Evening Press	1882	Eastleigh Weekly News	1892
Worthing Gazette	1883	Farnham Herald	1892
Slough Observer	1883	Evening Courier (Halifax)	1892
Rossendale Free Press	1883	Littlehampton Gazette	1893
Petersfield Post	1883	Lincolnshire Echo	1893
Gainsborough Evening News	1883	Darwen Advertiser and News	1893
Faversham News	1883	Wimbledon News	1894
Dalton News	1883	Aldershot News	1894
Thurrock Gazette	1884	Consett Guardian Chronicle	1894
Millom News	1884	Eastwood and Kimberley Advertiser	1894
Isle of Wight County Press	1884	Runcorn Weekly News	1894
Padiham Advertiser	1884	Woking News and Mail	1894
Ulverston News	1885	Western Evening Herald (Plymouth)	1895
Notts Free Press	1885	Horley Advertiser	1895
Northwich Chronicle	1885	Haslemere Herald	1895
Evening Chronicle (Newcastle-on-Tyne)	1885	Formby Times	1895
Liverpool Weekly News	1885	Crosby Herald	1895
Leek Post and Times	1885	Ashbourne News Telegraph	1895
Evening Star (Ipswich)	1885	Brentford and Chiswick Times	1895
The Daily Mail (Hull)	1885	Daily Mail	1896
Horncastle News	1885	Belper News	1896
Henley Standard	1885	Bexhill-on-Sea Observer	1896
Clitheroe Advertiser	1885	Cheadle and Tean Times	1896
Alton Gazette	1885	Keswick Reminder	1896
Wandsworth Borough News	1885	Leamington and District Morning News	1896
Thames Valley Times	1885	Romsey Advertiser	1896
Richmond, Twickenham and Barnes Herald	1885	Colne Valley Guardian	1896
Lancashire Evening Telegraph	1886	Worksop Guardian	1896
Somerset Standard/Somerset Guardian	1886	Salford City Reporter	1897
Holmfirth Express	1886	Northamptonshire Evening Telegraph	1897
Lancashire Evening Post	1886	Grimsby Evening Telegraph	1897
The Star (Sheffield)	1887	Dawlish Gazette	1897
Leatherhead Advertiser	1887	Camden and St. Pancras Chronicle	1898
Dorking Advertiser	1887	Ilford and Redbridge Pictorial	1898
Chichester Observer	1887	North-Western Evening Mail	1898
Brighouse Echo	1887	Burton Daily Mail	1898
Fulham Chronicle	1887	Burton Observer and Chronicle	1898
Financial Times	1888	Saturday Telegraph	1898
Beckenham and Penge Advertiser	1888	Evening Advertiser (Swindon)	1898
Cambridge Evening News	1888	Wallasey News	1899
Haverhill Echo	1888	St. Ives Times and Echo	1899
Hinckley Times	1888	Radcliffe Times	1899
Southern Evening Echo (Southampton)	1888	South Notts Echo	1899
Wisbech Standard	1888	Alton Herald	1899
Stockport Express	1889	Ilford Recorder	1899
Scunthorpe Star Series	1889	Daily Express	1900
Ripon Gazette and Observer	1889	Evening Echo (Bournemouth)	1900
Ripley News	1889	Heanor Observer	1900
Hoylake News and Advertiser	1889	North East Kent Times	1900
East Frinton Gazette	1889		
Bucks Examiner	1889		
Brigg Star	1889		
Evening Post (Leeds)	1890		
Nelson Leader	1890		
Staines and Egham News	1891		
Loughborough Echo	1891		

Newspaper Illustration

Harmsworth's rejection of illustrations in the *Daily Mail* was true to the newspaper heritage of his time. Journalism had to do with words. Papers were designed to appeal to a readership that enjoyed the élite status of literacy in a largely illiterate population. Those who had mastered the skill of reading would not wish to share their understanding with those who could only look at pictures.

The *Northampton Mercury* was among the first of a small numbers of papers to experiment with illustrations. In December 1720 three political cartoons were published on the 5th, 12th, and 26th. The drawing was crude and roughly done. The wooden blocks used had only a short life. Inserting the block into the frame together with the text slowed down production when time was already too short for reliability. And the reaction of readers was one of only mild interest.

Illustrations faded from the pages of the journals and did not return until the 1840s. Then, it was not in the multitude of dailies that pictures were presented but in a limited number of 'Illustrated' weekly papers. Of these, one of the first that still survives is the *Illustrated London News* (June, 1842). Others, no longer with us, were the *Illustrated London Life* (1843), *Illustrated Weekly Times* (1843), and *The Graphic* (1869). Among the provincial papers were the *Oxfordshire Illustrated Telegraph* (1859), and the *Illustrated Midland News* (1869).

All these papers were hybrids, reverting to the formulae of the seventeenth century. Part newspaper, part magazine, fiction was included on their pages, together with reviews, articles of general information, some humour and poetry. They dealt with scientific and technical matters, political affairs, foreign news, the social and cultural scene, personality and geographical sketches, finance and commerce.

This formula was virtually imposed on them by their use of illustrations. Although a primitive type of photography existed from the mid-1830s, illustrations had in general to be supplied by artists. There were virtually no technical resources available. When a man was sent to the scene of a story, he could do no more than sketch what he saw with speed and precision, interview eye-witnesses and make drawings from their reports, and then bring these back to the office for publication. Newspaper editors were thereby vulnerable to every vicissitude of travel, transport and human frailty. To ensure an adequate supply of pictures for their pages, it was necessary to include long-term 'institutional' subjects for which there was no time pressure and on which an artist could work for as long as necessary.

Sometimes an artist might be assigned to spend several months touring a remote region, such as China. Publication would probably have to wait until the man brought his material home to England with him. Unless, he had been fortunate enough to get it on board a reliable English ship in some distant port to which he had access.

If the Queen went on tour, a man was sent to follow her, sketching as he went. A team of artists might be despatched to capture the variety of moods on race day at Epsom. Illustrations were commissioned of inventions such as flying machines and submarines, or proposed installations, as a tunnel under the Thames. Lavish care would be bestowed on a drawing of the building of the Houses of Parliament. To this galaxy of back-up material, illustrations of hard news could be added as an overlay.

The period which this book covers ends in 1900. But it is worth breaking that boundary by a few years, for, in a sense, it was the illiterates who were finally to have their say. Pictures began to appear in popular daily papers in response to a competitive conditioning that began with the silent cinema.

From the mid-nineteenth century illustrated lantern lectures had become a popular form of entertainment all over the country. Then, in the 1900s, ordinary people began to flock to the weekly cinema. There they saw news reels. Their literacy was one of pictures, not words. Their expectation came to be that of seeing things, reading about them was an amplification. So it was the illustrated papers who paved the way, after all. The others, after some seventy-odd years, just followed suit.

Actuality

When, in the summer of 1842, Queen Victoria toured Scotland the *Illustrated London News* sent an artist to follow in her train. The resulting sketches were published in two double-page spreads on 3 and 24 September. The drawing is meticulous and a serious attempt has been made to design attractive page layouts. Similarly, the same year, many careful drawings were published, resulting from a visit to China. Some are obviously reworked drawings, others composites of many smaller notebook sketches. In the destroying of Chinese war junks by the Nemesis Steamer an attempt has been made at an 'action' technique – one that captures an instant of time. Apparently it was compiled from a sketch made by an eye-witness. In the drawing of the Chinese artillery gun one assumes a certain artist's licence in the drawing of the men.

In the *Illustrated London Life*, the following summer, there came several pages of lightning studies of 'types' and 'scenes'. The page design is much less ambitious, only a tenuous connection with the text is intended.

Some thirty years later, *The Graphic*'s presentation of its Arctic Supplement is both cruder and more lively. There is less attention to detail in the drawing, but some attempt is made to convey the impression of movement.

ARCH ON THE SIDE OF LOCH EARN.

THE ROYAL PARTY ON LOCH TAY.

TAYMOUTH CASTLE—THE MARQUIS OF BREADALBANE'S.

THE QUEEN AND PRINCE LANDING AT AUCHMORE.

THE QUEEN AND PRINCE ALBERT AT LOCH EARN HEAD,
(CHANGING HORSES.)

THE ROYAL BARGE.—LOCH TAY.

AUCHMORE HOUSE.—KILLIN.

STEPS ERECTED FOR THE QUEEN'S LANDING, AT AUCHMORE,
(MADE OF HEATHER AND BROOM.)

HER MAJESTY'S VISIT TO SCOTLAND.

In the proper department of our journal will be found a continuation of the account of the royal visit through a portion of Scotland up to the auspicious return of her Majesty, even to her ancient castle of Windsor; and some portion of her happy route homeward, is still to be illustrated in the columns of this paper. In the present number, however, our artist has presented a splendid collection of subjects, connected with the tour itself; and, more particularly, that portion of it, in the beautiful Highlands of Scotland, which was marked by such an enthusiastic display of loyalty on the part of the people, and such a magnificent series of festivities on that of the old nobility of the land. The detail of the royal journey, and the incidents contingent upon its progress through these inter-

(Continued on page 316.)

The English Newspaper

have come in to make their salaam to him. Heavy rain and much wind on the 2nd; the thermometer fell 20 degrees."

"Camp, Gundamuck, Sept. 5, 1842.

"On the morning of the 3rd inst. Sale's brigade arrived. This morning Monteith's brigade joined us, and to give you an idea of the scarcity of cattle, the 1st brigade had to send back cattle to assist Sale's brigade, which in its turn sent back cattle to meet Monteath. God knows how we are to manage to carry our things through the Pass, as we are to make our first march to-morrow on Cabul in two divisions. The first division only starts to-morrow, commanded by General Pollock in person.

Such of our readers as have not been furnished with a map of the seat of war in India will find an excellent one in our fifth number, which has been already reprinted three times.

CHINA.

Our last news comprised the capture of the city of Chapoo, a large place, carrying on an extensive trade with Japan; and we have now to announce further important successes. The extensive batteries at the mouth, and on the banks, of the Woo-sung river have been taken and destroyed, and the

CHINESE GUN WITH BAMBOO SIGHT.

Our casualties were numerous, two men being killed and twenty-five wounded, but confined entirely to the naval arm of the expedition. The enemy are said to have lost about eighty killed and a proportionate number wounded. They served their guns extremely well, and some of the vessels (particularly her Majesty's ship Blonde, and the steamers Nemesis and Sesostris) suffered a great deal from the heavy and destructive fire. The Nemesis' rigging was cut to pieces; an artilleryman belonging to her was obliged to have his right arm amputated at the shoulder joint; another man,

city of Shang-hae occupied by our troops, its public buildings burnt, and its rich granaries, the property of the government, given up to the people. The opposition offered at the entrance of the river was considerable, an incessant cannonade being kept up for two hours ere the enemy showed any symptoms of submission. This engagement took place on the 9th June; and, on the following day, some of the lighter vessels of the squadron advanced up the river, and captured a deserted battery mounting fifty-five guns. The city was taken on the 19th, the Chinese deserting it after receiving two broadsides. The operations were concluded on the 20th, by the capture of two additional field works, at a place some fifty miles higher up, whither the admiral had himself proceeded, with two iron steamers, for the purpose of reconnoitring.

Two hundred and fifty-three guns (thirty-two of them brass) were taken in the batteries, most of them of heavy calibre, and upwards of eleven feet long. The whole were mounted on pivot carriages of new and efficient construction, and it was likewise observed that they were fitted with bamboo sights.

We are here enabled to present our readers with the following sketch of one of these guns, for which we are indebted to the courtesy of the authorities at the India House.

belonging to the Pluto, lost both his 'legs' at the ancles, and Lieutenant Hewett, R.N., of her Majesty's ship Blonde, lost his head by a round shot.

It will be remembered that the Nemesis, which is commanded by Lieut. Hall, distinguished herself in a very extraordinary manner, shortly after her arrival in the Chinese waters, by blowing up a number of the enemies' war junks, which created no little consternation amongst the Celestials. As this event invests the Nemesis with more than ordinary interest, we here present our readers with a sketch of her on the trying and critical occasion to which

THE NEMESIS STEAMER DESTROYING CHINESE WAR JUNKS, IN CANTON RIVER.
(From a sketch in the possession of the Hon. East India Company.)

we allude. The following brief narrative of this steamer's career since her launch will not be allowed by way of episode, and will prove not altogether unacceptable. The Nemesis was built by Mr. Laird, of Birkenhead Iron-works, near Liverpool, for the Hon. East India Company, and sailed for China in March, 1840, was the first iron steam-vessel that passed the Cape of Good Hope, and the first that appeared in China. Her services there have been since pretty generally known, and the following is an account of the destruction of the war-junks illustrated in our engraving:— Arrangements having been made by Commodore Sir J. J. G. Bremer, K.C.B., &c., for the capture of the Chuenpee forts, and the opposite one of Ty-kok-tow, the Nemesis, after disembarking the 37th Regiment Native Infantry, took up an advantageous position under the upper battery of Chuenpee, in company with the Hon. Company's ships Queen, and commenced throwing shot with good effect, lodging many within the walls, thereby enabling the troops to advance, and take possession, which they did in the most gallant style. This accomplished, she proceeded round the point to assist in silencing the lower fort, throwing in grape, canister, and musketry, thereby distracting the attention of the enemy on the sea-side, and giving the troops and some of the Hyacinth's crew, whom we observed scaling the walls, greater facilities for entering, which they speedily did, driving all before them. She then pushed on to attack the war-junks strongly moored at the mouth of a small and shallow river at the bottom of Anson's Bay; and, when within 100 yards, commenced a heavy fire of shot and shell on the four largest, which was returned by them. The first Congreve rocket fired by her took terrific and instantaneous effect—blowing up one of the largest, with all her crew. The others being soon silenced, after they despatched her boats, in company with those of her Majesty's ship Sulphur, and one or two others from the Larne, Calliope, and Hyacinth. Junk after junk was boarded and set fire to. The

whole, 11 in number, blew up as the fire reached their magazines, and thus were completely destroyed. She now proceeded to a town up the river, much to the astonishment of the natives, and brought away two junks, which were moored to the shore, without firing a shot or receiving any such was the consternation at her appearance above at a place only navigable for junks. We understand that the commodore expressed himself much pleased with what the Nemesis had accomplished; and a remark made by Captain Elliot, the Chief Superintendent, that the Nemesis had done the work of two line-of-battle ships, proves that her services have been most important; one shot only struck her, the others falling short or going over. On the 9th January, agreeably to the instructions from the commodore, the Nemesis, in company with two rocket-boats from her Majesty's ship Blenheim, took up a raking position, about 1100 yards distant from the Anung-hoy fort, mounting 50 guns, and commenced throwing shot, shell, and rockets with the greatest effect, which was not returned, from the peculiarity of the position she was enabled to take up from her light draught of water; indeed the enemy could only bring four guns to bear on her, and these were of small calibre. Ten minutes, or thereabouts, after commencing firing, she was recalled by the commodore, he having received a flag from the Chinese, which ended in his hoisting a flag of truce, and cessing operations for the day." At the taking of Canton, and, in fact, in every engagement in China of consequence since 1840, she has always been distinguished, her light draught of water enabling her to navigate rivers, and run close in shore, when other vessels could not approach near enough to do any service. She has been fortunate in having a commander who combines first-rate skill and seamanship, with the greatest bravery, and who never appears satisfied unless he is constantly employed in active service.

Letters from Canton, dated the 20th of July, mention that intelligence

had there been received of the fleet being at anchor at Kiang-ine, in the Yang-tze-Kiang (probably the Kaou-tchaou of the French maps), on the 4th of July. Kaou-tchaou is some distance above the Great Canal and the city of Ching-Kiang-foo, and no great distance below Nankin, and from that position we suppose the entrances of the canal, both northern and northern, to be under Canton for two Hong merchants and two linguists to go to Soo-chow, and the control of the forces, and Nankin at their mercy. "The Imperial Canal, one of the longest and most important of artificial navigations, was constructed by Kublai Khan and his successors. Virtually, as a line of Che-Kiang, to Pekin, the capital of the empire, which is a distance of about 700 British miles. In reality, however, the artificial canal, the Cha-ho, or river of flood-gates, as the Chinese term it, is considerably shorter; it begins to the southward of the Yellow River, where the natural navigation of a lake connected with the Blue River ends, and is carried onward to Lin-tsing, in the north-west of Shang-tung. Thence the navigation is continued by the Eu-ho and Pei-ho to Pekin." "We have thus described the 'Imperial Canal,' not only because it is the grand route for the conveyance of merchandise and the imperial revenues from the southern provinces to the capital, but also because it has been stated that, in case of an attempt upon China by sea, this canal could be easily taken possession of at some point, and the communications between the two parts of the empire cut off." Keppoo has sent to the Canton authorities have consequently ordered Samqua and Howqua's fifth and only surviving son on this errand, with what specific object was not known,—the two Hong merchants were to leave left Canton yesterday. It was originally intended to have sent Howqua himself, but his great age has at last exempted him from this duty; it is supposed by the Chekiang authorities that the Hong merchants, being accustomed to deal with the barbarians, will be of use to them in their negotiations with the English, although the merchants are aware that on a former occasion Sir Henry Pottinger refused to see them. We suppose that some observed these orders very reluctantly, for, independently of the great expense, and, probably, exposure to which this journey will expose them, the Hong merchants in the north are come away, and the reputation of their wealth will have preceded them, their liberty will be in some danger should they be employed in negotiations, and these terminate differently from what the Chinese authorities expect; in which case banishment to Ele may very likely be the end of their mission. It is said that their being sent is with reference to settling the terms for the ransom of Nankin. This is, however, we suppose, mere

PORCELAIN TOWER AT NANKIN.

conjecture. According to Chinese reports, the large city of Shang-hai has been taken by the British force, which is said to have from thence penetrated into the country as far as Soo-chow, and taken that town also. Shang-hai is one of the most important seaport towns in the empire, whose trade is said to employ an immense number of junks. We have no accounts whatever from the north to confirm these reports.

The progress and result of the conflict of the 16th of June will be found very fully detailed in the following passages from the official circular of Sir Henry Pottinger, her Majesty's Plenipotentiary:—

"After the necessary delay in destroying the batteries, magazines, foundries, barracks, and other public buildings, as well as the ordnance, arms, and ammunition, captured at Chapoo, the troops were re-embarked, and the expedition finally quitted that port on the 23rd of May, and arrived on the 29th off the Rugged Islands, where it remained until the 13th of June, on which day it crossed the Yang-tze-Kiang river in the point where the river is joined by the Woosung.

"At this point the Chinese authorities had erected immense lines of works to defend the entrance of both rivers, and seem to have been so confident of their ability to repel us, that they permitted a very close reconnoissance to be made in two of the small steamers by their Excellencies the Naval and Military Commanders-in-Chief on the 14th inst.; and even cheered and encouraged the boats which were sent in the same night to lay down buoys to guide the ships of war in their allotted positions of attack.

"At daylight on the morning of the 16th the squadron weighed anchor, and proceeded to take up their respective stations, which was scarcely done ere the batteries opened, and the cannonade on both sides was extremely heavy and unceasing for about two hours; that of the Chinese then began to slacken, and the seamen and marines were landed at once, under the fire from the ships, and drove the enemy out of the batteries before the troops could be disembarked and formed for advancing.

"Two hundred and fifty-three guns (thirty-two of them brass) were taken in the batteries, most of them of heavy calibre, and upwards of 11 feet long. The whole were mounted on pivot carriages of new and efficient construction, and it was likewise observed that they were fitted with bamboo sights.

"The casualties in the naval arm of the expedition amounted to 2 killed and 25 wounded, but the land forces had not a man touched. It appears almost miraculous that the casualties should not have been much greater, considering how well the Chinese served their guns. The Blonde frigate had 14 shots in her hull, the Sesostris steamer 11, and all the ships engaged more or less. The loss on the part of the enemy is supposed to have been about 90 killed, and a proportionate number wounded.

"On the 17th and 18th June some of the lighter vessels of the squadron advanced up the Woosung river, and found a battery deserted, mounting 55 guns, of which 17 were brass.

"On the 19th two more batteries close to the city of Shang-hai opened their guns on the advanced division of the light squadron, but, on receiving a couple of broadsides, the Chinese fled, and the batteries, which contained 40 guns (17 of them brass), were instantly occupied, and the troops took possession of the city, where the public buildings were destroyed, and the extensive Government granaries given to the people.

"His Excellency the Admiral proceeded up the river Woosung with two of the small iron steamers on the 20th inst., about 36 miles beyond the city of Shang-hai, and in this reconnoissance two additional field-works, each mounting four heavy guns, were taken and destroyed, bringing the total of ordnance captured in these operations up to the astonishing number of 300, of which 76 are of brass, and chiefly large handsome guns; many of the brass guns have devices showing that they have been cast lately; several of them have Chinese characters signifying 'the tamer and subduer of the barbarians,' and one particularly large one is dignified by the title of the barbarian."

"The Chinese high officers and troops are supposed to have fled in the direction of the cities of Soochow, Wang-chow-foo, and Nankin. The same high authorities have made another indirect attempt to retard active operations by an avowed wish to treat, and have given a satisfactory proof of their anxiety to conciliate by the release of 16 of her Majesty's subjects (Europeans and natives of India) who had been kidnapped; but, as the overtures were not grounded on the only basis on which they can be listened to, they were met by an intimation to that effect."

The results of this victory have been remarkable. The Mandarins in the two most fertile provinces in China were dreadfully alarmed lest Wang-chow-foo and Nankin should be taken and sacked and the mouth of the Great Canal seized. The approach of the expedition to the mouth of the

CANTON.

THE IMPERIAL CANAL, CHINA.

Great Canal, and the dangers that threaten Nankin, would, it was thought, induce the Emperor to make an equitable arangement; but doubts were still entertained of his being exactly informed of the truth.

Nankin, before its destruction by the Tartars, was probably the largest and most splendid city that ever existed, and it is still considerable, possesses a great deal of trade and many ingenious manufactures, and is regarded as the Athens of the empire.

The efforts of the Chinese authorities to make resistance have hitherto been

NANKIN.

very great. A proclamation issued by the Emperor in the beginning of June breathes the most decided hostility to the "barbarians," but does not brag of the valour of his generals and soldiers. This proclamation, it ought to be remarked, is dated prior to the attack on Shang-hai.

It is worthy of remark that while Russia is described as busy, not only in exciting the Chinese against the just demands of Great Britain, but in assisting them with officers, the United States and France have sent their ships of war to watch our proceedings with that anomalous race, and, as it is openly declared, with the intention of demanding all the advantages that we may obtain by the expenditure of so much blood and money. The American and French frigates have sailed from the Canton river to the northern ports of China, which their ships were never before permitted to enter.

The intelligence from Canton is not unimportant, it appearing that preparations are again being actively made for the defence of the city and province. The Chinese have erected a fort of considerable size, some distance below Whampoa, on a parallel branch of the river, and large quantities of

WHAMPOA.

cannon are said to be cast for the use of the Government, at a foundry near the foreign factories at Shaming, which is ostensibly private property. They have also obtained shells of foreign manufacture for Paixhans guns.

Considerable sensations have been caused in the city by the renewal of the horrible system of poisoning. Howqua (the Hong merchant) issued a notice to the effect that the Hoonan (Tartar) soldiers had poisoned some of the wells, and that as many as twenty Chinese had died through inadvertently drinking the water. It is necessary, therefore, for foreigners to use much caution, as, though the Chinese are the intended victims of this atrocious design, its effects may not be confined to them alone. The greatest animosity appears to prevail between these Tartar troops and the inhabitants of the province of Canton, and several encounters, attended with much bloodshed, have taken place in the neighbourhood.

The American commander, Commodore Kearney, has demanded and obtained from the provincial government compensation for the losses of American citizens during the attack of the British force on Canton, but these gentlemen, it appears, expressed dissatisfaction at the sum received, although it was a larger one than the commodore was at first authorised to claim.

Kidnapping still prevails to a great extent, and many persons, the victims of former seizures, remain in the hands of the enemy. Complaints are everywhere made of the neglect of the authorities, in taking no measures of a stringent nature for the release of these unfortunate captives, and the prevention of further outrage; and it has been more than once plainly hinted that this is owing to the humble condition of the prisoners. It is satisfactory, however, to know that most of them are alive and in safety. When the fleet arrived off Chapoo, it was intimated to General Gough that several persons who had been kidnapped would be delivered up, if the threatened assault were abandoned. This proposition could not of course be listened to; but the desire to conciliate, thus evinced, was deemed a favourable sign, and there can be no doubt that the captives will be reserved, in the hope of gaining advantageous terms by their release hereafter.

The licentious conduct of the Manilla men belonging to the opium vessels has long been a fertile source of annoyance; and recently one of these villains, more daring than the rest, murdered a Chinese on Dane's Island. An explanation of the affair was demanded by the Hong merchants, who called all the foreign merchants together at the Consoo-house, for the purpose of investigation. The result we have not heard; but it is most obvious that if natives of China are allowed to be maltreated and slaughtered with impunity, by parties belonging to vessels which sail under the British flag, the Chinese have some show of justice for terming their outrages on our people warrantable retaliations.

Very little trade, it is said, is now carried on at Hong-Kong; and Macao, apparently, will still be the chief theatre for commercial operations. To show how little good has been done by the partial and most inefficient blockade on the coasts of China, it may be mentioned that the number of Chinese junks which have arrived at Singapore during the last season is greater than in any preceding year.

The Plenipotentiary (who left Hong-Kong on the 13th of June) reached the expedition previous to the operations at Woosung, and most of the ships of war and transports lately arrived from England must likewise have joined the force. Her Majesty's ship Vindictive reached Hong-Kong on the 19th of June, after a ninety-days' passage.

We have no news of importance from Amoy or Chusan; Ningpo and Chinghae have been evacuated, with the exception of a fortified height near the entrance of the river leading to the latter place, where a garrison has been left.

It now appears that Pekin is not the destination of the expedition, at least this year. The towns at the mouth of the great river Yang-tze-Kiang, the most magnificent river in China, have been captured by our troops, and the whole force was, by the latest accounts, moving upon the city of Nankin, intelligence of the capture of which was daily expected at Macao—indeed, there were abundance of Chinese rumours flying about Canton, Macao, and Hong-Kong, that it had been taken by our troops.

Nankin being captured, what is to be done next? On this point we are all in the dark. Will the occupation of that city—the southern capital of the empire—lead to a treaty? If not, will our authorities determine on the permanent retention of territory in the central provinces, or a movement on Pekin next year? Will time be attempted to be gained in fruitless negotiations; and if so, will the Plenipotentiary, after the experience of the last three years, allow himself to be duped? Some are of opinion that the occupation of Nankin, by giving us the command of the Great Canal, the artery by which the northern provinces are supplied with food, and placing at our disposal the resources of the flourishing province of Keang-nan, will dispose the Emperor to peace, and obviate the necessity of a visit to Pekin, which, for many reasons, it appears judicious to avoid, if possible. That the Emperor, on our approach to the capital, will betake himself to Tartary is more than possible, and we must then either winter at Pekin or abandon it. To winter at Pekin, a hundred miles from the fleet, would expose the army to no inconsiderable risk. The ships have no secure anchorage in the shallow waters of the Gulf of Pe-che-lee during the winter months; and the rigours of a Pekin winter, from the vicinity of the Tartarian mountains, are well known to be severe.

A very curious edict has been sent, showing, by its altered tone, that the Chinese authorities find it necessary at length to bend to the storm. The following is the despatch:—

"The English barbarians are now creating disturbances in the provinces of Keangsoo and Cheesang; and day by day their ships are increasing in number, and we are apprehensive that they will, ratlike, sneak into other places; we therefore desire to enlighten them by the principles of reason, and clearly to explain to them the formidable calamities (they are bringing on the country).

"At present it is difficult to find interpreters. On examination we have found that hitherto the English have reposed the greatest confidence in the Hong merchant Howqua, and we have heard that the said Hong merchant is more than eighty years of age, and we fear he will not be able to come. So immediately select either his younger brother, son, or nephew, who are able to hold converse with the foreigners on business.

"Let, after consultation, one or two of these men hasten to Keangsoo with the rapidity of a shooting star; we shall hold ourselves fortunate if a day is not lost. When the said younger brother, son, or nephew, obey the orders and hurry to Keangsoo, they will give lasting proofs of their loyalty, and perform an essential service to their country; and we, the said Great Minister and General, will certainly make an extraordinary report (to the Emperor).

"We have sent a report to the Emperor at the same moment that we forward this flying despatch: it is absolutely necessary that they be at our command to use as interpreters. There must not be a moment's delay."

But the most remarkable document is a proclamation from the Emperor himself, relating to the management of the affairs of the barbarians. It is dated 5th of June, 1842, and is published in the *Pekin Gazette*, the official organ of the Chinese Government, which circulates through every corner of the empire, and regulates the tone of public feeling. It gives the Emperor's own version of the cause and progress of the war. He traces it to the "opium flowing like poison into China;" and the idea of the miseries inflicted on his people by these outside barbarians, these robbers, as he styles them, melts his heart, and he exclaims, "What crimes have my people committed that they should be afflicted by such calamities?" The defeat of his troops at the Bogue forts is acknowledged, as also that his "black-haired race on the coast was troubled." The ransom of Canton is merely styled the repayment of the debts of the Hong merchants, six millions of dollars, "a very slight matter, and which he did not grudge." But this remarkable proclamation should be read *in extenso*. There appears no reason, judging from its contents, to look for any spirit of concession from the [illegible] but it is evident that the voice of truth has at length been allowed to approach the Imperial throne; there is a strange medley of despondency and hope, of intense hostility to the "hated race," to whom the spirits of his tooops "are not equal." "Still, if they will do their duty," adds his Majesty, "we can yet exclude the barbarian worthless sprouts, sweeping them into the depths of the wide ocean, and restore to the people of the empire the blessings of peace and tranquillity."

The approaches to the northern capital, which in 1840 were quite defenceless, are now strongly fortified, and vigorous exertions were being made to render them "quite impregnable," in order to check all advances of the "rebellious barbarians."

From the mouth of the Peiho to Teentsin numerous and strong defences have been thrown up, and large bodies of troops assembled. The Governor of Pechele, the Imperial province, represents to the Emperor the great importance of still larger appropriations being made for strengthening these fortifications; and his Majesty, in a personal interview with the high officers of the Chekeang army, has ordered them to make strenuous exertions for the erection of founderies and the casting of cannon, and that the guns be sent with flying despatch to Chekeang. These immense preparations must bear very hard on the imperial treasury; and this is at length made manifest in the official gazettes, three millions of taels having been advanced from it for expenses in Chekeang, and a fourth ordered from the neighbouring provinces.

Further accounts from the northward are looked forward to with great interest.

CANTON—MACAO—HONG-KONG.

The intelligence by the March overland mail has occasioned a total suspension of all buildings at Hong-Kong, and most of the foreign community continued at Macao and Canton. Little trade has been carried on at the new settlement in anything but opium, and nearly the whole of that branch of business had been removed to Whampoa, where there was a fine fleet of smugglers—ten or twelve sail in all—bearing the English flag. A Portuguese vessel lately came among them, but, being considered an interloper, was taken and towed out of the fleet. They were on the very best terms with the people, and, to say the least, were let alone by the Mandarins. The factories were still more than half deserted, and some were in utter ruins, and the number of foreigners in Canton did not exceed fifty or sixty. The people were quiet, and offered no molestation to them in the streets. Howqua did not often go abroad, and appeared desirous of keeping clear of all business. All this, of course, is prior to Admiral Cochrane's entrance within the river, the result of which is not yet known. The waters in the neighbourhood of Hong-Kong were infested by pirates, some of whom had been captured. Three foreign men-of-war, two American and one French, were in China, and either had proceeded, or were about to proceed, to the northward, to watch our operations there. Captain Campbell, of her Majesty's 55th Regiment, died at Chapoo on the 27th of May, of wounds in the head, received at the capture of that city, after lingering nine days. The Hong-Kong newspaper does not seem much to relish the present rather unfavourable decline of what it calls the "capital of the Anglo-Chinese empire." As an inducement to settlers, it says that three years' rental of a house or warehouse at Macao will suffice to construct an equal accommodation of a stable character at Hong-Kong; and that the charges for landing goods and discharging cargo amount to about one-fourth of the customary rates at Macao.

The *Gazette* of Tuesday evening contained the official details of the operations of the army in India and China, which will be found collated from a more graphic but not less authentic source in another part of our paper. We are indebted to the kindness of a British officer in China for several spirited and faithful sketches of important and commanding positions in that interesting country, which we this day present to our readers with the China news.

We learn from a report of the progress of the operations at the Thames Tunnel, that this magnificent undertaking is rapidly advancing to completion. The staircase of the shaft on the Rotherhithe side of the river has been finished several days. The entrance for the public from the south side is not expected to be opened before December next.

VIEW OF NINGPO.

VIEW OF THE CANTON RIVER.

CHINESE ARTILLERYMEN AND GUN.

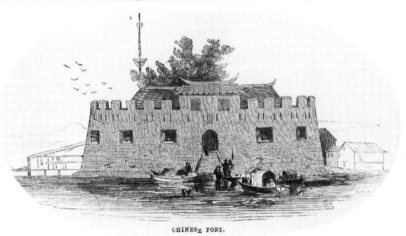

CHINESE FORT.

VIEW OF AMOY.

ILLUSTRATED LONDON LIFE.

No. 13.]　　　　　　　LONDON, JUNE 4, 1843.　　　　　　　[PRICE SIXPENCE.

EPSOM RACES.

THERE are certain things that happen to every man—being born is one of them: an event, almost as inevitable to the happy denizen of London, is going to the Derby. It is so long since we read "The Whole Duty of Man," that we forget whether the visitation in question is therein enjoined; that it *should be*, we feel.

It is now sixty-three years since the Earl of Derby instituted the race that perpetuates his name. A writer of the year 1777, speaks thus :—" It is well known, among the polite circles, that the late Lady Derby, formerly Lady Elizabeth Hamilton, had given an absolute refusal to proposals of marriage from the present lord, in hopes of winning the heart of his Grace of Dorset ; but no sooner were they baffled, by attentions to the house of Stanley, than she brought about a renewal of those addresses she had rejected, and yielded to them. However, to compensate in some degree for not being a duchess, she was resolved to signalise her nuptials with a scene of pleasure and entertainment unparalleled in expense and elegance. A *fête champetre* was contrived, which embarrassed the curiosity of the whole nation. The Duchess of Hamilton, her mother, was much blamed for not exerting her authority to prevent such an enormous expense ; but her grace found an excuse in that maternal vanity which, as it is generally supposed to be mingled with affection, softens the language of censure. A little female ostentation also checked General Burgoyne's prudence on the occasion : *it was that of his muse ;* for the darling pleasure of figuring as a man of taste and literary character, suppressed every other consideration. It is well known that the preparations for this unmeaning ceremonial astonished even the most extravagant. However, the extent of the proposed plan of operations was kept a profound secret from the earl's father, who, having been informed that something of a fete was to grace the nuptials, greatly approved of it, and declared to everybody that he should give a couple of hundreds towards the expense. Poor old man ! if he had known how many thousands were unprofitably lavished away on the occasion, he would, in all probability, have new-modelled his will, and not have left him the keys of his coffers."

The earl was married on the 9th of June, 1777 ; and at the *fête champetre*, a musical drama (written by General Burgoyne, of Saratoga celebrity) was produced. This sketch was entitled the "Maid of the Oaks." Hence the Oaks race, in 1779 ; and, by the reciprocity of the lady, the Derby in the year 1780.

We could be very dull and very historical, did we choose to dive into the history of Epsom ; but as LIFE is our motto, we will but skim its surface. Bede, whom myriads term the Venerable, they know not why, says it was famous for

THE DURDANS.

nuns, whose chastity is recorded, " they having, with their abbess Ebba, cut off their noses and lips, to save themselves from violation by the Danes, who, nevertheless, burnt them and their houses." We must append to this Ingoldsby's verdict, and say " It sarved 'em right." We prize our virtue highly, but should never dream of cutting off our noses to preserve it.

That Epsom was once celebrated for its spa everybody knows. George, Prince of Denmark (Queen Anne's *Albert*), made it a fashionable resort. Seats, villas, &c. &c., sprung up in vast and beautiful variety ; amid them, the Durdans.

This was formerly in the possession of Lord Guildford ; its present occupant is Sir Gilbert Heathcote, a fine, true English gentleman ; a sportsman, in the best sense of that word ; the intimate friend of the late monarch of this country, and the tried friend of the poor in his vicinity.

The celebrated Colonel O'Kelly lived at Epsom, and on its Downs, Eclipse (the wonder of the turf) made his professional *début*. Eclipse was the first horse ever vanned. Sir C. Bunbury's Diomed won the first Derby, Sam Arnull being steersman.

Having opened with this dash of the antiquarian and histo-

RACE-HORSE VAN.

[Continued at page 136.

STARTING FOR THE RACE.

PORTRAIT OF JACK WILLMOTT.

rical, let us now break away for the road—the freak, the fun, of this good year 1843. To begin at the beginning, "here we are," as Tom Mathews says in the opening of a pantomime, "here we are at Renton Nicholson's,—The Garrick's Head—the emporium of all the wit and spirit of the metropolis—the —but let the artist speak for us, and exhibit the happy party starting for the race.

St! st!—we are off. We flash by the Police Station, astonish *Herbert*, galvanize the Globe, and amaze great Russell-street.

Away with magic speed we dash,
Lightning less rapid and less rash.

With a philanthropy inherent in our nature we patronize thy bridge, oh! Waterloo! The grateful toll-keeper gazes upon us with wonder and with pride;—the New-Cut comes out to gaze at the spicy lot. Miss Vincent kisses her pretty *dabs* to us from the *Victoria*, and St. George's in the Fields is driven into a delirium of delight. From our pride of place we look around us, and behold the masses. "Little Scott's bill board-cart stops the way." Oh! the glorious, the true demo-

KENNINGTON-GATE.

cracy of the road to the races. Peasant and peer, dustman and duke—all are upon an equality now—all have one purpose—all are level. Look at yon over-dressed shop-boy and that antiquated dame;—does that Cockney think he can drive? —and who has been cruel enough to lend that old gentleman a horse without tying him to the saddle? No matter, all are bent on enjoyment, and we are not the man to mar mirth. Flash away, tender young gentleman in green veils; fare forth ladies of yielding temperament, in your many-coloured garments. Woman! young, old, sinned against, or sinning, do we worship.

The bosom we press'd as an infant, adore,
And in our warm manhood but love thee the more,
Whatever the scene that may rise on our view,
Let WOMAN be there, there is *happiness* too.

The row now commences in real earnest. Coves on the tramp, ladies on the loose, horsemen and gig-men gather: The road is one ruck of vitality—everybody nudges everybody. That little tailor, four feet nothing in his stocking feet, does the pugilistic, and pitches into a drayman six two, at the least. Go it, tailor! look fierce, though you can't fight. It is to be noted, that men, who can't make a dent in a pound of butter, always imagine that the result of their blows must be either long sickness or sudden death. Stop! Here we are locked, crammed, jambed, gorged up, at Kennington Gate.

If the gentlemen who employ their leisure in receiving tolls at this locality would oblige us with a list of the epithets bestowed upon them, how marvellously it would improve our vocabulary! Now we move on; no we don't. The pole of the following carriage is through our back, but as our pole is through the, one preceding us, we are even at all events. Hurrah! once more in the open, and away we whirl with that "fine fluent" motion that belongs only to a four-in-hand. There go the lads: Pembroke, Chesterfield, Palmerston, Owen Swift—all great men in their way; flaxen-haired sailors, *minus* extremities; *k—c-l—mp-ck* men, wot mustn't drive their dogs; six-feet life-guardsmen *sidd*-ing rosy-cheeked wenches; hardy handicraftsmen, who will see a Derby, if they die for it; and the myriad and one indescribables who make up the Epsom mob. Mr. Brown's go-cart is in the ascendant, and its occupants of the right sort. The road is now at its best. No one is there that ought to be absent, no one absent that ought to be there. We have reached the pinnacle of perfectibility. Talk of the glorious first of June, the anniversary of Waterloo, or the far-famed day when Nelson conquered and fell at Tra-fal-*gar*, what are they all to the Derby! day not has it not been sung, and sang admirably and oft! Has not Vincent Dowling, Ruff, Harrison, and Chapman, our noble

self, and Carlton, described it a myriad times! Moreover, has it not awakened the lively fancy of one now hushed for ever, poor Nimrod—peace to his manes!—he has gone "where the wicked cease from troubling and the weary are at rest." Why do these reflections arise at such a moment? because it is in our scenes of mirth, that, having hearts in our bosoms, we remember the old familiar faces, and feel our thoughts flow backwards to those who

Made every scene of enjoyment more dear.

Nimrod, with all thy faults, thou wert a matchless writer; and so, brushing away a tear to thy memory, let us try the fluids at the Cock at Sutton. Here is what Pierce Egan called a congregation of row-de-dow-ation. Pull up, and whilst we moisten the dust in our throats, let us present to you the portrait of Jack Willmott.

Our readers, jolly Jack Willmott—Jack Willmott, our readers.

Good my lord; like this fellow.—SHAKSPERE.

Like him? you'll love him, you dear and gentle ones; and ye of the harder sex and rougher mould, will declare that a better fellow never handled the ribbons, or tooled a first-rate drag than Jack Willmott. But, psha! everybody knows him, and why waste we words; none but himself can be his parallel. "Now, *sir?*" We obey the signal, and through a lush and

THE SPREAD EAGLE INN

PRINTING OFFICE

Who shall endeavour to depict the thousands wedged together upon the course. Theobald, in his everlasting blue-coat and his undeniable leathern indescribables, Beaufort in his artificial plaid fur-for-shames, and Peel in his wrapper. There stands one of manifest importance at Epsom ; there stands the recorder of all the doings, but only of this week but of all weeks in the year at Epsom. Shall we describe him ? No—we leave that to our artist, who has daintily furnished a portrait of Mr. Dorling.

smother, dirt and din, pursue our way. Now, does it seem a week ago since we were at the last Derby ? Not it. There's the same fair-haired hazel-eyed, girl looking into our very heart from that first-floor window. What are the men about in this part of the world, that such a creature can't find a husband ? There are the old "dog" gates, the chrystal pool, and here come the identical card-sellers, not an hour older, not a morsel leaner or fatter, civiler or saucier, sadder or merrier, rougher or ragged-er, than they were at the races of eighteen forty-two. We have progressed to the south-east of Ewell, famed of yore for the one anticipated horrors of its one. We are within the hundreds of Copthorne and Effingham. On with you, Jack, and land us at the Spread Eagle. No sooner said than done ; and behold, welcoming us at that princely hostelry, stands

MRS. LUMLEY.

England has beauties far surpassing those of any clime. In that belief we have long lived, in that belief we shall die. Say not—sensitive and continental travelling readers—say not that we are oblivious of the beauty we have worshipped in the sunny south, of the graces of Greece, or the models in the Morea. Earth teems with loveliness, but where, save in this happy land, do we find such lovely mothers ! Youth has its own beauty, and that is universal, but in most lands, girlhood gone, the charm has fled with it. In England, our loveliest women are those who are the mothers of lovely ones. We will not be guilty of the impertinence of cataloguing the attractions of Mrs. Lumley—our artist has sketched her form and features. We may be permitted to add, that in that suavity of manner that renders a woman delightful, in that goodness of heart that bespeaks her angelic, the subject of our sketch is a perfect woman, Nature's sweetest, noblest work. As to her "worser" half, a better fellow does not exist ; a good sportsman and a good Christian : his home is the resort of all the lovers of life. The name of Lumley is, in a word, synonymous with good fellowship and right feeling. If we stand looking at Mrs. Lumley, and chattering about her liege lord, we shall never reach the course, so adieu to the Spread Eagle, and let us away to the course.

"The beautiful plantations of Garlands, the more stately groves of Durdans, and the ancient and magnificent trees of Woodcote, combine to give a richness to the scenery of the surrounding country, and present, either from the Downs of Cobham, the town of Epsom encircled in their foliage." Lovely is the view from the ground ; but it is not of the prodigality of nature that we have now to speak—

God the first garden made,
And the first city Cain.

We leave to the melodious and lazy Thomson the description of Nature's beauties, and take upon ourself the task of describing "Man's doings on the Downs." From what far countries come these myriads ! Russia, France, Italy, India, Germany, and Turkey, have sent their sons, and there stands the sluttish race—the wanderers of the earth—the tent-dwelling gypsies.

The rough unsatisfactory manner in which race-lists, returns, &c., had been rendered was long a subject of complaint ; need we say, that "Dorling came, and all was right." One hundred years since, a person named Grange printed the cards, &c.; he was succeeded by Old Lindsay ; and Mr. L. followed by Mr. Dorling, predecessor of the present perpetuator of the sports. Dorling's lists are the perfection of racing chronology—their importance to the getters-up of Derby lotteries is immense ; in fact, wherever and whenever racing flourishes, the name of Dorling must be remembered as that of a boon-giver.

Health above, that

Greatest gift that heav'n bestowed on man,

might make Epsom the resort of all England, for where is there a spot more famed for the longevity of its inhabitants. George the Third decayed his lungs in this vicinity. Charles the Second (according to an old tradition) was born there. Invigoration murmurs in the breeze, and strength rides upon the gale. Gaze upon the happy numbers now enjoying their

PROMENADE UPON THE COURSE.

Would you not imagine that care was a stranger to this our sea-girt isle, and that there was no grave upon earth ! Fair-haired girls, that would fire the heart of an anchorite, and rouse old St. Anthony himself ; brunettes, whose warm blood rollicks beneath the brilliant russet of their hue ; and Saxon beauties (the aborigines of our northern counties) that, by the power of their glances, could make sages fools, "but never make fools sage." All, all are there. It is said that the women of France well better than those of England—it may be so ; but do they look as well ! For our part, we are always too much enchanted with their faces to watch their feet.

Forms vying with Venus, and fairy-formed faces,
That 'tis madness to sigh for, but rapture to see ;
Oh ! all the gay scenes, and all the dear races,
That Britain can boast of, old Epsom for me.

We must curb our enthusiasm, and look to business. A [Continued at page 140.]

A mysterious race are they ; unblanched by the North, unsullied by the warm beams of the East, the Coopers and the Lees find favour in our eyes ; they are the poetry of British humanity. What eyes have their womankind, what limbs their men. Though it is notorious that we are the very model of morality, still do we own that, in our early days, when—

The hot blood ran riot in our veins,
And boyhood made us sanguine,

we yearned for one of these dusky traversers of the wild, and could have even flown from man's water to become even like one of them. There's old Gypsy Jack (Stevens) ; look at his beautiful children ; yonder is their mother having the last boy in the pond, yet what creatures of health they are. Stevey has a fine family by the lady, who does honour to his name. As to the "random impressions" to be found "here and there" about the country, we can only say that Stevens' lecture on heads has had a most extensive circulation ; but we forget, we are writing a race not an autobiography, so away with ye, you beautiful darkness, and let us see the family of John Bull en masse.

PORTRAIT OF MR. DORLING.

THE JOCKEY.

THE SADDLING.

white as a sheet ; ould Tommy Lye is lively as ever ; John Day junior, is summing up his antagonist's horses, and Chifney, that living skeleton in buckskin breeches, looks as leary as if he "knew the length" of everything in the field ; Heseltine, Templeman, Macdonald, Rogers, &c. &c., complete the group. The Clerk of the Course gathers his troop together. With hard held breath, and almost suspended animation, the myriads stand. "Go !" and the race commences.

Talk of training !—this is its perfection : not a superfluous ounce has he upon him. Look at his broad shoulders, his large lower arm, his slender, but muscular, legs—he was meant for a rider, commissioned by nature for the turf. Privation is his doom ; in the season, it is not for him to luxuriate at the feast or revel in a debauch ; but he has his reward in the shouts that attend his victories, or the health that his abstinence produces. Yonder is

THE RUBBING-HOUSE.

Long years since, it was a "public," and the famed resort of smugglers and along-shore men, who used to make their way from Hastings, over Epsom and Banstead Downs. One Mrs. Sanders kept it of yore, and she had two beauteous daughters—creatures to make or mar a man. We believe Epsom still possesses one or two old gentlemen who, in their early days, felt the fatal influence of their charms. Beside this same house, Timms, an old man, was killed many years since. At that period, the robberies committed at the races were of the most atrocious description ; now, thanks to the police, men walk about unmolested, and a robbery, with violence, is a thing almost unknown. Justice is administered on the ground, and peculators dealt with in a summary manner—the mass of them being committed as rogues and vagabonds—this spares the prosecutor from the expenditure of money, time, and trouble. Colonel Rowan's cage is upon the ground. This is the age of port-ability ; for we boast of portable soup for our seamen, and portable houses for foreign settlers, and, amid the novelties of the day, may be named, the Epsom

PORTABLE PRISON.

Barrington, Bill Soames, Jack Sheppard, and Huffy White, peace to your souls (if ye had souls), ye know not the luxury of Epsomic lock-up. Hughes, A 1, or wily Thornton, never clapped you into that carriage for convicts, that post-chaise for pickpockets.

"Card of the races—buy a card, sir." "Oh, give him sixpence ; his brogue's worth the money." Albeit the illustrious Paddy carrieth a brogue upon his tongue, but no brogues upon his feet. Here, in his scarlet, stands the little hero of a hundred runs—look at him ! his fine muscular limbs, his broad open feet were made for motion. Patrick, we fear, imbibeth fluid too frequently and too fast, but he is still agile, the longest day is not too long for him, nor the fleetest pace too fast. London is inundated with portraits of poets and peers, of statesmen and lawyers, why should not we render those of as notable, if not as noted, public characters. Colnaghi is, we believe, publishing the figure-head of Satan Montgomery, the poet and pumps let us present the lineaments of

PADDY THE RUNNER.

That little piece of feminine simplicity is Paddy's better-half, and many are the little sixpences that they mutually obtain. The lad of the Emerald isle could, we verily believe, extract a

DINING ON THE COURSE.

THE SWELL WOT DROVE HIS "LADY TO THE DARBY."

THE SPEELER.

set out. Horses are jaded, drivers are drunk; some have lost their money, many their temper; the careless and reckless ones drive against everything they *foller*—for there is literally nothing to *meet*. London gathers in her myriads by instalments; and, amid the enjoyments bygone, may be reckoned the Derby-day. A day, that for sixty-three years has been marked out as one of jubilee by all Londoners, and one that forms the great, the engrossing feature of EPSOM RACES.

Evening is beginning to put afternoon out of countenance, and we have only time for one other turn upon the course. A glance at the Prince of Wales's stand, and away. What a slice of eternity is the past! The Prince of Wales!—Back flies memory to the day when the Duke of York and his princely brother used to revel at Epsom; when Moira and freedom, Whitehead and Wyndham, were beside them, when we were juvenile and curly. Well, we have drank the wine of life, and won't murmur over the *lees*. In so long a journey it is natural to expect a break down.

Passenger.—Bob, your linch-pin's out.
Driver.—Never mind; it's used to it—it won't come off.

"I was never upset in my life," said a friend to Jack Mytton. "Were you not, by ——," said Jack, and *over went the buggy.* Now we *hate been* upset—by wine, by woman, by curricle, by coach; and our long experience teaches us that there is, in such a case, only one course to pursue, i. e., to grin and bear it; for, depend upon it, in all the misfortunes of life, it is far better to grin than to be grinned at.

The road home is, perhaps, a more stirring scene than the

A BREAK DOWN.

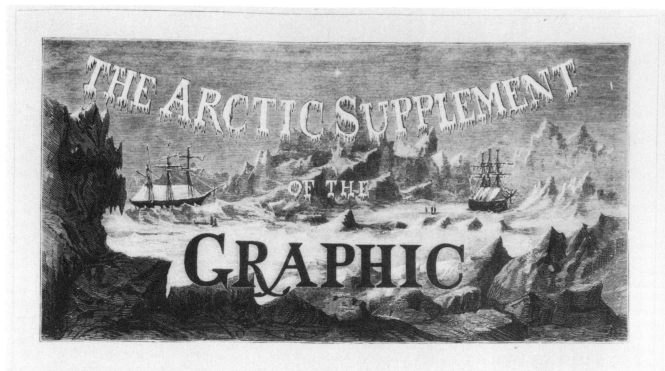

ESQUIMAUX WOMAN AND CHILD AT LIEVELY (OR GODHAVN) ON THE ISLAND OF DISCO

THE ARCTIC EXPEDITION—SERVING OUT LIME-JUICE ON BOARD THE "ALERT"

THE ARCTIC EXPEDITION—WATERING FROM AN ICEBERG

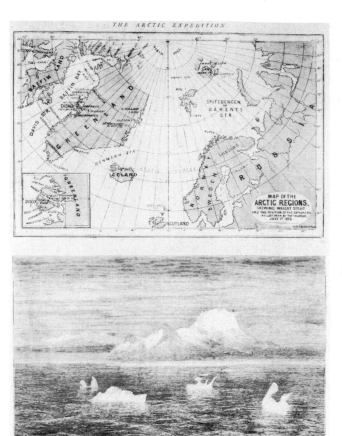

CAPE DESOLATION OR "SHARING CLOSE", WEST COAST OF GREENLAND

THE ARCTIC EXPEDITION

THE ARCTIC EXPEDITION—A MUSICAL EVENING ON THE LOWER DECK OF THE "ALERT"

THE ARCTIC EXPEDITION—THE "ALERT" NEAR HOLSTEINBORG, GREENLAND: STEAMING CUTTER OR IÇEBOAT ON SKIDS

Composite

Flooding offers a unique opportunity in reporting dramatic events. Unlike other disasters, the devastations of wide-spread flooding remain long enough for an artist to commit them to paper.

The front-page illustration of *The Graphic* (10 July 1875) is a good example of a composite made up of many smaller impressions. The subsequent treatment of the Toulouse floods can be compared with those dealing with floods in Monmouthshire and Budapest.

THE GRAPHIC

AN ILLUSTRATED WEEKLY NEWSPAPER

VOL. XII.—No. 294
Reg.d at General Post Office as a Newspaper]
SATURDAY, JULY 17, 1875
WITH EXTRA SUPPLEMENT [PRICE SIXPENCE
Or by Post Sixpence Halfpenny

1. A Railway Train stopped by the Waters.—2. The Sufferers Camping Out.—3. Marshal MacMahon visiting the Distressed Districts.—4. "Pour les Inondés!"

THE FLOODS IN FRANCE—SKETCHES AT TOULOUSE

THE FLOODS IN MONMOUTHSHIRE—AFTER THE SUBSIDENCE OF THE WATERS

INTERIOR OF THE NEUSTIFT CHURCH, BUDA

SQUARE IN RAITZENBAD—FIREMEN AND SOLDIERS WORKING IN THE RUINS

THE FLOODS IN BUDA-PESTH, HUNGARY

APARTMENT IN A COTTAGE NEAR THE RESERVOIR

BREACH IN THE RAILWAY NEAR THE RESERVOIR

THE FLOODS IN MONMOUTHSHIRE

Interpretation

Examining visual style, a distinction can be made between the drawing of events or places exactly as the artist saw them, and the imaginative interpretation of what has been seen.

In the Carriage Works at Oldbury, the Railway Catastrophe near Trent Junction, the Great Fair of Nijni Novgorod, Ventilation under the House of Commons, Building the House, Toulouse before the Floods, Pentonville, Nelson's Column and the Trial of the 81-ton Gun, one has the impression of direct,

accurate representation with little or no embellishment.

But there has been some fairly obvious visual development in the Shocking Accident at the Odd Fellows' Hall, Locomotive Fire Engine, Ploughing by Steam, Post Office on the Steamer 'Pekin', Events in Ireland, Royal Visit to Sheffield, Regent Circus – Oxford Street, Collision in the Solent, Interior of St. Paul's Cathedral, Oxford and Cambridge Cutter Match, Laying Pneumatic Tubes and the Newspaper Market in Paris.

THE MODEL PRISON AT PENTONVILLE.

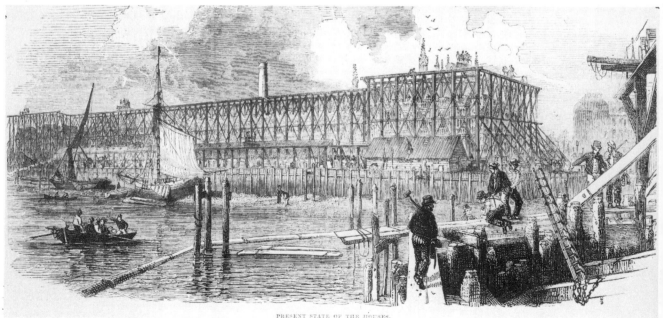

PRESENT STATE OF THE HOUSES.

ON THE WAY TO INDIA — HOT WORK; THE POST-OFFICE ON BOARD THE P. AND O. STEAMER "PEKIN"
FROM A SKETCH BY ONE OF OUR SPECIAL ARTISTS

NELSON'S COLUMN.

RAILWAY CARRIAGE WORKS AT OLDBURY.—THE CARRIAGE SHOP. (See page 22.)

PLOUGHING BY STEAM.

RAILWAY CARRIAGE WORKS AT OLDBURY.—THE FORGE. (See page 22.)

PLOUGHING BY STEAM.

MR. H. T. RICKETTS, of the Castle Foundry, Buckinghamshire, has patented an invention by which it is proposed to construct implements for cultivating or turning over the land by means of tines set round a cylinder or rotating axle in such a way as to act more advantageously than those hitherto employed. The frame of the implement runs on two or more wheels, and its rotating axle on which the pins are set when moving over the land comes only a small distance above the surface of the soil. The implement is arranged to be moved by locomotive power, as shown in our illustration. The tines of the implement are all similar in form to each other, and are set one after the other around the axle or shaft in such a manner as to cut or enter the land in succession, having the appearance when on the

owing to the failure of the attempts to deliver them is about 1 in 300, and of newspapers 1 in 124.

With regard to money-orders the report states 127 new offices were opened, making the total 2,960. The number of orders issued was 6,589,396 for a total of £17,602,185 (showing an increase of 4 per cent.), and the commission received was £111,591, which left a profit of £23,996. The money-order system, although now productive of a large profit in England and Scotland, is still carried on at a loss in Ireland, owing, in the latter case, to the smallness of the individual sums.

THE OXFORD AND CAMBRIDGE CUTTER MATCH, OFF LAMBETH PALACE.

1. LOADING — 2. POWDER CARTRIDGE — 3. POWDER TRUCK — 4. EXTRACTING THE VENT CAP 5. PRESS BOLT — 6. DIGGING OUT THE SHOT — 7. AFTER THE DISCHARGE
TRIAL OF THE 81-TON GUN AT WOOLWICH

THE NEWSPAPER MARKET AT PARIS. (See page 202.)

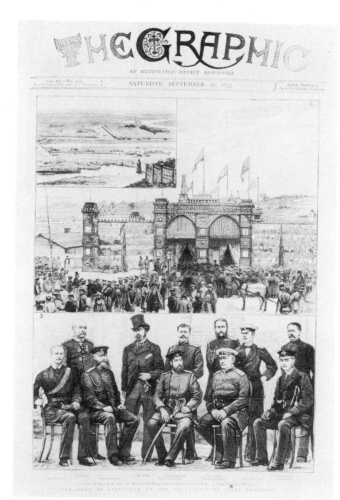

1. Cooling Chamber in front of Air Machine : Placing Ice in Position.—2. Air Intake on East side of House : Spray Jets for Washing and Cooling Air.—3. Battery Chamber : Canvas Strainers and Draught Excluders.—4. Chamber beneath Floor of House : Taking Temperature over Grating.—5. Air Furnace in Upcast Shaft of Clock Tower.

SKETCHES IN THE VENTILATION DEPARTMENT UNDER THE HOUSE OF COMMONS

THE NEW TELEGRAPH ARRANGEMENTS AT BIRMINGHAM.—LAYING PNEUMATIC TUBES IN THE SNOWSTORM. *(See next page.)*

SHOCKING ACCIDENT AT THE ODD FELLOWS' HALL, TEMPLE-STREET, BIRMINGHAM. *(See page 85.)*

Deception

More elaborate forms of artistic 'deception' (the term used in the nicest sense) can be seen in Town and Harbour of Cherbourg, Submarine Boat, West India Steam Navigation, New Aërial Ship, New Flag of the Republic, Carriage Works at Oldbury (compare with the pictures on p. 100), Cleopatra's Needle – Alexandria, Twin steamship 'Castalia', Statue of Liberty, Balloons, and Tunnel under the Thames.

The four pictures of Hereford Ox, Drain-tile Machine, Cattle-feeding Apparatus and Sheep-dipping Apparatus are an interesting combination of visual information and attractive design.

THE TOWN AND HARBOUR OF CHERBOURG.

THE NEW FLAG OF THE REPUBLIC.

STATUE OF LIBERTY TO BE ERECTED IN NEW YORK HARBOUR
TO BE PRESENTED TO THE UNITED STATES BY THE FRANCO-AMERICAN UNION IN COMMEMORATION OF THE CENTENNIAL ANNIVERSARY OF AMERICAN INDEPENDENCE

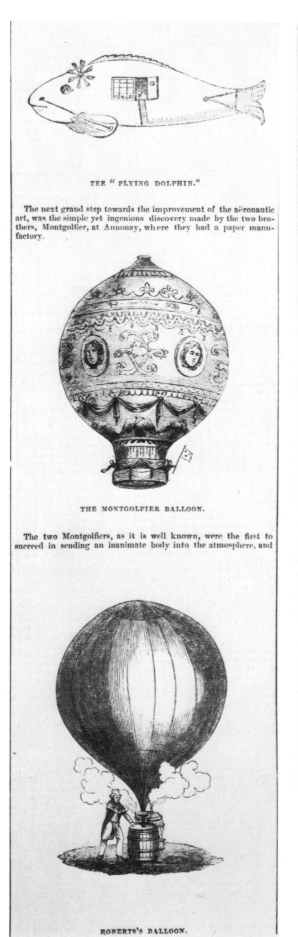

TEE " FLYING DOLPHIN."

The next grand step towards the improvement of the aëronautic art, was the simple yet ingenious discovery made by the two brothers, Montgolfier, at Annonay, where they had a paper manufactory.

THE MONTGOLFIER BALLOON.

The two Montgolfiers, as it is well known, were the first to succeed in sending an inanimate body into the atmosphere, and

ROBERTS'S BALLOON.

SIR W. WARE'S 4 YEARS AND 10 MONTHS OLD HEREFORD OX.

DRAIN-TILE MACHINE.

CATTLE-FEEDING APPARATUS.

SHEEP-DIPPING APPARATUS.

BIRD'S EYE VIEW OF THE RAILWAY CARRIAGE WORKS AT OLDBURY. *(See page 23.)*

The English Newspaper

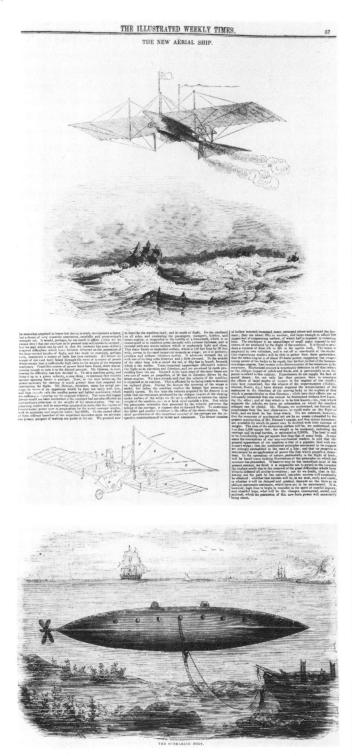

THE NEW AERIAL SHIP.

THE SUBMARINE BOAT.

WEST INDIA AND ATLANTIC STEAM NAVIGATION.

CLEOPATRA'S NEEDLE, ALEXANDRIA, PRESENTED TO ENGLAND BY MEHEMET ALI PASHA, BEING EXAMINED BY SIR JAMES ALEXANDER.

THE GRAPHIC

AN ILLUSTRATED WEEKLY NEWSPAPER

VOL. XII.—No. 298
Regd. at General Post Office as a Newspaper

SATURDAY, AUGUST 14, 1875

PRICE SIXPENCE
Or by Post Sixpence Halfpenny

THE CHANNEL PASSAGE—THE TWIN STEAM-SHIP "CASTALIA" LEAVING DOVER FOR CALAIS

Action

The 'action' picture presents the artist with the technical problem of 'frozen' movement – of capturing an instant of time. Some interesting variations of technique are represented in Collision in the Solent (compare with pp. 98–104), Attempted assassination of Queen Victoria, Attack on Potatoe Store, Riots at New Cross, Preston – Attack on the Military, Accident to Thunder Steamer, Catching a Whale, Collision between the Prince Patrick Steamer and the Elfin Schooner, Frozen-out Gold-diggers, Explosion at Hounslow Powder Mills, Irish Renegades, Crossing the Niagara, Disaster near Trent Junction and Destroying a Railway.

THE DISASTER NEAR TRENT JUNCTION: SCENE IMMEDIATELY AFTER THE ACCIDENT. (See page 126.)

COLLISION BETWEEN THE PRINCE PATRICK STEAMER AND THE ELFIN SCHOONER.

[OCTOBER 23, 1869.]   THE ILLUSTRATED MIDLAND NEWS.   125

THE RAILWAY CATASTROPHE NEAR TRENT JUNCTION.
(See page 119.)

THE SHEET SHED AT TRENT.

THE FUNERALS AT LEICESTER CEMETERY.

CLEARING THE LINE AFTER THE ACCIDENT.

DRILLING IN IRELAND.

MAKING PIKES.

RIFLE PRACTISING.

PIKE MAKING IN IRELAND.

Urged by curiosity, says the reporter of the "Morning Chronicle," I recently visited the establishment of the celebrated David Hyland, who exhibits on a sign-board, "Pike-maker to the Castle;" and I confess I was rather surprised to find that the statements which I had heard and read with regard to the open and undisguised sale of the "national weapons" were far from being exaggerated. At the moment I happened to call, the shop, which by the way is not very capacious, was completely crowded, and outside were congregated several individuals awaiting their turn to be supplied. Having expressed a desire to see a sample of these essential Hibernian implements of warfare, Mrs. Hyland, who was busily employed as door-keeper to prevent too great a pressure of customers, a task which she fulfilled with as much fidelity as a due regard to her interest would permit, kindly made way for me and gratified my inclination by showing me several samples of these truly formidable implements of destruction. It appears that the original mode of constructing pikes, that is with a small hatchet on one side, and a crook on the other, has been superseded, and the modern one is simply a spear, something like the sergeants' halberts some years since in use in the British army, but much longer, the blade being about eighteen inches in length. Mrs. Hyland informed me, in answer to a question, that her husband had about sixteen men at work in this peculiar branch of Irish industry, and that each man was able to turn out from six to eight pikes per day; there are, accordingly, close on six hundred pikes weekly circulated by this factory alone.

St. George's School of Medicine, Grosvenor-place.—The distribution of prizes took place on Monday, Sir J. Clark in the chair.—Anatomy Senior : Silver medals, R. E. Price and H. Brown ; cert. of honour, Finnimore and Turner.—Anatomy Junior : Bronze medal, T. Ball ; certs., Bullock, Goodall, and V. Jones.—Medicine : Prize, Allen, cert., G. Fast.—Chemistry : Prize, Ball ; certs., V. Jones, Warden, and Bullock.—Materia Medica : Prize, V. Jones ; certs., Ball and Bullock.—Surgery : Prize, R. E. Price ; cert., Turner.—Midwifery : Prize, R. E. Price ; cert., Turner.—Practical Midwifery : Set of instruments, J. S. Gundry ; cert., Gatliffe.—Medical Jurisprudence : Prize, R. E. Price ; cert., Turner.—Botany : Prize, R. E. Price ; certs., Bullock and Turner.—Practical Chemistry : Prize, H. Brown ; certs., W. Blosen and R. E. Price.—Clinical Surgery : Prize, P. Allen ; cert., Finnimore.

Fires in Edinburgh and Suffocation of Five Persons.—A fire took place on Sunday morning at the Sciennes (in the southern environs of Edinburgh), which has occasioned the loss of five lives. The tenement in which the occurrence took place is occupied by families of the humblest rank. The apartment which was the immediate scene of the event is situated on the ground floor, and was occupied by an old woman named Ann Taber, 72 years of age, with whom a grandchild, Ann Liddle, five years old, resided. This poor woman, in order to eke out a subsistence, also boarded three boys from the West Church Parochial Board, of the names of Jas. Peffry, aged seven ; Joseph Adams, six ; and Robert Melville, eight years. The whole of the inmates slept in two beds, in a close and confined room, and they had retired to rest with their customary regularity on Saturday evening. About half-past nine o'clock on Sunday morning thick smoke was observed to fill the apartment, which was entered, when the bodies of Mrs. Taber and her grandchild, Ann Liddle, were found lying on the floor, and the boys on the bed, all quite dead. The origin of the fire has not been ascertained, and the damage consists in the destruction of the two beds, several chairs, and a quantity of clothing, while a portion of a partition was also burned down. The fire had obviously been burning for some hours, though, from want of air, and the closeness of the apartment, its rapid progress had been prevented. Parts of some of the bodies were scorched by the flames, and the remains of a feather bed have been found, the odour from which must have been overpowering, and contributed greatly to produce this lamentable occurrence. The second fire, which took place about one o'clock on Saturday morning, was in the roof of a thrashing mill attached to the farm of Redenlaw, about six miles westward of Edinburgh, occupied by Mr. Browne, farmer. It is supposed to have been caused by a spark from a locomotive engine on the Edinburgh and Glasgow railway, from which the farm-steading is distant about one hundred yards, and its existence was discovered by an Irishman who had been sleeping in one of the outhouses.

Newspaper Taxes.—It is reported (but we do not believe the report) that government intend to reduce the newspaper stamp to the price of one farthing, and also to bring down the advertisement duty from eighteenpence to sixpence.—Derby Mercury.

The Burners of the Railway Bridges.—The Court of Assize of the Seine has just been occupied for two days with the trial of seventeen persons for the burning of the Rouen railway bridge over the Seine at Asnières. The jury, after a most patient hearing, brought in a verdict of acquittal, with respect to all the prisoners, except one, a young man named Violet, whom it declared guilty. The prisoner, a person of gentlemanlike exterior, and, it is said, of some property, protested in the most solemn manner that he was innocent ; that, far from having had any design to do harm, he had attempted to dissuade the rioters from their intention, and that at last, when he found that they were bent on mischief, he directed their attention to the bridge rather than to the village of Asnières, which they at first seemed inclined to set fire to. This statement was, however, quite at variance with the evidence given by the witnesses, and the court sentenced him to five years' imprisonment. The members of the jury and the court signed a petition to the provisional government in favour of the prisoner.

IRISH REPEAL MEETING BY TORCHLIGHT.

PRESTON—ATTACK ON THE MILITARY.—TWO RIOTERS SHOT.—*See* p. 233.

IRELAND.

ATTACK ON A POTATOE STORE.

CROSSING NIAGARA ON A VELOCIPEDE.

ACCIDENT TO THE THUNDER STEAMER AT BATTERSEA BRIDGE.

CATCHING A WHALE, OFF DEPTFORD PIER.

THE SPANISH INSURRECTION; INSURGENTS DESTROYING A RAILWAY.

THE FROZEN-OUT GOLD-DIGGERS.

Maps

Maps are a specialised form of illustration. An early, simple, example has already been shown on page 92. Compare this with these two later examples of 1842 (Afghan Country) and 1859 (Italy).

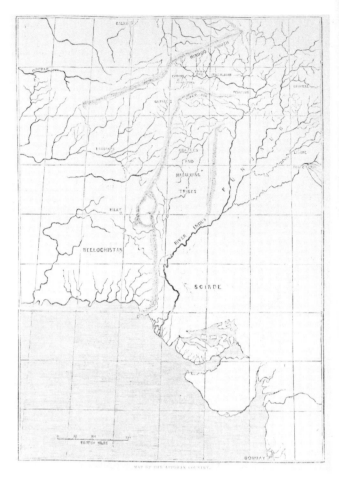

Decoration

From time to time editors indulge in the use of illustrations purely as a decorative feature. Sketches of Old London is one example. A Trip up the River Thames is another.

Coaching in the Highlands and German Character Sketches are examples of decoration coupled with amusement.

Six O'clock at the GPO is in the cartoon style.

Another curious form is a page of Royal autographs.

The decorative style comes to a peak at Christmas time when it may result in pages of popular music, evocative festive scenes, or others that range from the maudlin to the prophetic.

VIEW OF OLD LONDON, LOOKING EASTWARD FROM THE STRAND.

SUPPLEMENT TO THE ILLUSTRATED LONDON NEWS.   547

Leaving Old London Bridge, let us go westward, and see what St. James's Park looked like in the time of Charles II., contrasting it with the park of our day, as displayed in the foreground of the Colosseum Print.

All the representations of the park in this reign give us the long rows of young elms, surrounded by palings.

"We are able, from various sources, plans, engravings, and incidental notices in books, to form a tolerably accurate notion of the aspect which the Park assumed in the course of these operations. At the end nearest Whitehall was a line of buildings occupying nearly the site of the present range of Government offices.

Wallingford House stood on the site of the Admiralty; the old Horse Guards, the Tennis-yard, Cock-pit, and other appendages of Whitehall, on the sites of the present Horse Guards, Treasury, and offices of the Secretaries of State. The buildings then occupied by the Admiralty stood where the gate entering from Great George Street now is. From Wallingford House towards Pall Mall were the Spring Gardens, opening as we have seen into the Park."

St. James's Palace may not unaptly find place here, and afford another opportunity of contrasting things past and present.

Not far from St. James's, we have Whitehall; of which

"London" affords us a view, as it appeared before the fire which destroyed it.

This old palace was the residence of Cromwell and his family, and subsequently the scene of the dissipations of Charles II. The choir of the chapel royal was celebrated for its music, and produced, amongst other composers, Henry Purcell. Evelyn, speaking of Whitehall just before its destruction, says :—"I can never forget the inexpressible luxury and profaneness, gaming and all dissoluteness, and, as it were, total forgetfulness

ST. JAMES'S PARK, IN THE TIME OF CHARLES II.

ST. JAMES'S PALACE, FROM A PAINTING BY HOLLAR.

of God (it being Sunday evening), which this day se'nnight I was witness of ; the King sitting and toying with his concubines, Portsmouth, Cleaveland, and Mazarine, &c.; a French boy singing love songs in that glorious gallery, whilst about twenty of the great courtiers and other dissolute persons were

at basset round a large table, a bank of at least £2000 in gold before them ; upon which two gentlemen who were with me made reflections with astonishment. Six days after all was in the dust."

Few places are richer in historical associations than West-

minster, and still fewer portions of the metropolis have preserved to themselves uninjured their ancient monuments. The great fire destroyed the cathedral of London, together with the majority of relics which time had spared to the city ; and thus in the heart of London we have few buildings of an earlier

WESTMINSTER, ABOUT 1660.

WHITEHALL, AS IT APPEARED BEFORE THE FIRE OF 1691.

1. Taking in Provisions.—2. Cooking Dinner. Anxious Enquiries: "How long will it be?"—3. An Envious Sight—Another Fellow's Camp —4. The Early Morning Shave.—5. Taking it Easy: A Fair Breeze.—6. Camping Out: Boat made Snug for the Night: The Last Pipe.

A TRIP UP THE RIVER THAMES

SNOWBALLING.—BY H. WOODS.   (See the Verses.)

BEACONS OF THE NINETEENTH CENTURY.—BY E. BUCKMAN.   (See page 271.)

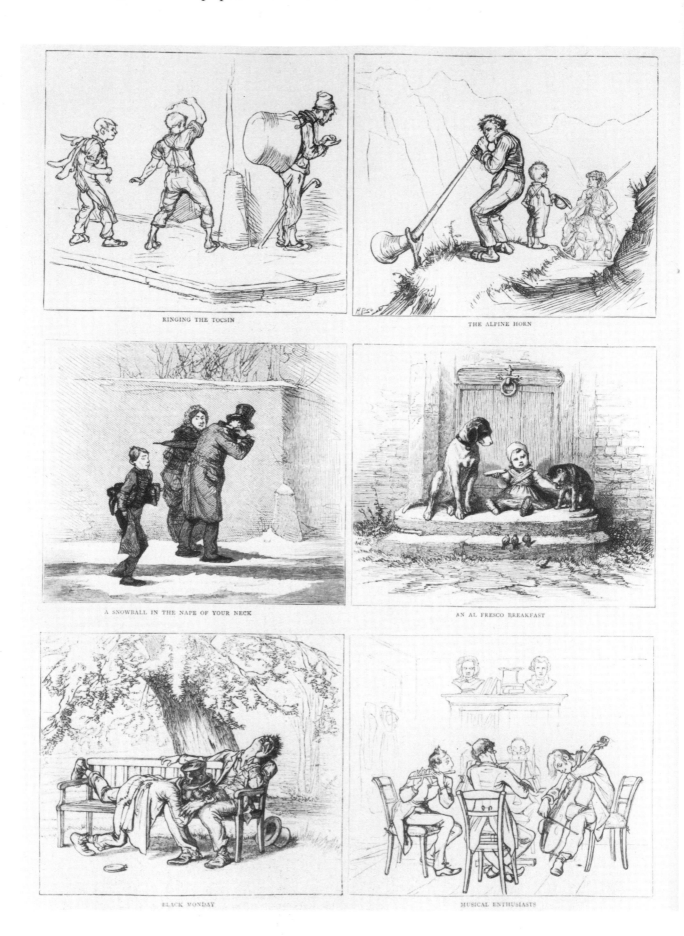

RINGING THE TOCSIN

THE ALPINE HORN

A SNOWBALL IN THE NAPE OF YOUR NECK

AN AL FRESCO BREAKFAST

BLACK MONDAY

MUSICAL ENTHUSIASTS

SUPPLEMENT.   SATURDAY, DECEMBER 18, 1869.   THREEPENCE.

BRINGING IN CHRISTMAS.—BY F. ELTZE. (See "Modern Christmas," page 269.)

SIX O'CLOCK AT THE GENERAL POST-OFFICE.

COACHING IN THE HIGHLANDS.

CHRISTMAS EVE IN ENGLAND: SNAPDRAGON.—BY F. W. LAWSON. (See page 278).

TWELFTH NIGHT IN PARIS: DRAWING THE PRIZES.—BY F. LIX. (See page 278).

The English Newspaper

Bibliography

The Beginnings of the English Newspaper, Joseph Frank, Harvard 1961

A History of English Journalism to the Foundations of The Gazette, J. B. Williams. London 1908

The Freedom of the Press in England 1476–1776, F. S. Siebert. Urbana 1952

Government and the Press 1695–1763, Laurence Hanson. Oxford 1936

The English Newspaper, Stanley Morison. Cambridge 1932

The Yorkshire Post, Mildred Gibb and Frank Beckwith. Yorkshire Conservative Newspaper Co. 1954

Guardian – Biography of a Newspaper, David Ayerst. Collins 1975

A History of the London Gazette 1665–1965, P. M. Handover. HMSO 1965

The Development of the Provincial Newspaper 1700–1760, G. A. Cranfield. Oxford University Press 1962.

Acknowledged with thanks

During the writing of this book, I have been in touch with many hundreds of editors who have patiently answered my queries. It would require another book to thank them all – but I would like to extend particular thanks to a few and hope that this may stand for them all.

P. Beck, Editor of Berrow's *Worcester Journal*
Mike Connor, Editor of *Lloyd's List*
E. G. B. Atkinson (retired) of Meynell Langley
K. R. Nutt, Associate Editor, *Mercury and Herald* (Northampton)
Mrs D. Young, Officer in Charge, the *London Gazette*
Mr Philipps, Librarian, *The Times*
G. G. Thomason, Managing Director, *Middlesex Chronicle*
M. J. Lansdown, Editor, *The Wiltshire Times and Chippenham News*
R. R. Waterhouse, Editor, *The Craven Herald*
Mrs Barbara Birkett, Secretary to the Editor, *The Newcastle Journal*
Jacqueline M. Alo, Marketing and External Relations Adviser, The Newspaper Publishers Association Ltd.
A. L. Smith, Assistant Editor, *Southern Evening Echo*
Gerald Isaaman, Editor, *Hampstead and Highgate Express*
John Little, Editor, *The Wells Journal*

E. Pannell, Editor, *Darlington and Stockton Times*
David Newton, History Editor, East Midland Allied Press
John King, Head Librarian, Beaverbrook Newspapers
Jack Lawrie, *The Sunday Times* Inquiry Desk
H. R. Pratt Boorman, Director, *Kent Messenger*
P. L. Whitehurst, Editor, *Windsor, Slough and Eton Express*
Roger Harrison, General Manager, *The Observer*
Mrs Monica Woodhouse, Managing Director, *Hampshire Chronicle*
John Edwards, Editor, *Yorkshire Post*
W. Sanders, Director and Editor, *Salisbury Journal*
W. G. Garner, Editor, *Reading Chronicle and Berkshire Mercury*
Jackie Beal, Information Department, The Newspaper Society
D. J. Tempero, Editor, *Andover Advertiser*

The publisher acknowledges with grateful thanks the illustrations supplied by many organisations, and in particular, the *London Gazette* (Great Fire of London), *Lloyd's List*, East Midland Allied Press (Duty Stamps – *Stamford Mercury*), *Reading Mercury*, *Hartford Mercury*, *The Observer* (Illustrated Crime Story), Berrow's *Worcester Journal* (title page), *Lichfield Mercury* (title page), *Wilts and Gloucestershire Standard* (title page), *Lynn Advertiser* (title page), *Southport Visiter* (title page), *Bedford Times* (title page), *Northampton Mercury* (title page).

Index of Newspapers

Index of Persons